W9-ARX-589

STEADFAST IN FAITH

Steadfast in Faith

Catholicism and the Challenges of Secularism

David G. Bonagura, Jr.

CLUNY MEDIA

Cluny Media edition, 2019

For more information regarding this title
or any other Cluny Media publication,
please write to info@clunymedia.com, or to
Cluny Media, P.O. Box 1664, Providence, RI, 02901

VISIT US ONLINE AT WWW.CLUNYMEDIA.COM

Nihil obstat:
REVEREND WALTER F. KEDJIERSKI, PH.D., *Censor deputatus*

Imprimatur:
MOST REVEREND JOHN O. BARRES, S.T.D., *Bishop of Rockville Centre*

December 10, 2018

Library of Congress Control Number: 2018964295

ISBN: 978-1949899597

Cover design by Clarke & Clarke
Cover image: Giuseppe de Fabris, *Statue of Saint Peter
in Front of Saint Peter's Basilica*, Rome, 1838–1840
Courtesy of Wikimedia Commons

CONTENTS

To Amanda, my dearest wife and best friend

❧ Acknowledgements

This book has had a long gestation, and I am deeply grateful for the many selfless people who have helped along the way. First, I would like to thank my parents, Dave and Diane Bonagura, who passed on the Catholic faith to me and my siblings, saw to it that I was educated in this faith, and supported me even as my career path veered from what they had anticipated for me. Thanks also goes to Dr. Charles Howlett, who many years ago was the first to encourage me to write for publication. I am particularly grateful to two individuals who helped me find a home within the world of ideas: Mr. Gerald Russello, editor of *The University Bookman* and my friend of many years, and the Most Rev. William Murphy, Bishop Emeritus of the Diocese of Rockville Centre, who appointed me to teach at the Seminary of the Immaculate Conception in 2010.

More immediate to the production of this book, I would like to thank Dr. Robert Royal, president of the Faith and Reason Institute and editor of *The Catholic Thing* website, which was the initial platform for some of the themes found in these pages. This book benefitted from the support, encouragement, and suggestions that I received from three friends in particular: Rev. Joseph Scolaro,

Rev. Dennis Suglia, and Dr. Joshua Hren. I owe a profound debt to my mentor and friend Dr. Lee Oser, who thoughtfully read and critiqued each chapter as it appeared; his numerous corrections and suggestions have made this a better book than could have appeared without his guidance. I would also like to thank my editors at Cluny Media, Leo Clarke and John Clarke, for their thoughtful revisions, wise counsel, and hard work throughout the publication process. Any errors that remain are my own.

As an author who is first a teacher, I am blessed to have been associated with some very fine Catholic educational institutions that have been directed by faith-filled individuals. In no particular order, I would like to thank the Most Rev. John O. Barres, Bishop of Rockville Centre; Sister Mary Louise Brink of the Seminary of the Immaculate Conception; Rev. Msgr. Peter Viccari, Rev. Kevin O'Reilly, and Dr. Donna Eschenauer of St. Joseph's Seminary; Dr. Peter Brown and Mrs. Judy Welsh of Catholic Distance University; Rev. Daniel Lahart, SJ, Dr. Gary Tocchet, and Mr. Pedro Acosta of Regis High School; Brother Kenneth Hoagland, S.M., and Mr. Kenneth Conrade of Kellenberg Memorial High School.

Even more important than institutional support is spiritual support. I would like to express my sincere gratitude to Rev. Thomas Fusco and Rev. Christopher Sullivan of Our Lady of Victory Church, as well as to Rev. Piotr Rosek and Rev. Msgr. Edward Wawerski of St. Hedwig's Church, for the devoted pastoral care they provide for me and for my family.

Cicero called friendship "a harmony of all things, human and divine, joined with good will and affection." It is a great blessing to share a harmony in faith with John Connelly, Blaise Nagy, John Donodeo, Greg Weston, A. J. Chianese, Nikolas Churik, Jay Barry, Dan Sullivan, Steve and Janet McIntyre, Jim and Joan Krug, Steve and Kathy Waldow, Kevin and Sophie Oriani, Matt and Maggie

Knox, Mike and Carolina Toth, Rev. Msgr. Frank Caldwell, Rev. Eric Fasano, and Rev. Brandon O'Brien.

Lastly, I would like to thank my children, Joseph, Charlie, Stephen, Anthony, and Maggie, who supported me in this project and willingly sacrificed many hours of ball playing to allow me to write. But the greatest thanks of all goes to my saintly and patient wife, Amanda, for her constant support and encouragement. Without her love and generosity, what follows on these pages would not exist.

PART I
PRELIMINARIES TO FAITH

❧ INTRODUCTION

Faith in Jesus Christ has encountered opposition from the very beginning. All but one of Jesus' apostles suffered violent deaths because they professed Jesus' name and taught others to do the same. For the first three centuries of its existence, Christianity was derisively viewed as a pernicious superstition by the ruling Roman authorities. Once Christianity was finally accepted within the Roman Empire, brave and faithful Christians, conscious of their duty to preach the Gospel to all nations, journeyed across the globe and risked their lives to transmit faith to peoples who had yet to hear the name of Christ. The multitude of Christians across the globe today owe their faith to the zeal, courage, and even the blood of these missionaries who knew that the ultimate gift they could bestow upon their fellow human beings was salvation in Jesus Christ.

Today, new opponents, infatuated with themselves and with the technocratic power at their disposal, are assailing not just Christianity itself but also any expression of belief in God. For decades they have tried to limit the extent and influence of faith within society through legal claims and public disparagement. At the same time, a convergence of other factors has led to a crisis of faith in the Western world, throughout which there has been a general abatement of religious practice and a rejection of the Christian moral code. This erosion of faith from without and from within has been called secularization, a condition whereby the world increasingly operates as if God did not exist. At present, the land that was once sought by millions of Christians as a place to worship God freely has been dubbed "post-Christian America."

Now as much as ever, those who believe need support as they carry on within a world that is growing indifferent and even hostile to faith and to them. Believers need fellowship with one another so they know that they are not alone; they need assurance of the content of their beliefs so that they may remain firm in their faith; and they need knowledge of the faith they profess so that they may engage non-believers in the public square.

This book, intended for teenagers, young adults, parents, grandparents, teachers, and those seeking to deepen their faith, is an attempt at meeting these needs. It seeks to address all of the questions and challenges that contemporary secular culture has put to Catholics who are trying their best to practice their faith in an increasingly hostile world: Why should we believe in the first place? What does it mean to have faith in God? What if I have doubts? What is the relationship between faith and science? Why do I not feel anything when I pray? Why do I need the Church when I am already a spiritual person? What makes Catholicism more special than other religions? Can I, or anyone else, really be saved? How can faith in God and the reality of evil and suffering coexist?

In responding to these questions, this book serves as an apology for faith in Jesus Christ, true God and true man, upon whom we are right to build our lives, our families, and our societies. "Apology" here does not mean "to be sorry," a condition into which too many Christians are being forced today. Rather it means "defense," a defense of faith as a justifiable, worthwhile, and necessary way of knowing, being, and living.

Contrary to the claims of those hostile to faith, to believe in God is inherently reasonable, even if the basis of faith lies beyond purely rational calculation. Faith in itself is a legitimate form of human knowledge, and so it coexists with science, reason, and experience. It is also deeply personal because it is the way in which human beings relate directly to God, our creator and ultimate end. Faith, therefore, is constitutive of our very existence, and to deny it is to deny the very core of what it means to be human.

By exploring the nature of faith in light of the particular challenges presented by twenty-first-century secularity, we hope to improve our understanding, to deepen our piety, and to grow in fortitude. These are gifts of the Holy Spirit, the guarantor of faith, who comes to us to spark a new Pentecost in a world so desperate to recover the sense of God's presence within it.

❧ Chapter 1

Faith in the World Today

Faith is a reality in the lives of all human beings, often in ways that we do not realize. Whenever we accept the story or account of another person and do not verify her story for ourselves, we make an act of faith. Faith is the relationship of trust that exists between us and the person speaking to us, one that is expressed when we say, "I have faith in you" or "I believe you." Since we trust the person, we also trust her account; we assume that she is telling us the truth not because we plan to investigate the claim at a later date, but because we believe the person is authentic and credible.

We make acts of faith in this generic sense all the time. When we read the newspaper or watch the broadcast news, we accept that what is reported to us is a true story of events. When we learn about the discoveries of science—that the universe is in fact expanding, or that matter is composed of tiny subatomic particles invisible even to microscopes—we believe that what we are told is true because we trust the scientific endeavor and the scientists who study the world. When we travel to an unknown place, we trust that our GPS is guiding us in the right direction as we drive, and as a result we make every turn it commands. When a friend or colleague tells us what happened to her over the weekend, we automatically assume her story is true because we have a relationship with this colleague and we deem her trustworthy. Of course, the inverse situation also applies: we may have another colleague who has been deceitful in the past and has a propensity for telling tall tales. In this instance, we doubt his story that he rode a bull over the weekend because we do not trust him as a credible person. We do not have faith in him, and therefore we do not believe his story.

Faith, then, is an authentic form of knowledge. It is clearly different from empirical knowledge, by which we are able to verify claims through our own observation, and from rational knowledge, by which we verify claims through abstract reasoning, but faith-based knowledge is legitimate in its own right. In fact, most of our knowledge about history, about the world, about our friends and our families comes to us through faith, that is, through our willful assent to what other trustworthy people have told us is true. We do not consider our knowledge of American government faulty because we have never been to Washington, DC, or have never read the countless volumes in the Library of Congress. Rather, by trusting the information we have learned through books and stories from a variety of sources, we can say that we know what the American government is, how it functions, and what it has accomplished.

Christian religious faith consists of this same act of trust in another person, whereby we accept as true what is told to us. The difference is that with Christian faith the person we trust is God, whom we do not see, and what we accept is God's revelation—His testimony about Himself and His plan for us. In the words of Blessed John Henry Newman, "When faith is said to be a religious principle, it is...the things believed, not the act of believing them, which is peculiar to religion."[1] At its most basic level, then, Christian religious faith is the personal relationship of trust we have with God and our acceptance of what He has revealed.

In the world today faith is often assailed as irrational or outdated amidst so much science, technology, and access to information on the Internet. But faith in the general sense of trust is, as mentioned, natural to human beings, and so much of our lives is predicated upon it. In fact, as Newman writes, "we know little more than that we exist, and that there is an Unseen Power whom we are bound to obey. Beyond this we must *trust*; and first our senses, memory, and reasoning powers; then other authorities:—so that, in fact, almost all we do, every day of our lives, is on trust, i.e. *faith*."[2]

In reality, then, the assailants of religious faith—that is, faith in a creator God to whom we owe our lives—attack not the act of faith itself, but the person toward whom religious faith is directed, God, and the acceptance of His word. Both factors—the act of faith itself and faith in God in particular—can and must be justified if Christian believers are to remain confident in their faith among so many vociferous detractors, and to maintain their rightful place in American society and in American civil discourse.

Religion and Faith in America Today

Religious faith in twenty-first-century America finds its expression in a multitude of beliefs and practices. Statistics have depicted some discernible trends in recent years, especially regarding the practice of Christianity in general and Roman Catholicism in particular. In 1900, approximately 90 percent of Americans called themselves Christians.[3] By 2007, that number had fallen to 78.4 percent, only to fall substantially further just seven years later: In 2014, 70.6 percent of the American population identified as Christian.[4] The population of American Catholics, always a minority, has also dropped: At the time of World War II American Catholics made up about 25 percent of the country, only to slip in 2014 to 20.8 percent, for a total of approximately 51 million

American Catholics.[5] With the decrease in those identifying themselves as Catholics has come a consequent decline in Mass attendance among the Catholic population at large. In 1974, 47 percent of Catholics attended Mass every Sunday; that percentage had fallen to 24 percent in 2012.[6]

At the same time, the percentage of Americans claiming no religious affiliation has risen sharply: In 1957 only 3 percent of Americans claimed no religious affiliation according to a government survey.[7] By 1990 this percentage grew to 7 percent, and then soared to 16.1 percent in 2007 and to 22.8 percent in 2014.[8] This rapidly growing group that now comprises more than one out of every five Americans has been dubbed the "Nones," and they comprise approximately 46 million people—just five million less than the number of American Catholics. Yet only a third of Nones claimed to be atheist or agnostic; by contrast, 68 percent of Nones believe in God, 37 percent claim to be "spiritual but not religious," and 21 percent pray every day.[9] When viewed by age, young people under age 30 form the largest percentage of Nones at 32 percent, while 21 percent of 30–49 year olds rank themselves among the Nones. Most noteworthy, however, is that 30 percent of Nones were raised Catholic but no longer identify as such.[10] For every convert received into the Catholic Church, there are six former Catholics who no longer practice or identify with the Catholic faith.[11]

On the whole, Americans have generally retained a mindset that is open to God. What has changed over the last several decades is that many increasingly want to relate to God on their own individual terms rather than through an official religion, including the Catholic Church, which, as will be seen later, claims a critical role in transmitting faith and facilitating a personal relationship between God and man. Among the categories denoted in the most recent surveys, some amount of fluidity exists between groups, as some Americans change religious affiliations more than once over their lifetimes, or they join the ranks of the Nones before returning to an institutional religion again.[12] Yet it seems that Americans' approach to God, to religion, and to faith is being increasingly determined by individual preference rather than familial, communal, or institutional considerations.

In addition to growing individualism, a phenomenon that will be examined later, several factors have contributed to the weakening of religious practice in America. One factor has been the conscious decision by certain proponents of the Scientific Revolution and the Enlightenment Project, which began in the seventeenth and eighteenth centuries, to use their newfound knowledge to discredit religion and the existence of God. Discoveries in science and growth in human beings' abilities to control our lives and our environment have been wrongly interpreted as signs that God does not control as much as we once thought "before we knew better," that is, before the development of science. In the fields of cosmology and evolution in particular, the discovery of multiple galaxies and the theory of man developing from other animals have been interpreted as signs that human beings are not the unique center of God's plan but are insignificant parts of a series of chance happenings. At the same time, those who lived in the Middle Ages (500–1400) have been denigrated as simpletons who, so enthralled by their faith and so ignorant of science, thought that the world was flat and worried instead about how many angels could dance on the pin of a needle. The fact that both of these claims are completely false Enlightenment-era fabrications, yet are widespread in the public imagination, shows the extent to which science has been misused by certain parties to attack, rather than complement, religious faith. By darkening religion with this unjustly cast shadow, belief in God is now wrongly perceived as being anti-science. Few people today, with science so powerfully prevalent, would want to put themselves in such a camp.

A second factor contributing to waning religious practice has been the sweeping force of technological advancement in America and in the "first world" that has created countless material goods and modern conveniences. Of course, creature comforts are good things and not necessarily inimical to religious faith and practice; there have always been devout believers who have been wealthy. Yet Jesus saw the danger that material goods can present to the spiritual life when He warned, "It is easier for a camel to pass through the eye of a needle than for a rich man to enter the kingdom of God" (Matt. 19:24).[13]

Modern goods and technology can lay claim to a host of wondrous accomplishments: the eradication of certain diseases, the control of potentially damaging natural phenomena, the widespread availability of clean water, and the augmentation of the food supply. But these goods can also be used negatively to banish God and anoint ourselves masters of the universe, as can happen with nuclear power, reproductive technologies, and human genome experimentation. In these and other cases, such tantalizingly powerful materials can lead to materialism—the belief that only what is physical and tangible has any real significance for our lives.

In a famous homily delivered in Reykjavik, Iceland, Pope St. John Paul II explained how physical and social comforts, if not rightly used, have the potential to lead us away from God:

> In a highly developed society such as yours, where everyone has enough to eat, where education and health care are available to all, and where a high level of social justice has been achieved, it is easy to lose sight of the Creator, from whose

loving hands all things come. *It is easy to live as if God did not exist.* Indeed, there is a powerful attraction to such an attitude, for it might seem that acknowledging God as the origin and end of all things lessens human independence and places unacceptable limits on human action. But when we forget God we soon lose sight of the deeper meaning of our existence, we no longer know who we are. Is this not an important part of *the dissatisfaction* that is common in highly developed societies?[14]

A third factor has been a steady increase of political and cultural efforts to limit the presence and influence of religion in the public square. Disputes over whether prayer can be part of public fora and school sponsored events have played out acrimoniously in communities and in politics, with some disputants seeking recourse to the judicial system for resolution. Some have sought the removal of the phrase "under God" from the Pledge of Allegiance on the grounds that it violates the separation between church and state. Students and professors have been disciplined and even dismissed for their support of marriage as a union of one man and one woman. An organization called the Freedom from Religion Foundation, which exists "to promote the constitutional principle of separation of state and church, and to educate the public on matters relating to nontheism," boasts on its website that it "keeps several challenges in the courts at all times, and has ended a variety of violations of the First Amendment."[15] Religious-based groups have not been exempt from political and legal interference within their own internal affairs: Much has been made in recent years about political attempts to limit the constitutional right to the "free exercise of religion" by recasting it as a "freedom to worship" that should not be showcased outside the church building. Increasingly, those who have remained strong in their religious faith are finding themselves marginalized by a public opinion that has become skeptical of faith and its role in society.

A Secular World

The waning of religious practice and the attacks on religion itself are the most recent developments of what we have come to call "secularity." The adjective "secular" means "belonging to this world." Hence the noun "secularity" refers to the status or condition of a world that considers only what is of the demonstrable natural order as constitutive of society and public life. References to the divine or to faith are deliberately excluded from public life in this view. "Secularism" is the belief that only the realities of the natural world should have any bearing on our conduct and political life; a secular world, therefore, functions as if God did not exist. For example, according to the U.K.'s National Secular Society, "separation of religion and state is the foundation of secularism.... Secularism ensures that the right of individuals to freedom of religion is always balanced by the right to be free *from* religion."[16]

Three other terms are often involved with this general understanding of secularity. "Secularization" literally means "the process of becoming secular," and it refers to the process of transitioning from a situation of religious influence to one where the state or some other nonreligious entity becomes the dominant influence, such as when a Catholic hospital or school closes and is reopened by the government.[17] Or, as one more forceful commentator put it, secularization is "the loosing of the world from religious and quasi-religious understandings of itself, the dispelling of all closed world-views, the breaking of all supernatural myths and sacred symbols.... Secularization is man turning his attention away from worlds beyond and toward this world and this time."[18]

12

A "secularist" is a person who espouses secularity as an ideal way of living. Finally, "secular humanism" refers to an ethical way of human and humane living according to natural order principles that do not acknowledge any divinity as its arbiter, motivator, or foundation. In the words of a proponent, secular humanism is "a comprehensive nonreligious life stance that incorporates a naturalistic philosophy, a cosmic outlook rooted in science, and a consequentialist ethical system."[19]

Faith and the Presumption of Unbelief

In the twenty-first century we are compelled to live the life of faith within this secular world, and since faith is always influenced by the surrounding culture, it is of the utmost importance that we understand what secularity is and what it means for faith. For insights into contemporary secularity, we shall turn briefly to Charles Taylor's magisterial study *A Secular Age*. For Taylor, "a secular age is one in which the eclipse of all goals beyond human flourishing becomes conceivable; or better, it falls within the range of an imaginable life for masses of people."[20] In late Antiquity, the Middle Ages, and the early Modern period the culture in which Christians lived helped foster and nourish faith: "belief was the default option" in the face of cultural challenges or new situations.[21] In our own time, however, "the presumption of unbelief has become dominant in more and more of these [cultural] milieux; and has achieved hegemony in certain crucial ones, in the academic and intellectual life, for instance; whence it can more easily extend itself to others."[22]

One very real way we have seen this shift to a "presumption of unbelief" is in the replacement of the greeting "Merry Christmas," along with Christmas's attendant religious symbols, with "Happy Holidays," and its use of generic symbols of winter: by using the latter greeting, we implicitly assume that our interlocutor does not believe. Further, Taylor adds that the disposition toward belief, once esteemed in itself, has been pejoratively labeled "naïve" while the presumption of unbelief is now considered "reflective."[23] Hence believers are perceived as simpletons while unbelievers are assumed to be intelligent and willing to use their own minds to figure out the world.

The presumption of unbelief has become possible because we now live in what Taylor calls an "immanent frame," that is, a world that only considers what is natural and rational, as opposed to what is supernatural or transcendent, as real.[24] It is within this frame that secularity's "purely self-sufficient humanism" accepts "no final goals beyond human flourishing, nor any allegiance to anything else beyond this flourishing. Of no previous society was this true."[25]

For 1900 years, Catholics have been challenged by rivals—pagans in the Roman Empire, barbarians in Europe, Muslims in Africa and the Middle East, native peoples in Asia and the New World, Protestants in America—but these rivals had beliefs of their own; they simply rejected the *Catholic faith in particular*. Now, for the first time in history, an increasing number of people are rejecting *faith itself*, and they are doing so largely not from spite, but from apathy. In this environment it is very challenging to maintain a life of religious faith and to share that faith with others. Just as seeds need proper conditions in order to develop into plants, so, too, does faith develop best in a culture conducive to belief and to religion.

Unlike seeds, faith can still grow and persevere in hostile environments—the entire history of Christianity certainly proves this. But since faith is a relationship of trust, it requires constant nourishment and support, both internally through the efforts of the individual and externally through the help of others, to remain strong and vital. If there are too many external factors constantly undermining the reality of faith, then it becomes more likely that the believer may lose confidence in that relationship.

Let us consider the examples of three individuals to contextualize our current situation. Holly, a 15-year-old Catholic and a sophomore at a well-regarded public high school, is a typical teenager growing up in America today. Her parents insist that religion is important, and that she attend Mass every Sunday, but she was never taught why. Aside from these two influences, the remainder of Holly's week is saturated with worldly tasks, good in themselves, but they all take place within the immanent frame that Taylor described: not once has anyone told her that she should live her life and perform her tasks for the glory of God in fulfillment of His will. Holly studies diligently and receives high marks. Her favorite class is biology, where she has learned that the existence of human beings is the result of random mutations and unplanned evolution. She has learned about the importance of strong self-esteem and of having "values," although the latter word has never been defined, and she has never been told how to form these values. She has been told repeatedly to be tolerant and accepting of all people regardless of how they look or how they behave. After school, she plays on the junior varsity soccer team. Two days a week after practice she goes to her local dance studio to rehearse for her upcoming recital. Upon returning home, she completes her homework and spends several hours consumed by social media, following her friends as well as a number of celebrities, her favorite being singer Katy Perry, whose songs "I Kissed a Girl" and "UR So Gay" she has memorized. Her 24-year-old sister recently moved in with her boyfriend and has stopped attending Mass. Few of her friends or classmates go to church on Sunday; religion is never discussed or considered, and God is mentioned only when His name is invoked in vain.

Absorbed in this secular environment, it is very difficult for Holly to have a genuine relationship with God. She only encounters Him briefly at Sunday Mass, which seems to her as just a boring activity to be endured in the midst of a busy weekend filled with more pressing and exciting things. Any attempts to discuss with her the critical importance of faith for a happy life are met not with hostility, but with incomprehension: she simply cannot see a reason, living as she does in this environment, why God should have a larger role in her life—she is happy in her life as it is now.

In this secular existence Holly lives generally unaware of God and the importance of faith. Andrea, a contemporary of Holly and a child of devout parents, is struggling mightily within the same conditions. Although Andrea has a strong faith, prays alone and with her family, and is involved in parish spiritual activities, she is painfully aware that she is the only person in her class who is. She tries not to make her friends aware of her religiosity, and she becomes uncomfortable whenever anyone mentions religion or her participation in it. Occasionally she questions her own beliefs, not because she doubts them, but because she wonders why she is the only one who thinks they are worthwhile. Whereas she once happily attended many religious activities with her parents, in the last couple of years her willingness to participate has dwindled: Why, she thinks, should she be the only high school student at the Stations of the Cross on Friday?

Despite the difficulties they face, Holly and Andrea are fortunate enough to have parents who insist that they attend Mass. As the statistics outlined above make clear, not all children are as blessed: more and more parents have gravitated, in reality if not officially, toward the Nones, and, naturally, if parents do not attend church, their children do not attend either. Larry, a 49-year-old father of three and insurance broker at a medium-sized firm, is one such father. He has not been to church since his youngest son, now 13, made his first holy communion five years ago. Larry's drift away from Catholic practice was gradual and developed not from a particular incident, but from a growing indifference. After attending Mass with his family weekly through his teenage years, Larry first started skipping Mass on occasion while a student at a Catholic university: there were certain weekends when he just did not have time to attend. Upon graduating he found an entry-level job and rented an apartment in a suburb, where he played on a men's softball team each Sunday morning. He considered softball more fun and more important for his integration into his new neighborhood, so he stopped attending Mass except on Christmas and Easter. At age 27 Larry married a woman whose slow drift away from the Catholic faith over her adolescent years mirrored his own. They married in the Catholic Church and had their three children baptized. Their children were enrolled in their parish's religious education program, through which they received their first holy communion and confirmation, but they did not attend Mass on Sunday. Early in their family life they attended Mass on Christmas and Easter, but as the children grew into their teenage years, they started to miss even on these days because they were so busy. Although Larry's wife occasionally pops into church for a parish event, Larry himself, at this point in his life, sees no need for God or for religion. He is content enough with his current existence, and he considers himself a good person: he does not think church can make him any better. His children, despite having attend a religious education program for several years each, are essentially unchurched.

The growing number of people like Holly, Andrea, and Larry unwittingly contribute to the "presumption of unbelief" in our secular world today, although they are as much the product of our secular world as contributors to it. Believers gradually are finding less support from acquaintances, colleagues, and media not only for belief in general, but also for any intellectual position in the public square that can be supported by a faith-based perspective, especially regarding marriage, human sexuality, and family life. The proliferation of discussions about the need for laws protecting religious freedom indicates the defensive position into which believers have been thrust.

There is more to secularism than the belief that God or the transcendent ought to be excluded from public life. Secularity is expressed in several prevailing philosophies and worldviews. In particular, four component beliefs have both contributed to secularity's development and have remained features of its continued existence. But before we examine each of these in terms of their impact on religious faith, we will briefly consider the view of the world that the Catholic faith espouses as a point of contrast.

❧ CHAPTER 2

The Catholic Worldview

A "worldview" is a theory about the meaning and philosophical underpinnings of life and of the world. There is a Catholic worldview, and it developed beginning in the first century of Christianity from the fusion of biblical Hebrew culture with Greek Hellenistic culture. Its critical foundation lies in the account of creation in the Book of Genesis: God freely created the world of His own volition, and He did so simply by willing it into existence—of no other explanation of the cosmos, from antiquity to modern secular theories, can this be said.[1] The world, therefore, and everything natural in it is good because it was created by God, the ultimate Good. The world is also reasonable and ordered because it is created by God, who is pure rationality Himself, a fact we know from the beginning of John's Gospel: "In the beginning was the Word, and the Word was with God, and the Word was God" (John 1:1). And since the world is reasonable, we can study it, and in doing so, we learn about its creator.[2]

The crown of God's creation is humanity since human beings alone are made in His image and likeness in order to share in His love. Unlike all other creatures, human beings are in the image of God because we possess an intellect and a will: the former gives us the ability to think rationally and relate to God our creator, while the latter gives us freedom to choose. But the first human beings used their free will to sin against God: their sin is usually viewed as one of pride, but it can also be viewed as a sin against faith—they lost their trust in God and chose to trust in themselves instead. From this single act of distrust, the world and its creatures fell from grace and were left in a weakened state. This state is what Catholics call the human condition that is a consequence of original sin.

Rather than leave human beings to wallow in the misery they made for themselves, God chose not to remake the world, but to redeem it—literally, to buy it back—by becoming a man. The incarnation of the Son of God, the eternal Word of the Father, Jesus Christ, is the expression of God's love *par excellence*, for through it "man, by entering into communion with the Word and thus receiving his divine sonship, might become a son of God."[3] Our redemption was wrought when in our place Christ, "whom God put forward as an expiation by his blood," died on the cross in an act "to be received by faith" (Rom. 3:25). This act of sacrificial love is re-presented at every Mass, through which we come into direct communion with Christ, the Son of God. Through the Eucharist Christ remains incarnate among us, and our task as believers is to form a personal relationship with Him. This is the essence of faith, as we will see later.

It is by these three events, now presented to us as doctrines—the creation, the incarnation, and the redemption—that the Catholic worldview is molded. Because the world was created good and then redeemed by God, it has a purpose, as do human beings and the rest of His creatures. Christians have long understood this purpose by way of an analogy: God is the father of a family whose collective destiny is to return to God in Heaven after its earthly sojourn. Like any human father, God lovingly cares and provides for us, an action which we call God's providence. He instituted the Church and the sacraments to provide for us spiritually, and He gave us the ability and ingenuity to take care of our own physical needs. Also like any human father, God desires our happiness and what is best for us: He reveals His law and will so that we may know how to return back to Him. The Fathers of the Church referred to God's providential work of creating, redeeming, and guiding the world as the "divine economy," from the Greek *oikonomia*, meaning the ordering of a household. Unfortunately, like all human children, we often think we know better than our Father and insist on doing things our own way—we sin. But as a loving Father, God is ready and willing to forgive us: we need only confess that we have wronged Him and express our sorrow.

Further, a necessary consequence of the goodness of creation and the revelation of God's will for us is that the world is real, and we can really know things about it. It seems strange to make this ostensibly obvious point, but we will see its significance shortly. The existence of the world is self-evident; our knowledge of it comes from our senses. Our intellect then processes and makes judgments about what we have experienced. In this way, St. Thomas Aquinas teaches that "[w]hen...things are the measure and rule of the mind," truth is defined as "the equation of the mind to the thing."[4] In other words, the world itself is constitutive of what is real and true; we come to know things as true when we turn our minds toward what already exists in the world. Through the powers of sensation and intellection, we are able to apprehend universal characteristics in our experiences of particular objects, and we, in turn, know about a particular object through our knowledge of its universal characteristics.[5] This understanding of the world as we experience it as determinate of reality and of truth is called realism, and it finds its best expression in St. Thomas Aquinas's philosophy.

Realism is a necessary part of the Catholic worldview because it ensures the facts of creation, of God's plan for the world, and of our participation in His plan. It is also essential to the moral life, which concerns how we treat our world and our fellow human beings. The precepts of morality that come from our reflections on the nature and purpose of the world comprise the natural law, which, as the *Catechism of the Catholic Church* explains, "expresses the original moral sense which enables man to discern by reason the good and the evil, the truth and the lie."[6] In the Catholic worldview, therefore, morality is objective, that is, it is determined by factors that exist in the world, and not by a person's own subjective understanding of what he thinks is good or bad. Realism is also the philosophical underpinning of the primary transmission of God's grace, the sacraments, whose entire system hinges on the use of real, knowable things to effect real grace in the lives of believers, especially with regard to the Eucharist.

This worldview shapes the way Catholics live and interact in the world. It does not limit individual freedom or call for a uniform way to behave and think. Rather, it forms the foundation upon which individual Catholics can pursue their own unique interests and tasks. It fosters not uniformity among believers but *universality*—the sharing by diverse peoples in the oneness of God and in His plan for us.

With this background in mind, we can now examine from the perspective of the Catholic faith the four principal components of secularity and how they impact the life of faith today. These components are individualism, relativism, pluralism, and scientific naturalism.

Secular Worldviews and Challenges to Faith

The first major philosophical component of secularity is individualism, the belief that each individual is the ultimate arbiter of his or her own existence, behavior, and decisions. Of course there is nothing wrong with individual expression and fulfillment. The issue here is that contemporary individualism hinges on a radical understanding of freedom that pits the individual in opposition to all other people and entities. Since achievement of the individual's desires is the most important goal, no institution or rule can stand in his way. Freedom, in this view, is *freedom from* encroachments extraneous to the individual's personal whims. A 1992 Supreme Court opinion perfectly expressed how this conception of freedom can lead to an unbridled and inherently self-centered worldview: "At the heart of liberty is the right to define one's own concept of existence, of meaning, of the universe, and of the mystery of human life."[7]

Individualism of this sort is a great threat to religious faith, which, as we will see later, depends wholly on other people who not only pass down faith but also live it themselves. Since Catholicism expresses the truth about God, it espouses a ritual form of worship that both fosters and protects our faith in Him. This sort of belief and practice is directly challenged by a secular world that perceives institutions and rituals as shackles on individual expression. Individualism is the foundation of the decision of many Nones to be "spiritual but not religious," that is, they believe in God or a higher power but prefer to relate to Him on their own terms rather than through the communal experience of an institutional religion such as Catholicism. Hence individualism presents a challenge not to the content of faith but to the perceived limits it places upon the person. And as evidenced in the quotation above from Pope St. John Paul II, sometimes God is wrongly perceived as limiting human freedom by presenting a moral law for human beings to follow.

This understanding of individualism and freedom is clearly detrimental to communal living because it does not acknowledge a fundamental truth valid for all human beings upon which freedom can be established. We saw above, for example, that the U.K.'s National Secular Society seeks to answer claims of freedom of religion with a corresponding claim of freedom from religion. When two individuals or groups have a competing claim without a common standard to which they can appeal, as is happening right now in American courts concerning religious liberty issues, and each party argues that it has a right to be free from coercion by the other, how is the claim to be adjudicated? In this view, freedom ironically becomes imprisoned by the opposing desires of the two parties: freedom from the other requires the confinement of the other.

By contrast, the Catholic worldview understands freedom as directed toward the fulfillment of goals established by God through creation. Rather than wrap oneself in a cocoon so as to be free from all desires that are not one's own, freedom in the Catholic view is *freedom for* accomplishing what is true and good in accordance with God's will. Without truth to direct it, freedom collapses into selfishness and narcissism, paralyzed by its inability to see beyond the caprice of the individual. Hence, as St. John Paul articulates in a seeming paradox, "human freedom finds its authentic and complete fulfillment precisely in the acceptance of [God's moral] law."[8] The moral law becomes a compass whereby we can find the proper and healthy ways to live as human beings. And like all mechanical things, when human beings function according to the way they were intended, they function more happily and efficiently.

The second philosophical component of secularity is relativism, which denies the existence of an objective truth that is binding for everyone across all cultures, particularly in matters of morality. Relativism instead holds that moral claims can apply only to individuals or groups, not to humanity as a whole, and these claims are determined by subjective criteria, such as emotion, preference, or cultural standards. With relativism no action can be deemed true or correct in itself: it can only be "right for me" or "right for you" depending on circumstances and desires. Relativism is the moral philosophy of the individualist: it asserts that what one desires is necessarily right simply because he desires it.

The prevalence of relativism within America today can be seen by a subtle yet significant shift in vocabulary in recent decades. In public discourse we rarely hear discussions of "morality" or "morals"; instead we hear about "values." Morals imply standards and binding rules, but values are subjective, such as the price value of a good for sale, and therefore imply variance and even disagreement.

If the assessment of actions is purely subjective, then it becomes exceedingly difficult to prohibit certain behaviors in public life. Movements to reject such strictures often include an accusation: "Don't impose your values on me." Conversely, the same rationale is used to justify any type of behavior and demand that the behavior be accepted by others in the name of tolerance. As a result, in a relativistic society, since no independent standard exists to measure action, every law or rule of behavior is perceived as an imposition by the ruling power on the rest of the population. St. John Paul clearly perceives the dangers that power unchecked by objective moral laws presents to society:

> Authentic democracy is possible only in a State ruled by law, and on the basis of a correct conception of the human person.... Nowadays there is a tendency to claim that agnosticism and skeptical relativism are the philosophy and the basic attitude which correspond to democratic forms of political life. Those who are convinced that they know the

truth and firmly adhere to it are considered unreliable from a democratic point of view, since they do not accept that truth is determined by the majority, or that it is subject to variation according to different political trends. It must be observed in this regard that *if there is no ultimate truth to guide and direct political activity, then ideas and convictions can easily be manipulated for reasons of power.*[9]

Relativism challenges faith directly by denying the universality of truth. The Catholic faith is *catholic* precisely because it is *universal*—true and valid for all people, regardless of time or culture. Further, if truth cannot be known, it follows that God cannot be known, since, in this view, non-scientific knowledge is a purely subjective matter. This view reduces religious faith to an individual, feel-good exercise rather than an expression of a real relationship with the real God.

As with individualism, the Catholic worldview counters the whim-driven nature of relativism with its understanding of the world as created with a purpose discernible by all and of human beings as created in the image of God. Without this foundation, the order of society collapses under the weight of the group strong enough to impose its desires on everyone else. Far from constraining the moral life, the Catholic worldview provides a clear and fair playing field in which free will and moral choice can be exercised in a way that allows human beings to flourish, by analogy, as children in God's loving family.

The third prevalent philosophy in our secular world is pluralism. In the general sense, a plurality is a state in which multiple expressions exist within a single entity, and this can be a good thing. In politics, for example, a plurality exists when there are several different political parties all trying to meet the single goal of helping the nation, each in its own way. Within the Catholic Church there is a genuine plurality of expression of the one faith by different regions: the Latin (Western) Church, the Byzantine Church, and the Syro-Malabar (Indian) Church all have distinct liturgies and religious practices that express the same faith through their different cultural heritages. Plurality is also seen in the hundreds of religious orders that exist within the Church, from mendicant friars, to cloistered contemplatives, to religious teachers, to hospital chaplains: each group carries on the work of Jesus Christ in its own unique way. As Joseph Ratzinger wrote before becoming Pope Benedict XVI, "The truth of the faith resonates not as a mono-phony, but as a sym-phony, not as a homophonic, but as a polyphonic melody composed of the many apparently quite discordant strains in the contrapuntal interplay of law, prophets, Gospels, and apostles."[10]

But because contemporary secularity has rejected the existence of truth which previously bound into one the diverse expressions of different groups, plurality has morphed into pluralism. Pluralism is similar in nature to individualism, except it applies to associated groups of people. To its extreme, pluralism allows different groups to express their respective opinions without reference to a common whole or common truth, with each group demanding respect and tolerance for its own ideas and practices within the public square by virtue of its existence, not by the validity of its ideas. Since no truth exists, each group is equal. And it seems that the heading under which the greatest number of different groups dispute is religion.

The seemingly unlimited quantity of religions without reference to a shared truth or goal for them leads to the perception that all religions are equal. Membership in a particular church becomes perceived not as the pursuit of truth or a response to God, but as the personal preference of a particular individual, akin to joining a club or a gym. If there are so many religions to choose from, why should it matter to which one belongs? And why should any of them receive any special privileges in society, such as tax breaks or a public voice over moral and community issues, if they are just another group?

From the Catholic viewpoint, the problem of pluralism is the same as that of individualism and relativism: the denial of truth in the world and of purpose in nature as the directors of our lives and our societies. Such a denial is contrary to our own experiences of the world, which dictate to us what we must do as we encounter it, and not the other way around. A human being who jumps from a tall building seeking to fly by waving his arms learns a painful lesson about human nature. It is also worth noting that individualism, relativism, and pluralism exist because of a prior skepticism: adherents of these views doubt that truth can be known, so, in a certain sense, their skepticism forces them into these positions. But, in a strange irony, since there are no scientific proofs that can verify these three beliefs, to hold any one of them is an exercise of faith, trusting implicitly that they are in fact correct views of the world and how we live.

The fourth and final component of secularity is scientific naturalism, the belief that the universe and everything in it can be explained solely by natural causes that are ascertainable by science. Scientific naturalism sees the universe as a "closed system," meaning the universe's fullness is contained within itself: there is no divinity or supernatural force inserting its will or effects into the universe from beyond. Hence what is real is only what can be measured by science. This theory can be taken a step further to claim that science can and should answer all of life's questions, not just the quantifiable ones. This belief is called "scientism."

Harvard psychology professor Steven Pinker has articulated the essence of scientism—as well as scientism's challenges to religion—as forcefully as anyone.[11] Scientism in the "good sense," he argues, rests on two ideals that should be the foundation of the intellectual life: the intelligibility of the universe, which can be explained (or will be someday) by science, and the difficulty of acquiring knowledge. He also asserts that science's power can do more than make the world intelligible: it can serve as the basis for social and political life.

> The facts of science, *by exposing the absence of purpose in the laws governing the universe*, force us to take responsibility for the welfare of ourselves, our species, and our planet.... [T]he scientific facts militate toward a defensible morality, *namely adhering to principles that maximize the flourishing of humans and other sentient beings*. This humanism, which is inextricable from a scientific understanding of the world, is becoming the de facto morality of modern democracies, international organizations, and liberalizing religions, and its unfulfilled promises define the moral imperatives we face today.[12]

Pinker's explicit denial of purpose in the world is directly counter to the Catholic worldview. And his understanding of secular humanism is exactly as Taylor described: it is concerned with human flourishing in this life, and nothing more.

To this assertion Pinker adds a further point: "Most of the traditional causes of belief—faith, revelation, dogma, authority...—are generators of error and should be dismissed as sources of knowledge." It is science, not religion, he declares emphatically, that should be our guide for "the deepest questions about who we are, where we came from, and how we define the meaning and purpose of our lives." In fact, "[t]he moral worldview of any scientifically literate person—one who is not blinkered by fundamentalism—requires a radical break from religious conceptions of meaning and value."

As Pinker makes clear, scientific naturalism presents three deliberate challenges to religious faith. First, it denies the legitimacy of faith itself, relegating it to a superstition whose usefulness has been displaced by the capabilities of science. Second, as mentioned, it denies that there is an order and purpose to the universe; our lives, and everything that happens in them, are instead the products of chance probabilities that we cannot explain. Third, it declares itself the lone authority in all moral and political matters in society with the right to determine the content of the common good.

Before considering these challenges directly, it is important to point out that these claims of scientific naturalism are all claims of faith in the generic sense of trust, as we noted in Chapter 1. There is no scientific or demonstrable proof for any of Pinker's claims. In this worldview the entity trusted is "Science," now deified as an absolute power, and the content of belief is the findings of science, which are conflated into something greater than mere measurements of the world. Scientific naturalists have essentially turned science into a god, the deciding arbiter and power of the universe. Where science has yet to establish empirical certainty, it is left to human beings, as Pinker states, to invent for themselves their own truth and the best course of action in matters of morality and politics according to their own caprice. They are left in this situation because by denying purpose to and in the world, they deny that truth can be found. In the Catholic view, truth is that which is, that which exists, according to the nature and purpose of the universe. For scientific naturalists, by contrast, truth is reduced to meaning, which is constructed from our experiences and our interactions with others, with each person forming his or her own meaning. Truth thus becomes a tool manipulated to improve our collective lots as human beings.[13]

In the scientific naturalist worldview, what is to prevent the principle of "might makes right" from being imposed on innocent people and minority groups in the name of science? History is replete with horrific examples of what happens when human beings take law and morality into their own hands after having rejected or deliberately manipulated God's laws and the natural laws of the world. But if we place our faith in science rather than God, innocents and minorities no longer have a universal standard to which they can at least point for protection: the ruling powers will act under their own interests, claiming that what they have manufactured in the name of science is the new truth to which all must conform. As Joseph Ratzinger writes, "When the human person is no longer seen as standing under God's protection and bearing God's breath, then the human being begins to be viewed in utilitarian fashion. It is then that the barbarity appears that tramples upon human dignity."[14]

The basis of faith, therefore, whether in God or in Science, is intrinsically tied, from the human vantage point, to the notion of purpose. We have already seen how purpose is inherent within the Catholic worldview. As Pinker notes, scientific naturalists deny that there is purpose or order in the universe. This belief—and it is a belief, since there is no demonstrable proof for it—stems from Darwinism, which holds that the organisms of the world are a product of the unplanned confluence of random mutation and natural selection that seemingly occur without any purpose at all. And because in their view life is allegedly *generated* without an ultimate purpose, scientific naturalists reason by extension that organisms *live* without an ultimate purpose.

This is a striking assumption, since it extends well beyond the limits of what science can measure. It also ignores that fact that all human beings act for a purpose in everything that they do. Hence it is equally fair for believers to reason that, in the case of human beings, the countless actions they perform for a multitude of purposes facilitate a broader purpose—that of their lives. Surely the fact that so many human beings routinely search for meaning and purpose in their lives suggests an inherent orientation of life toward this end. When human beings turn to science to learn more about the world in which they live, they are presupposing that the world has a discernible order, and they engage in the scientific endeavor to serve certain purposes they have in mind. In fact, every act of science, from hypothesis to conclusion, is done for a deliberate purpose.

The scientific naturalist, then, must explain how such purpose-driven beings fit into a supposedly purposeless world. To cite chance mutations facilitated by the mechanism of natural selection is really to cite nothing at all: as Howard P. Kainz notes, chance "is simply an event or effect for which we don't know the cause.... As applied to nature, the anomalies and quirks and exceptions that we seem to witness are not the result of chance, but simply evidence of the fact that nature is purposeful, in the sense that it acts in certain ways 'for the most part.'"[15] This turns on its head the notion that our faith in God's providence and answered prayers ultimately reflects the discrepancy between the world and our understanding of it: Perhaps the presumption of a purposeless world is the result of a discrepancy between the development of organisms and our under-standing of this development. As Kainz concludes, "The human mind is constituted to look for causes; but to say that our species has been caused by multiple chance mutations is an abdication of reason equivalent to saying vacuously that it has been caused by multiple 'I-know-not-whats.'"[16]

The supposed claims of secularity's most potent threat to reli-gious faith, scientific naturalism, are, upon examination, much closer to faith claims than to scientific statements. In fact, all four major philosophical components of secularity promise more than they deliver. They are certainly not more appealing or beneficial for individuals and society than the Catholic worldview.

Faith v. Reason?

Along with others who share the secular worldview, Pinker sees religious faith as a superstition, and, therefore, as something irrational. The Catholic worldview is not fazed by such facile criticism: Catholics assert both the rationality of faith itself and the belief that faith and reason are profoundly interrelated. In fact, the Church proposes for the world a beautiful vision of faith and reason as the twofold means by which we come to know God and the truth:

> Faith and reason are like two wings on which the human spirit rises to the contemplation of truth; and God has placed in the human heart a desire to know the truth—in a word, to know himself—so that, by knowing and loving God, men and women may also come to the fullness of truth about themselves.[17]

Today's secular world, by contrast, not only rejects faith and the God who is faith's end, but it also has become suspicious of reason and truth itself. As we have seen, contemporary relativism and pluralism are the result of a society that has willfully turned its back on truth. Truth itself still exists; but, blinded by truth's grandeur, frustrated by an inability to comprehend it fully, and inconvenienced by the demands it makes, the secular world has declared by its own authority that truth cannot be known, and, therefore, might as well not exist. If reason does not have truth to seek, it becomes like a ship on the sea without a rudder or compass: lost and unsure what to do—or worse, susceptible to any wind that blows.

In other words, by rejecting truth, the secular world has lost its faith in reason—it no longer believes that reason can know things definitively, and so it has rejected reason. Without the faith—the trust—that human reason can know the truth, we are left with a world whose only truth is that there is no truth. And when we no longer have truth toward which we can direct our lives, what enters in its place is nihilism, a philosophy that believes nothing really exists or can be known. Nihilism is the de facto position of those who believe life has no meaning or purpose. For those "in the nihilist interpretation," writes St. John Paul, "life is no more than an occasion for sensations and experiences in which the ephemeral has pride of place. Nihilism is at the root of the widespread mentality which claims that a definitive commitment should no longer be made because everything is fleeting and provisional."[18]

Nihilism and the eclipse of reason adversely impact human nature, which is inclined to know and to seek after the causes and truth of things. The proof of this is found in our daily living: when the phone rings, or when we see a notice that we have an email or text message waiting for us, we instantly and instinctively seek after the truth: Who is contacting us? What does this person want? If we are surprised by the message, we automatically wonder why the person said or wrote what she did, especially if it is accusatory or offensive in some way. We may even go so far as to question the veracity of the message if the circumstances prompt us. And, should the means for delivering the message malfunction in some way, we wonder with frustration why it failed to work and how we can fix it.

Our natural inclinations and scientific achievements point us to the existence of truth that is external to ourselves and to our ability to find it using reason. The entire enterprise of technological advancement, to select just one example, depends on a myriad amount of rational presuppositions about how things work within the world. The workings of technology depend on our use of reason and on the existence of truth, without which the gadgets could not function. GPS, to name just one example, depends on a complex working of multiple satellites, all of which presuppose a synchronization of time, geographical coordinates, orbits, and mathematical algorithms in order to function. If any one of these were even slightly miscalculated, the entire GPS system could not work. And in order to calculate anything, there has to be truth toward which the calculation can arrive.

And it is not just the mechanistic workings that point to truth: our automatic reactions to their workings and failings point to the union of factual and moral truth. When we ask why or how something is the case and then respond accordingly, we show how the things of the world direct our moral actions—how what something is guides what we ought to do. With GPS, we have the ability to locate anything on the globe. Questions immediately follow: Should we use it to spy on another country or our neighbor? Should we use it to drop precision bombs on an enemy? The fact that we can disagree on how exactly we ought to act does not negate the inherent connection between what something is and how we should act in light of it.

From our own daily experience, then, we know that reason is indeed worthy of our faith. It is wrong to say, as some secularists assert, that faith is contrary to reason, since reason presupposes our faith in rationality as such. We have faith that reason can find the truth about things, about actions, and about meaning. It is not an accident that contemporary secularity's crisis of reason has followed four centuries of philosophical attacks on religion: the culture of suspicion toward God, the foundation of order and truth within the universe, has turned on itself, so much so that some thinkers deny that we can know anything of substance or meaning at all. Without faith reason cannot function; and if reason cannot function, then our very humanity is denied.

Hence, for the secular world to recover the use of reason and an understanding of the truth, it must first accept the need for faith, for trust in the created order, and, by extension, for trust in the creator of this order. In this way, religious faith serves as "the convinced and convincing advocate of reason" because it "stirs reason to move beyond all isolation and willingly to run risks so that it may attain whatever is beautiful, good and true."[19] That is, faith aids reason by calling the latter away from navel gazing and back toward its ultimate end that is the truth. And when reason is homed in on the truth, it leads to God.

Faith and reason, then, are inherently intertwined, since they mutually presuppose and depend upon the other. Faith, in addition to providing reason with confidence in its own abilities, also functions as "a purifying force for reason itself."[20] Reason, explains Benedict XVI, "can never be completely free of the danger of a certain ethical blindness caused by the dazzling effect of power and special interests."[21] The advent of certain biotechnologies over the past half-century shows how reason, in love with its own power and potential, can collapse in on itself without faith to redirect its gaze back toward the broader truth it is intended to serve. Faith purifies reason by reminding it that, along with knowledge of the truth and the power to harness that truth, there arise corresponding moral and ethical concerns.

For example, for decades science has been taking human gametes to create human life in a laboratory. Now these same laboratories have modified the very DNA of these created embryos. By recalling reason to its role as servant—rather than fabricator—of truth, faith prevents reason from exercising power for power's sake.

What can potentially be done by science or reason's power should not necessarily be done, and it should not be done if it will violate the truths of nature or the human person.

This is not to say that faith or religion are to control the workings of reason or science—far from it. Faith respects the autonomy of reason and science to work according to their own internal principles. To be sure, reason and science have produced tremendous benefits for humanity, from antibiotics to x-rays, from airplanes to telecommunications. When these products of human reason are used for the enrichment of human life according to the truth of the natural law and the proper ends of humanity, we applaud them as expressions of the talents God has given us, talents that ultimately point us back to Him. But when these products transgress the natural law, faith calls upon reason to reconsider or even to halt its workings lest a grave wrong be committed.

It is the nature of truth itself that allows faith and reason to work together in this complementary fashion. "God is Truth itself,"[22] declares the *Catechism of the Catholic Church*. Therefore, faith and reason both lead to the same end by their respective means.

[T]he God of creation is also the God of salvation history. It is the one and the same God who establishes and guarantees the intelligibility and reasonableness of the natural order of things upon which scientists confidently depend, and who reveals himself as the Father of our Lord Jesus Christ. This unity of truth, natural and revealed, is embodied in a living and personal way in Christ... He is the *eternal Word* in whom all things were created, and he is the *incarnate Word* who in his entire person reveals the Father. What human reason seeks without knowing it can be found only through Christ: what is revealed in him is the full truth of everything which was created in him and through him and which therefore in him finds its fulfilment.[23]

Here we also see the foundational way in which reason aids faith, for reason is the means by which God speaks to us, both in Sacred Scripture and in the person of His Son, the eternal and incarnate Word. Faith is reasonable by its nature because God is the author and end of reason, and He has given us the natural ability to understand rationally His revelation to us. And since all human beings have the ability to reason, God's revelation can be heard, understood, and believed by all people, regardless of ethnicity, nationality, or geography. Christ is the Word spoken eternally by God the Father for all human beings to hear and respond in faith.

By extension, reason enables the enterprise of theology, the rational study of God and His revelation. Theology is, in the famous definition of St. Anselm, faith seeking understanding. We have already seen how reflecting on creation points to the existence of God, the creator. When applied to God Himself, theological reasoning helps us understand in rational terms God's revelation to us and the nature of our relationship to Him. Theology formulates the reality of faith into the dogmas and teachings that help us comprehend who God is and how He has acted in history. Transubstantiation, for example, is a philosophical term that helps us grasp how the bread and wine of the Eucharist are, in fact, the body and blood of Christ. At the same time, we also recognize the limits of reason when discussing the mysteries of God: whatever we say in human terms, even in the most profound theological books, barely catches a glimpse of the immeasurable splendor of these divine realities.

Since reason helps us express the essence of faith, it keeps faith from the constant temptation to turn its attention away from God and squarely onto ourselves. This happens when faith allows itself to be consumed by feelings and emotions, or by fantasies about idealized humanity and human accomplishments that are divorced from the limits imposed by human nature and understood by human reason. St. John Paul clearly identifies the danger of faith enclosed on itself: "Deprived of reason, faith has stressed feeling and experience, and so run the risk of no longer being a universal proposition. It is an illusion to think that faith, tied to weak reasoning, might be more penetrating; on the contrary, faith then runs the grave risk of withering into myth or superstition."[24]

Finally, reason can purify religion when the latter misdirects its perspective toward something that is evil. It is reason that corrects the heinous notion that violence against innocents can be perpetrated in the name of God. Reason teaches us that God would never authorize an action or behavior that is contrary to the nature and the natural law that He created, and violence against innocents is a flagrant violation of the life God Himself created. We glimpse this through faith as well as through reason.

For centuries, thinkers from Tertullian to Martin Luther to Karl Barth have questioned the role that reason plays in faith, viewing it as a foreign incursion into the purity of God's revelation. In fact, reason is as equally inseparable from God's revelation as it is from our nature as human beings. It is because of reason that we can have faith in the first place, and it is as the Word, the incarnate expression of truth and rationality itself, that God speaks to us. Without the twin wings of faith and reason working in tandem, we will never rise to glimpse the fullness of truth.

The Catholic worldview is not just a choice, equal in value to secularity or any other worldview. It presents the truth about who human beings are and how they should live. This truth, as we shall see, is also far more compelling than anything that secularity has to offer. It hinges upon a prior, foundational truth: the existence of God. To this truth we now turn.

❦ CHAPTER 3

The Existence of God

In 1870 the First Vatican Council forcefully proclaimed the existence of God:

> The holy, catholic, apostolic, Roman Church believes and confesses there is one God, true and living, Creator and Lord of heaven and earth, almighty, eternal, immense, incomprehensible, infinite in his intellect and will, and in all perfection. As he is one, unique, and spiritual substance, entirely simple and unchangeable, we must proclaim him distinct from the world in existence and essence....
>
> The same Holy Mother Church holds and teaches that God, the beginning and end of all things, can be known with certainty from the things that were created through the natural light of human reason, for "ever since the creation of the world his invisible nature...has been clearly perceived in the things that have been made" (Romans 1:20); but it pleased His wisdom and goodness to reveal Himself and the eternal decrees of His will [to the human race] in another and a supernatural way, as the apostle [Paul] says: "In many and

41

various ways God spoke of old to our fathers by the prophets; but in these last days he has spoken to us by a Son" (Hebrews 1:1–2).[1]

The confidence and clarity of this proclamation is somewhat startling to us, who have become accustomed to hearing God's existence questioned, if not rejected outright, by many in our secular society. This confidence should be instructive as we begin to consider the existence of God: belief in God is not an absurd proposition or superstition. There are numerous reasons for not only believing that God exists, but also trusting confidently that He cares for us as individual human beings.

Before delving into these reasons, let us underscore four points in the declaration from the First Vatican Council. First, there is only one God who is real and exists distinct from the universe, which was created by and is contingent upon Him. Second, this God is pure spirit and, unlike corporeal human beings with their finite nature, is all-powerful and eternal, that is, everlasting and not subject to limits of space and time. Third, God's existence can be known by the use of human reason alone. Fourth, God willed that purely natural knowledge of Him was not enough, so He revealed Himself gradually over time in a way that can only be known through faith. The culmination of this revelation is the incarnation of the Son of God, Jesus Christ. When it comes to questions about God's existence, it is this third point that generates the most interest and will be our main focus.

As mentioned in the first chapter, the difference between faith in general and religious faith is not the act of believing, but the things believed. Knowledge based on faith—on our trust in another person and her account—is perfectly normal and legitimate. In the case of religious faith, we believe in God, who, as a pure spirit existing independent of the universe, cannot be tested or examined empirically by measurement and observation. Instead, as St. Thomas Aquinas explained, we know through reason that God exists by His effects, which are the ways by which He makes Himself known.[2] These effects are seen and felt both in the external world and in the internal workings of our hearts. Since we are beginning from effects to an unseen cause, we cannot "prove" God's existence the way that we can prove certain truths in geometry or mathematics; with these latter truths, their existence becomes readily apparent, as when we add two apples to three oranges to total five pieces of fruit. Because we cannot see God, to show His existence we proceed like a doctor making a diagnosis: the patient has several symptoms, the effects of being sick, and from these symptoms the doctor determines the particular illness, which is the cause of the symptoms. Hence in choosing to believe in God, we are making a judgment based on the evidence for His existence. We then trust that our judgment is correct.

This is why belief in God is ultimately a matter of faith, not empirical knowledge, and therefore a choice of the believer: the evidence points toward God's existence, but, since He cannot be seen or examined directly, the evidence cannot coerce the mind toward acceptance of the truth of God in the manner of a math problem or science experiment. Two added to three will always equal five: this is a truth that we cannot rationally deny. But when considering the existence of God, it is still possible, despite the evidence presented, not to believe in Him, not to trust that He is real. This is one of the factors that make faith a different sort of knowledge from empirical knowledge: faith cannot be compelled, because it presupposes the freedom of the believer in making a choice to believe, as we will see later. This is an important point to keep in mind as we consider the rational evidence for God's existence—we can know with certitude that God exists, but we do so ultimately through faith, not through reason. A second important point will follow as we examine arguments against God's existence: the insights of science and reason also depend upon faith, upon trust in certain ideas or prior assumptions, for their function.

Knowing God and Showing God's Existence

Evidence for God's existence apart from His revelation to us is intimately bound with the question of how we are aware of God, a purely spiritual being whom we cannot see, in the first place. The Catholic Church has long taught that "the desire for God is written in the human heart, because man is created by God and for God; and God never ceases to draw man to himself."[3] God "hardwired" human beings to know Him in the very act of creation. We become aware of God through the act of self-reflection by considering who we are, what is surrounding us, and what is happening to us. By reasoning in this manner, therefore, we become aware of God's existence through five general approaches, two pertaining to the external world and three pertaining to our personal experience, as outlined by the late Cardinal Avery Dulles: contingency, design, conscience, our own natural restlessness as human beings, and religious experience.[4] Of these five, the first two demonstrate the reasonableness of belief in God; the latter three are, for most people, the more convincing reasons for accepting the gift of faith. None of these arguments is intended to be sufficient on its own: it is their collective force that cogently points to the truth of God's existence.

First, the contingency, or dependence, of everything we encounter in the world is a fact determined by our own experience: everything we encounter in our daily lives has been made by something prior. These things, from mountain peaks to manufactured goods, had a specific origin, and they are constantly in flux, as eventually, from the eroded mountain peak to the malfunctioning dishwasher, they breakdown. When we consider the earth itself along with the other heavenly bodies, the solar system, and the universe, we see the same evidence of a specific origin and constant change. It stands to reason that these, too, were made by something prior. But what? We cannot reason causes backward to infinite regress: there must be something distinct from this chain of events and uncaused in itself. In the words of Cardinal Dulles, "[t]here could be no contingent beings unless there were at least one self-sufficient Necessary Being, from whom all the others directly or indirectly derive their existence."[5] As distinct from the chain of events, this Necessary Being whom we call God is wholly unlike any created reality with which we are familiar. Since the entire universe is distinct from and contingent upon this Being, we reason that God must be omnipotent and everlasting, without beginning or end. He is the Unmoved Mover, the Uncaused Cause who Himself must be the fullness of existence.

Biologist Richard Dawkins, the most vociferous and most prominent atheist attacking religion today, vehemently rejects the argument of contingency in his book *The God Delusion*. Dawkins asserts that contingency arguments for God's existence "make the entirely unwarranted assumption that God himself is immune to regress."[6] A "terminator to an infinite regress" is a "dubious luxury," and is problematic in his view "because the designer himself (herself/itself) immediately raises the bigger problem of his own origin.... Far from terminating the vicious regress, God aggravates it with a vengeance."[7]

Dawkins's criticisms are hampered by his naturalist worldview that denies the existence of realities that lie outside the capabilities of scientific verification. Since he cannot put God under a microscope or dissect God in a lab, Dawkins simply assumes that He does not exist; if God did exist, Dawkins surmises, He "would have to be complex and statistically improbable" to be capable of designing the universe.[8] In other words, Dawkins's argument depends on his prior faith that only what is empirically measurable is real. But there is no empirical proof for Dawkins's assertion. Rather, he approaches science in this way because his faith in his naturalist worldview has colored his scientific perspective.

The argument from contingency is based on philosophical reasoning, not scientific experimentation, and it hinges on a prior understanding—the nature of God Himself. Constrained by his purely scientific perspective, Dawkins cannot admit what God must be if He is the Uncaused Cause: God is the fullness of Being in and of Himself. He is *the reality* of the universe; everything else receives its existence from Him, the creator. He therefore must be, in the words of the First Vatican Council, "almighty, eternal, immense, incomprehensible, infinite in his intellect and will, and in all perfection," existing without corporeity and transcending the limits of space and time. If God were not so, then He would indeed be contingent and part of the chain of regression as Dawkins insists. But God is not the object of science—He is the prior reality without which science cannot exist.

Hence to acknowledge the existence of God we do not use scientific knowledge with its measuring of physical things, but metaphysical knowledge, that is, philosophical knowledge of things' natures in themselves. Metaphysical knowledge exceeds the limits of scientific knowledge because it seeks not just how something works, but why it works. Metaphysical knowledge includes reasoning about realities such as courage, love, happiness, sadness, and even existence itself. And reasoning about existence brings us directly into the mystery of God.

The ancient Greeks were as aware as we are that something cannot come from nothing. In our experience, we do not encounter things that cause their own existence. Through reason we induce that God is the source and origin of the universe and everything in it. Later in this chapter we will see how revelation shows that God is also far more than the mere postulated answer to a philosophical problem.

The second argument for the existence of God is that of design, which points to the intricate order of and within the cosmos. Every natural object and living thing is an enormously complex entity whose component parts are so delicately ordered that they suggest a prior designer, an intelligent planner, who in a manner unknown to us, has "arranged all things by measure and number and weight" (Wis. 11:20). From the heavenly bodies with their exact laws of motion, to human beings whose existence hinges upon the coordinated and simultaneous movement of dozens of biological processes, to the immense variety of life in the animal kingdom and in nature at large, it is an utter marvel how they all have come to work, and to work so efficiently. In fact, the workings of heavenly bodies and living things depend on a great number of prior, underlying factors that, if altered in any way, the planets would collapse and life on Earth would come to a swift end. The extraordinary complexity and intricately refined nature of the universe, for example, has been enumerated starkly by the late theologian and physicist Stanley Jaki:

> If gravity had been stronger by one part in 10^{40}, the universe would have long ago undergone a catastrophic collapse instead of a systematic expansion. Again, if the strength of the initial explosion, or Big Bang, had been different by one part in 10^{60}, the universe would have taken on a very different

evolutionary course. If [the ratio of the combined masses of proton and electron to the mass of the neutron] had been slightly less, hydrogen atoms would become unstable and the sun would have long ago faded.

Again a slightly different ratio of the respective strengths of the electromagnetic and nuclear forces would prevent the formation in supernovae of that very element carbon, which is the mainstay of organic life as we know it. Further, a mere five percent decrease in the strength of nuclear force would prevent the formation of deuterium which has a key role in the nuclear chain reaction within the sun and makes it possible for the sun to become a stable, long-lived star. As to neutrinos, the lightest of all fundamental particles, if their mass had been ten times larger than their actual value, or 10^{-34} kg, they would have, because of their very large number, caused a gravitational collapse of the universe.[9]

This radically precise and extremely fragile universe strongly suggests the existence of a God who has "tuned" all its aspects to join together in one cosmic symphony. The same goes for living creatures, and above all human beings, whose biological complexity and unique ability to reason also suggest that they were designed by God. As Joseph Ratzinger writes, "The more we know of the universe the more profoundly we are struck by a Reason whose ways we can only contemplate with astonishment. In pursuing them we can see anew that creating Intelligence to whom we owe our own reason.... In what is most vast, in the world of heavenly bodies, we see revealed a powerful Reason that holds the universe together."[10]

Yet the argument from design is also vehemently rejected by Dawkins, who argues that evolution's theory of natural selection "shatters the illusion of design within the domain of biology, and teaches us to be suspicious of any kind of design hypothesis in physics and cosmology as well."[11] The theory of evolution by means of natural selection holds that chance mutations in genetic development which are advantageous to an organism are passed down to offspring, and these offspring are, by these advantageous mutations, made more "fit" for survival than their fellow organisms. These offspring that survive also pass on the mutations, called now adaptations by virtue of their success, and they surpass their rivals, which die out in the wild world: this survive or die motif is the mechanism of natural selection. This theory, made popular by Charles Darwin in the late nineteenth century, maintains that evolution occurs on two levels: microevolution, which refers to the adaptations that occur of organisms within a species, such as the changing of birds' beaks; and macroevolution, which is the changing of one species into another, genetically different species. According to the theory, both types of evolution occur by means of the natural selection just described. Since natural selection unfolds according to a determinate set of probabilities "without any deliberate guidance,"[12] Dawkins asserts this theory as grounds for denying that God has designed the cosmos.

When looked at more closely, Dawkins's relationship to Darwinism seems to exhibit a great deal of faith—his trust in the theory exceeds what science allows. For example, to explain the origins of life and of the universe he turns to the anthropic principle, which he says "has a faintly Darwinian feel."[13] The anthropic principle holds that "the fundamental constants of physics had to be in their respective Goldilocks zones" for life to come into existence, and Earth happens to be one planet out of a billion others where the infinitesimally small odds of hosting life exist.[14] "The anthropic principle kicks in to explain that we have to be in one of those universes (presumably a minority) whose by-laws happened to be propitious to our eventual evolution and hence contemplation of the problem."[15]

The anthropic principle is essentially a circular argument: Life could exist on earth, so therefore it does, and only because the conditions of Earth made life statistically possible. This theory sheds no light whatsoever on how exactly or why life came to be in the first place. It amounts to an explanation that "life exists because it could," which is hardly a scientific answer. Dawkins claims that the theistic answer to the origins of the cosmos—that God created it by His own will—"is deeply unsatisfying, because it leaves the existence of God unexplained."[16] At least the theist makes an attempt at an explanation: it is really Dawkins's anthropic principle that fails to satisfy.

There is much more faith, in the generic sense of trust, involved in the enterprise of science than Dawkins and his fellow scientific naturalists care to admit. For one, evolutionary science cannot empirically measure evolution the way that physics can measure acceleration of a projectile or chemistry can measure the quantity of hydrogen molecules in an ounce of water. Rather, evolutionary science is an exercise of inductive reasoning, and therefore proceeds in the exact same manner as the demonstrations for God's existence: from effects to an unseen cause. Just as there can be no definitive proof for God's existence, so, too, there is no definitive proof for evolution: its veracity as a theory depends on the trust that individuals have in the evidence for its claim. Hence Dawkins himself acknowledges that someday we may find an explanation better than natural selection.[17]

Currently, science still does not know how exactly the world came to exist or how the first living organism came to be, and it may never know: there can only be hope that by trusting in the work of science this knowledge can be obtained eventually and somehow. Science, then, proceeds from a prior act of faith: that the universe is intelligible, and that through advances in scientific techniques more information about the world may follow. There is strong evidence, for example, that the universe and its content came to be through a massive explosion—a big bang—but that begs the question of how the explosion was caused, and where the material that preceded and followed the explosion came from. To exclude God's role in the creation of the world outright on the grounds that science will eventually find an explanation that does not require His existence is an act of faith parallel to that made by religion.

As regards the beginning of life, Dawkins writes that "[t]he origin of life was the chemical event, or series of events, whereby the vital conditions for natural selection first came about. The major ingredient was heredity, either DNA or (more probably) something that copies like DNA but less accurately, perhaps the related molecule RNA."[18] This rather unsettled thesis lacks the precision that scientific naturalism claims for itself, and also fails to explain how—or why—life came into existence. Dawkins boasts that "I shall not be surprised if, within the next few years, chemists report that they have successfully midwifed a new origin of life in the laboratory."[19] His boast conveys his deeply held faith in science, and a trust that exceeds what scientific evidence has found to date: no non-living thing has ever self-generated a living organism in recorded history. It is also ironic that Dawkins's particular act of faith in the chemists trusts that they, as intelligent designers, will be able to *create* the conditions for life.[20] It all sounds so much like the creation argument of theists, yet Dawkins rejects that argument root and branch.

Regardless of whether science ever finds the exact manner in which the world and life came to be, religious believers are justified in believing in God and His creation just as scientists are in believing in science. (And, of course, believers are right to trust science and its findings as well.) From the twin foundations of the metaphysical reasoning just described and of God's revelation to us, believers know that God created the world from nothing. Revelation tells us that human beings were deliberately willed by Him to share in His love and were created as the pinnacle of His creation. No finding of science can contradict this because belief in the creation of the world is perfectly compatible with science, regardless of the content of scientific theories postulated to explain the world and human origins.

Revelation and religious faith do not claim to say *how exactly* God brought into being the cosmos and human life *in the precise physical sense.*[21] The cosmos and the first human couple could have been brought into their exact physical form by God in a number of ways, with a physiological evolution possible among them, and human beings are free to use their intellect and will to inquire after these ways—to seek God's imprint by the use of science and other means.[22] In fact, our innate inclination to inquire after our origins and into the nature of things is one way that God has oriented His creatures back to Himself, the author of all things.

This, then, is the purpose of science: to examine empirically the substance of God's creation. For this reason the Catholic Church, despite biased stereotypes to the contrary, has long promoted and fostered the study of nature: from her adoption of Greek philosophy in her first centuries, to her preservation of the pagan classics after the fall of the Roman Empire, to her founding of the world's first universities in the twelfth century, to her patronage of art and architecture, to the work of her own clergy in the field of science, to her contemporary pontifical academies for the study of various academic disciplines, the Church has been both a bulwark and a catalyst for the natural sciences. The more we know about the natural world the more we can appreciate the sheer brilliance of its supernatural origins.

Religious faith has nothing to fear from scientific inquiry, for, as Pope Leo XIII taught at the end of the nineteenth century, "truth cannot contradict truth."[23] As chemist Stacy Trasancos explains, *"Faith and science are two different manifestations of the same reality. When they seem to have conflicting conclusions, it is because our knowledge is not complete."*[24] The Church respects the province of science to explore the natural order. She cautions, however, that science ought not to overstep its bounds: that is, it ought not take its empirical knowledge and claim a monopoly on metaphysical knowledge from it, as scientific naturalists such as Dawkins and Pinker have done. Ratzinger writes,

> We cannot say: creation or evolution, inasmuch as these two things respond to two different realities. The story [in Genesis 2] of the dust of the earth and the breath of God...does not in fact explain how human persons come to be but rather what they are. It explains their inmost origin and casts light on the project that they are. And, vice versa, the theory of evolution seeks to understand and describe biological developments. But in doing so it cannot explain where the "project" of human persons comes from, nor their inner origin, nor their particular nature. *To that extent we are faced here with two complementary—rather than mutually exclusive—realities.*[25]

Dawkins rejects the complementarity of creation and evolutionary science advocated by Trasancos and Ratzinger. Instead, he argues that the two "are close to being irreconcilably different."[26]

Having rejected God along with the possibility of creation and design entirely, Dawkins uses the scientific theory of evolution via natural selection to make claims of metaphysical knowledge—such as "Darwin made it possible to be an intellectually fulfilled atheist."[27] Dawkins holds that natural selection allows for the gradual development of new species through macroevolution, and argues that slow and unguided natural selection destroys the notion of design in the universe. Whereas evolution is a scientific theory that can be scrutinized empirically, design and unguided natural selection are two distinct metaphysical claims that interpret the results of physical science. In other words, design and unguided natural selection are both interpretations that require faith.

The problem facing Dawkins is that despite his claims to the contrary, unguided macroevolution requires a tremendous amount of faith that unplanned mutations and survival rates all end up harmonizing into working forms and passing on neatly to the next generation. When we consider the physical design of human beings in particular, and couple this physical reality with the existence of an immaterial human soul that is capable of reasoning and loving, it is very plausible to believe that some intelligent being—God—somehow, in a manner unknown to us, has deliberately directed any potential developments, including any evolutionary developments, so that they all end up in the symphony that is human biology and human reasoning. As Cardinal Dulles explains, "The argument [that God designed the universe] does not deny that natural selection could play a role in the development of higher forms of life. That which is unfit, no doubt, ceases to exist. But to account for the tendency of life to evolve to higher levels we need to postulate a purposiveness behind and within creation."[28]

The assertions of Dawkins and scientific naturalists notwithstanding, the theory of evolution in itself cannot cast doubt on

God's existence. Rather it is their faith in atheism that has colored their interpretation of the theory to exclude God's existence outright. Science contributes enormously and positively to our knowledge of the cosmos and of our physical make-up. But the sheer force of these epic realities points to something beyond themselves, and this is evidence to help believers assent firmly to God's existence.

The arguments from contingency and design are rational, metaphysical approaches to demonstrating the existence of God. Together, by considering the world and its existence, they show that although we cannot see God or subject Him to scientific analysis, it is reasonable to believe that God is real. But since we are "hardwired" to know God, and since we are made in His image and likeness, we can also become aware of God's existence by looking at and within ourselves. There are three additional arguments of this kind.

The third argument for God's existence is the argument from conscience, which Cardinal Dulles explains as "the 'inner voice' that discloses the unconditional moral imperative"[29] to do good and avoid evil. An inner sense for this imperative is present in all human beings whose instant reaction after an action, either of shame and guilt or of joy and satisfaction, point to some standard that exists beyond themselves. Reflecting on this reaction, conscience enables us to see that there must be some higher authority to whom our actions, and by extension our own selves, are subject. This higher power must have the capacity to judge human actions and then reward or punish them accordingly, and in order to do so, the judge must possess the fullness of knowledge and power. Again we are brought back to the definition of the First Vatican Council with which we began this chapter: the reality of conscience points to the prior reality of God, who must be "omnipotent, eternal, immense, incomprehensible, infinite in intellect and will, and in every perfection."

The nature of conscience, with its innate sense for God's existence and for right action, has been attacked both by nonbelievers and by proponents of moral relativism. They claim that conscience is not innate but an external feeling of guilt imposed by society, and that as a result all morality is subjective, as we saw in the previous chapter. Dawkins himself sees our moral nature as the product of natural selection, and for this reason he denies any objective sanction of our altruistic or selfish genes.[30]

Blessed John Henry Newman helps us meet this objection by distinguishing a twofold feeling of conscience.[31] One is the "moral sense" that directs the mind toward the law and to what exactly ought to be done. The second is the perception of "the dictate of an authoritative monitor" that seemingly exists independent of the person; this is why we commonly speak of conscience as a "voice," someone other than ourselves who is speaking to us. Since each person's internal conscience experiences not just a rule, but the seeming presence of another person, conscience can stir our emotions, which respond to people, not to rules or societal expectations. Because of this emotional element Newman concludes that conscience

> always involves the recognition of a living object towards which it is directed. Inanimate things cannot stir our affections; these are correlative with persons. If, as is the case, we feel responsibility, are ashamed, are frightened, at transgressing the voice of conscience, this implies that there is One to whom we are responsible, before whom we are ashamed, whose claims upon us we fear. If, on doing wrong, we feel the same tearful, brokenhearted sorrow which overwhelms us on

hurting a mother; if, on doing right, we enjoy the same sunny serenity of mind, the same soothing, satisfactory delight which follows on our receiving praise from a father, we certainly have within us the image of some person, to whom our love and veneration look, in whose smile we find our happiness, for whom we yearn, towards whom we direct our pleading, in whose anger we are troubled and waste away. These feelings in us are such as require for their exciting cause an intelligent being.... If the cause of these emotions does not belong to this visible world, the Object to which [the malefactor's] perception is directed must be Supernatural and Divine; and thus the phenomena of Conscience, as a dictate, avail to impress the imagination with the picture of a Supreme Governor, a Judge, holy, just, powerful, all-seeing, retributive.[32]

Dawkins got half of the equation right: our moral sense is indeed hardwired in us as part of our nature. But he fails to see that this moral sense does not merely anchor us to our ancestral past: it opens us to God, toward whom all our actions and emotions are ultimately aimed. Our "Good Samaritan urges" to show mercy to a debtor or to adopt a child cannot be explained as "misfirings, Darwinian mistakes," as Dawkins alleges.[33] Rather they are our willed responses, born of emotional reactions and rational reflections, to the God whose voice calls us in the depths of our conscience to respond to Him.

The fourth approach to God's existence is "the restlessness of the human heart."[34] As the argument from conscience also reveals, human beings are created with an astonishing intellectual capacity that far exceeds even the most cunning of our fellow mammals. We have the ability to reason, to think abstractly about the past, present, and future as well as how we ought to act in a given situation.

Because of this ability it follows that we have freedom to act as we choose according to our own deliberations. Unlike all other animals, we have the power to choose actions that run counter to our instincts. And with freedom comes the extraordinary abilities to love, to serve, to sacrifice, and to worship.

These abilities make us "restless" since they are all directed to something outside of ourselves. St. John Paul explains that "[i]n this creative restlessness beats and pulsates what is most deeply human: the search for truth, the insatiable need for the good, hunger for freedom, nostalgia for the beautiful, and the voice of conscience."[35] Only the infinite and unlimited God is capable of fully satisfying these infinite human desires. St. Augustine's prayer to God is the most famous expression of this reality: "[Y]ou have made us for yourself, and our heart is restless until it rests in you."[36] We can see this truth when we see the change in disposition and behavior of someone who has converted or returned to the Catholic faith after a life of dissipation: after years of restlessness from seeking happiness in the wrong places, the person has found inner peace by rejecting those activities and choosing to follow God.

It is with our hearts, rather than our eyes, that we see God, a fact that leads us to the final approach to knowing that God exists: we experience Him ourselves. After Jesus rose from the dead He could only be recognized by those with faith: the disciples on the road to Emmaus and the apostles fishing in the Sea of Tiberias saw the risen Jesus but they did not recognize Him until their hearts were opened by the gift of faith. Religious experience is a genuine encounter with the God whom we cannot see but is nonetheless real, and this experience is the most convincing manner by which people assent to the truth of God's existence.

Much religious experience is seemingly quite ordinary. The series of events that work out too well to be a mere coincidence, the sudden feeling of calm in the midst of a tense situation, and the surprise encounter with the very person we had prayed about earlier in the day are just a few of the ways that we encounter God and experience His providence. As William James explained in his study of this issue, religious experience "is as if there were in the human consciousness a sense of reality, a feeling of objective presence, a perception of what we may call 'something there.'"[37]

As just one example, let us consider the vocation story of a young religious sister, who, between her junior and senior years of college, was discerning whether to join her desired religious order immediately or return to finish her university education.[38] She had many thousands of dollars in student loans at this point, and she could not enter the order until her debt was paid. She prayed for a sign to help her choose. Shortly after confiding her dilemma to her pastor, she received a phone call: a parishioner had just died, and he had left a large sum of money to the parish. The deceased's daughter, having been informed of the young woman's dilemma by the pastor, decided to send the money to pay the young woman's debt so she could enter the order. Using a series of seemingly ordinary human events, God had given her the sign she needed.

Dawkins claims that religious experience is "the least convincing" argument for God because it can be discounted by knowledge of psychology.[39] It is true that not every claimed religious experience is in fact one, and it is true that some have tried to claim religious experience as a justification for their heinous actions. But the abuse of something does not negate its use. The apostles saw Jesus risen from the dead; so certain were they of their experience that they were violently killed for it. The same can be said for the countless martyrs in the two thousand years since: they were certain that their experience of God, and His promise of eternal life to come with Him, was worth more than their very lives. The witness of the martyrs is a powerful validation of our own religious experiences: there have been very many martyrs in very many circumstances in very many years, yet they all died for a single reason: they all knew the same God.

But Dawkins, or the worldview he represents, will not allow for anything to exist outside of his scientific naturalist worldview: so when he confronts the experience that 70,000 people had in Fatima, Portugal, in 1917, of the sun dramatically dropping in the sky, he is forced to dismiss it. Now, suddenly, Dawkins wants us to ignore psychology, which teaches that 70,000 people cannot hallucinate the exact same thing.[40] From the experiences of the apostles, to those at Fatima, to our own, psychology cannot simply explain away the possibility of a true encounter with God, even if Dawkins does not want to believe it.

Miracles represent the religious experience *par excellence*. Dawkins dismisses the possibility of miracles because they "violate the principles of science."[41] In the Gospels of Matthew, Mark, and Luke, the word for miracle is *dynamis*, meaning an act of power, and it is the source of our own "dynamic" and "dynamite"; the world "miracle" is literally "something to be wondered at." Jesus' miracles were wondered at because they were astonishing acts of divine power. They did not overturn any laws of reason: they did not square the circle, nor did they violate the principle of non-contradiction. Rather they manifested the power that God the creator has over His creation, so much so that they transcended the very limits of nature. By walking on water, by turning water into wine, by giving sight to the blind, by cleansing lepers, and by raising the dead, Jesus invited us to believe in Him, for His actions were only possible because of His divinity.

Miracles do challenge the limits of scientific knowledge, which is often left speechless at their occurrence—perhaps this is the real reason that Dawkins does not want to take them seriously. But miracles in the form of inexplicable healings of debilitating physical ailments as well as miraculous events have continued from the time of Jesus through our own times. Today, when the Catholic Church acknowledges the occurrence of a miracle due to the intercession of a saint or some other cause, she does so only after a team of medical or other secular officials conclude after exhaustive research that no rational or scientific explanation can account for what has happened. Three examples of the general types of documented miracles will here suffice.

First, there are the miracles, generally involving the healing of illnesses, associated with the direct intercession of a saint on behalf of the living. To name just one of the most famous and recent canonizations, in 2016 the Church canonized Mother Theresa of Calcutta, the famous foundress of the Missionaries of Charity who worked with the poorest of the poor in India's slums. Although she was widely acclaimed for her heroic sanctity in her lifetime, Mother Theresa still needed two miraculous healings attributed to her intercession in order to be declared a saint. Two healings were indeed examined medically and deemed inexplicable: the complete disappearance of a tumor of a non-Christian Indian woman, and the reversal of a terminal coma of an electrical engineer in Brazil. In both instances the intercession of Mother Theresa before God was directly sought through the prayers of caretakers asking for healing despite the medical odds against it.[42]

Second, there are miracles occurring within nature as well as physical healings associated with appearances of the Blessed Virgin Mary. To name but one, in 1858, a beautiful young woman appeared to fourteen-year-old Bernadette Soubiroux on eighteen occasions in a grotto in France. When asked by Bernadette to identify herself, the woman gave an unusual, ungrammatical response:

"I am the Immaculate Conception." Prompted by the woman, whom no one else could see, Bernadette dug into the ground where she stood and discovered flowing spring water. The woman also asked that a chapel be built at this spot. After several years of skepticism and examination, it was concluded that the woman was the Blessed Virgin Mary, and a chapel was built there. Since then the waters of Our Lady of Lourdes have been sought by millions of pilgrims from all over the world because of their reported healing powers. While untold numbers of spiritual healings have taken place here, there have been sixty-nine inexplicable healings of all sorts of physical ailments.[43] These healings have been attributed to Our Lady of Lourdes.

Third, there are miraculous events that cannot be explained by reason alone. One famous instance occurred in Italy in the eighth century: at Mass, a priest, plagued by misgivings over whether Jesus was truly present in the Eucharist, saw the newly consecrated bread and wine change into live flesh and live blood before his eyes. The astonished priest showed the transformed elements to the people present, who quickly ran to spread the news to the villagers of Lanciano. To this day the miracle endures: the host-flesh remains as human flesh not decayed, and the blood has coagulated into five globules; both of these remain on display in the church in Lanciano. Both the host-flesh and the blood have been tested in labs by scientists, with comprehensive examinations occurring in the 1970s. Lab analysis has confirmed that the host-flesh is indeed muscular tissue of a human heart that has not suffered any decay despite the passage of over a thousand years and of exposure to the atmosphere. The blood contains minerals common to human blood, and it also contains proteins in the same proportions as found in the blood of living human beings. Both the host-flesh and the blood have the same AB blood type; this is the same type as is found stained on the Shroud of Turin, which is believed to be the burial cloth of Jesus. Upon publishing the findings of their investigation, the scientists of the United Nations' World Health Organization declared that the origin and composition of these elements in Lanciano are completely unique and have no scientific explanation.[44]

For these and countless other miracles, careful medical and scientific evaluations of each case have taken place, and in each instance, doctors and scientists were unable to find a natural cause of the cures or events. As was the case with Jesus' miracles, the principles of science stand in awe of these acts of God. But as with the other demonstrations of God's existence, the miracles themselves do not coerce belief. It is perfectly possible for someone like Dawkins, who refuses to admit the possibility of any occurrence outside the province of science, to assert that science, somehow and someway, will be able to explain what we now think is inexplicable. The actual act of God in these miracles remains unseen: we see only the effect that is the cure, the event, or the transformation. Like the apostles before the risen Christ, we need faith—trust with a willing, docile heart—to see the reality of God and His infinite power working within the world He Himself created.

God Cares for His People

From these demonstrations we can conclude two things. First, the noble enterprise of science includes not just purely rational and experimental knowledge, but also a great deal of faith-based knowledge. So much of the scientific endeavor proceeds from countless acts of trust: trust that the universe has an order and can be known, trust that reason and experimentation are effective and reliable, trust that we can obtain meaningful knowledge from science. Second, the faith-based knowledge that believers in God possess is entirely reasonable, even if this knowledge cannot be proven empirically. The attributes of God as enumerated by the First Vatican Council make rational sense.

If we were left with these divine attributes alone, we would have "the philosophers' God," the God who is the rational necessity for explaining the origins of existence and the world. Over the centuries some have professed that this infinite God exists as the Unmoved Mover, but either they have assumed that God would want nothing to do with us, or they have refused to allow the possibility of any religious or personal relationship with Him. In the United States, the most prominent group among these was the seventeenth- and eighteenth-century Deists, who count Thomas Jefferson and other Founding Fathers among their adherents. Deists held that God is a disinterested "Watchmaker" who set the world into motion, but He has no interest in His creation and He does not intervene in the world in anyway. For the Deists there is no personal revelation of God, no miracles, and no interaction between God and human beings in this world.

Implicit in this notion of a purely philosophical God who is disinterested in human affairs are two assumptions.[45] First, the Fullness of Being itself is too great to concern Himself with small, finite things such as human beings. This assumption is still present in popular contemporary thought: writing about the decline of religious belief in *The New Yorker*, Adam Gopnik declares that if God is the fullness of existence, then "[s]omething *that* much bigger than Phil [or any human being] is so remote from Phil's problems that he might as well not be there for Phil at all."[46] Joseph Ratzinger offers a correction to this assumption: precisely because God is absolute, the fullness of existence in Himself, He encompasses not just the greatest things, but also the smallest.[47] Jesus expressed this reality during His ministry: "Even the hairs of your head are all numbered"; "So the last will be first, and the first last;" and likewise, "Let the children come to me, and do not hinder them; for to such belongs the kingdom of God" (Luke 12:7, Matt. 20:16, Luke 18:16). So far from being insignificant, human beings are the centerpiece of God's creation precisely because the infinite God elevates His creation toward Himself.

The second assumption of the purely philosophical God, related to the first, is that He is pure thought, completely enclosed upon Himself. Ratzinger counters that because God encompasses the whole of creation, reaching out even to the most seemingly insignificant aspects of it, the highest form of Being includes relationship, not isolation. Being is diffusive of itself. From revelation we know this to be true because God is Triune, that is, He is relational in His very essence. Even the act of creation is relational: God shares His goodness with what He chooses to bring into existence.

We can conclude, then, that God, the infinite and absolute supreme being, is not a distant Watchmaker of pure thought enclosed upon itself. He is rather a creative and relational intelligence, and since He creates, He is free. As Ratzinger puts it, since God "upholds and encompasses everything, [and] is consciousness, freedom, and love, then it follows automatically that the supreme factor in the world is not cosmic necessity"—nor is it science, nor evolution, nor mathematics—"but freedom."[48] God created freely, and made human beings free: only in this way could we enter into a relationship with Him.

This brings us to the limits of what purely rational knowledge can tell us about God. Beyond this, we depend upon God's own revelation of Himself, which He did in history, since He decided, for reasons known only to Himself, as the First Vatican Council explained, "to reveal Himself and the eternal decrees of His will to the human race in another and supernatural way." The act of God's self-revelation in time is called salvation history, which is recorded for us in Sacred Scripture and is passed on to us through the Sacred Tradition of the Church. Divine revelation confirms and surpasses what we are able to know about God through reason; hence most of our limited knowledge of God comes from the Bible.

Perhaps the most important event in the Bible that links God's revelation with the reasoning just described is God's encounter with Moses in the burning bush. There God reveals two things about Himself: "I am the God of your father, the God of Abraham, the God of Isaac, and the God of Jacob.... I am who I am" (Ex. 3:6, 14). God tells Moses that He is Being itself, He simply exists—"I AM"—without qualification. At the same time, He is the God of individual men—Abraham, Isaac, and Jacob. He who is Being itself is also relational, personal, and cares for His creation. The "I am" of Exodus is expressed by St. John the Evangelist as *Logos*, that is, creative and loving reason, the Word of God: "In the beginning was the Word, and the Word was with God, and the Word was God" (John 1:1).[49]

We know, then, that the God of the Bible—the God who is love, who cares for His people as a loving father, who is perfect justice and perfect mercy—is the eternal, infinite God who upholds the entire universe. The philosophers' God of the universe and the personal God of love are one and the same. We also know from Scripture that this Word, who was with God and who was God, "became flesh and dwelt among us" (John 1:14). The Word made flesh is Jesus Christ, the eternal Son, who came to teach us that God is the ultimate loving Father. In salvation history, Christ was God's final revelation, His final "Word" to be given: He had no reason to speak further because in Christ He revealed His very self. Christ, by His words and by His actions, testified that the essence of God is love and showed us what love is—the complete gift of self to another. It was love that prompted God to send His Son to redeem the human race, destitute from the effects of sin. It was love that led the Son, in obedience to the Father, to sacrifice Himself on the cross to atone for our sins. And it is love that we are called to give to God and to one another in this life so we can be happy with Him forever in the next life. This love is the essence of Christian life.

Through the incarnation God not only redeems us for eternal life, but He also reveals how we ought to live this life. As the Second Vatican Council teaches, Christ "fully reveals man to himself and makes his supreme calling clear."

> He Who is "the image of the invisible God" (Col. 1:15) is Himself the perfect man. To the sons of Adam He restores the divine likeness which had been disfigured from the first sin onward. Since human nature as He assumed it was not annulled, by that very fact it has been raised up to a divine dignity in our respect too. For by His incarnation the Son of God has united Himself in some fashion with every man. He worked with human hands, He thought with a human mind, acted by human choice and loved with a human heart. Born of the Virgin Mary, He has truly been made one of us, like us in all things except sin....
>
> By suffering for us He not only provided us with an example for our imitation, He blazed a trail, and if we follow it, life and death are made holy and take on a new meaning. The Christian man, conformed to the likeness of that Son Who is the firstborn of many brothers, received "the first-fruits of the Spirit" (Rom. 8:23) by which he becomes capable of discharging the new law of love. Through this Spirit, who

is "the pledge of our inheritance" (Eph. 1:14), the whole man is renewed from within, even to the achievement of "the redemption of the body" (Rom. 8:23).... Pressing upon the Christian to be sure, are the need and the duty to battle against evil through manifold tribulations and even to suffer death. But, linked with the paschal mystery and patterned on the dying Christ, he will hasten forward to resurrection in the strength which comes from hope.[50]

The restless hearts of human beings have their model and inspiration in the heart of Christ. Christ experienced both the joys and trials of life. He provides a model for us in our own lives to conform ourselves to the will of God at all times, even amidst suffering and death. Hence by imitating Christ "life and death are made holy and take on new meaning." Through the revelation of the Son of God, we receive and understand the very purpose of our lives: union with God forever.

Life Without God?

There have been countless philosophies and explanations of life and of how we ought to live. The Catholic account of life's meaning and purpose is the most beautiful and compelling one that exists, bar none. It is also true, and we know it is true because, of all rival accounts, it best speaks to the very center of the human heart and to all of life's deepest questions. The Catholic account comes directly from the experience of God and His revelation as just described and as transmitted to us in Sacred Scripture and Sacred Tradition. The Bible, so disparaged by Dawkins and his best-selling atheist colleagues, provides a comprehensive and unequaled account of the meaning of life. To paraphrase G. K. Chesterton, Jesus Christ's message is the "Good News" not just because it is good, but because it is "new."[51]

We are so familiar with Jesus' teachings that they no longer astonish us. But to astonish is exactly what they were intended to do. There is so much originality in the person and teachings of Jesus—from the love of "neighbor" understood as any human person, to the offering of the left cheek if someone strikes the right one, to the prohibition of divorce, to the Beatitudes, to His revelation of His unique relationship with God the Father, to His unprecedented status as God incarnate, crucified, and risen—that we can trust the authenticity of His message and of His status as the Son of God. No novelist or storywriter could have composed a story this unique, this coherent, and this powerful. With Christ, a true re-vel-ation, as in a pulling back of a veil, has occurred in making God known to humanity.[52] The truest and most comprehensive account of what it means to be human is appropriately authored by the creator of human beings.

While there certainly are nonbelievers living good, moral lives (many even are more attuned to the moral quality of their lives than some believers), the nonbeliever is hard pressed to present a compelling and comprehensive reason for living. Scientific naturalists such as Dawkins deny that life has any meaning or purpose at all: we "are biologically programmed to impute intentions to entities whose behaviour matters to us," states Dawkins, "[b]ut, like other brain mechanisms, these stances can misfire."[53] Seeking a greater purpose in actions or in life is a "misfire" for Dawkins. In fact, Dawkins dismisses the most fundamental of human questions—"Why?," which is asked by all human beings beginning as early as age two—as "a silly question."

> "Why?" in the sense of purpose is, in my opinion, not a meaningful question…. You can ask, "What are the factors

that led to something coming into existence?" That's a sensible question. But, "What is the purpose of the universe?" is a silly question. It has no meaning.[54]

Dawkins's reasoning is the exact opposite of Aristotle, who writes that "men do not think they know a thing till they have grasped the 'why' of it, which is to grasp its primary cause."[55] Dawkins is so absorbed by the dogmatic worldview of scientific naturalism, which denies the existence of purpose because it cannot be measured with instruments, that he deliberately rejects a fundamental dimension of our human nature.

How, then, shall human beings live according to the worldview of scientific naturalism? If "purpose questions are not good ones," then those who espouse this worldview cannot ask themselves about the meaning of life—they reject this possibility outright. Rather than ask, "Why am I here?" they instead are trapped in a suffocating dilemma: "I am alive here on earth. Yet I do not know why I am here and I cannot ask why. I know the biological factors that brought me into existence, but that does not at all satisfy the persistent desire within my heart for meaning. But, regardless, I must act or I will perish. How, then, shall I live? To what standards shall I appeal for direction?"

When scientific naturalists turn to the question of how human beings ought to live, they are confronting purpose questions. They may deny the existence of an ultimate purpose of life, but in fact they cannot devise an ordered society or ethical code without assuming the answers to some very fundamental "why" questions. As we saw in the previous chapter, to deny purpose is tantamount to denying the very ground that we stand upon. Without purpose and the possibility for a meaningful life we are left with Gopnik's deplorable vision for human happiness: "[B]y happiness we need mean only less of pain. You don't really have to pursue happiness; it is a subtractive quality. Anyone who has had a bad headache or a kidney stone or a toothache, and then hasn't had it, knows what happiness is."[56]

By investigating the grounds for believing in God, we have learned two things. First, it is perfectly reasonable to have faith in God. Second, science and the realm that today we normally ascribe to reason—morality, politics, human well-being—require faith: faith that they are reasonable enterprises, faith that these enterprises work and function effectively, and faith in the immeasurable assumptions that form the foundations of these enterprises. Society cannot, then, reasonably exclude perspectives on life, morality, politics, and human well-being that are shaped by religious faith, since the claims of the secularist and scientific naturalist also rest upon faith claims. The content of these perspectives, rather than their starting points, should determine their validity within the public square.

Since faith in God is reasonable, it remains to show what exactly faith entails. As mentioned at the outset of this chapter, the demonstrations for God's existence do not coerce faith. Still more is required, both of God and of us. We will now turn to what religious faith is and to what it means for us.

PART II
THE NATURE OF FAITH

❧ CHAPTER 4

What Does It Mean to Believe in God?

Believers and nonbelievers have two markedly distinct worldviews and ways of being. Ideally, believers try to live according to God's word, within a framework and according to standards that God has created, and with the hope that God is their ultimate goal at the end of this life. Nonbelievers settle for living according to the measures, standards, and hopes of their own devises that seem to be the logical path for human beings endowed with the gift of reason. But Pope Benedict XVI captures the necessary limitation of their attempts.

> Man left to himself, indifferent to God, proud of his absolute autonomy, eventually ends up following the idols of self-ishness, power, domination, polluting the relationship with himself and with others and taking paths that do not lead to life but death. The sad experience of history, especially of the last century, is a warning to all humanity.[1]

The lives of genuine believers are quantitatively and qualitatively different from nonbelievers. The quantitative difference is in the regular things believers do: attend church on Sunday, set aside time for prayer, celebrate religious holidays, abstain from certain foods during fast times, and live according to a certain moral code. It is the qualitative difference, however, that not only gives cause for the regular things that believers do, but also explains what it means to believe. In turning again to Benedict XVI, we see what belief provides for our lives.

[To believe] is a human way of taking up a stand in the totality of reality, a way that cannot be reduced to knowledge and is incommensurable with knowledge; it is the bestowal of meaning without which the totality of man would remain homeless, on which man's calculations and actions are based…because he can only do this in a context of meaning that bears him up. For in fact man does not live on the bread of practicability alone; he lives as man and, precisely in the intrinsically human part of his being, on the word, on love, on meaning. Meaning is the bread on which man, in the intrinsically human part of his being, subsists.[2]

To believe in God means that there is more to life than material goods and human caprice. To believe in God means that reality is not just comprised by what we can see; it is to know that reality is underpinned by God whom we cannot see. To believe in God means that our lives have meaning, a meaning that is imparted directly by Him and that leads directly to Him; and if our lives have meaning, they also have purpose. To believe in God means our lives are not just for making profits or experiencing pleasure, but for building relationships and expressing love.

For Christians, the meaning of life is not something subjective or man-made, as someone may say that he finds certain activities, events, or ideas meaningful. The meaning comes from God, who as we saw last chapter, is *Logos*, the creative and loving reason of the universe, the Word. Hence God Himself is meaning, He is the Word that we must come to understand.[3] And, if meaning can be analogously seen as bread which nourishes the soul of human beings, then it is all the more fitting that God became man to give Himself to us in the Eucharist as bread for the life of the world.

Belief in God, then, begins with an act of acceptance. Believers accept that there is more to the world than meets the eye, that there are spiritual, and not just physical or material, forces present in the universe, and that God who is our creator is our meaning and our end. As Benedict concludes, "faith in God appears as a holding on to God through which man gains a firm foothold for his life. Faith is thereby defined as taking up a position, as taking a stand trustfully on the ground of the word of God."[4]

To believe in God involves a second aspect that stems from this act of acceptance. As we saw in the last chapter, God is both Being itself, the eternal force and meaning of the cosmos, and the personal God of individual human beings. To believe in God, then, is to open ourselves to a real, personal relationship with Him. This relationship also adds to the qualitative dimension of believers' lives: relationships, be they marital, familial, social, or professional, can shape, for good or for ill, our personal outlook, demeanor, and overall happiness in ways that cannot be measured. Belief in God establishes a direct relationship between God and the individual believer. Like all relationships, communion with God can deepen over time, it can flourish at certain moments and languish at others, and it can become stale if the believer neglects to put her full energy into the relationship. An individual's relationship with God, although mediated through the community of the Church, is also intensely and intimately personal: no two people have the same relationship with God. And since relationship with God is built through faith, trust lies at the very center of this union.

Perhaps the simplest way to understand our relationship with God is in terms of friendship with His incarnate Son, Jesus, who began His ministry by building relationships with his apostles and first disciples by asking them to trust Him. Over the course of three years, Jesus earned their trust by His unprecedented teachings and by His miracles; through these actions He revealed His divine self to them. Just before He died, Jesus explained to His apostles how their relationship with Him had deepened: "This is my commandment, that you love one another as I have loved you. Greater love has no man than this, that a man lay down his life for his friends…. No longer do I call you servants, for the servant does not know what his master is doing; but I have called you friends, for all that I have heard from my Father I have made known to you" (John 15:12–13,15). Just as Jesus called his apostles to friendship, so He calls each believer to friendship with Him. The essence of this friendship, as Jesus Himself described, is love, and this love is proved by the complete gift of self to the other: Jesus gave Himself completely to us by laying down His life on the cross, and He invites us to lose our lives for Him in turn (Matt. 16:25).

Jesus established a friendship with each of His apostles—and He has established a friendship with each baptized believer ever since—in order to bring each one into union with Himself and with His Father. This union, which is destined to last forever in Heaven, begins not with death, but with a believer's first response to God's call. Jesus said, "This is eternal life, that they know you the only true God, and Jesus Christ whom you have sent" (John 17:3). For all believers, past and present, no relationship has ever offered more than the one begun with God. With knowledge and acceptance of Him, the relationship that is eternal life begins in this life. As Benedict XVI writes, the believer "has found life when he adheres to him who is Life.... The relationship to God in Jesus Christ is the source of a life that no death can take away."[5]

These two aspects of belief, acceptance and relationship, show that Christianity is not primarily about rules or doctrine, as critics so often allege. At root Christianity is about receiving a person and our relationship to Him. The rules and doctrines of the Church all emanate from this reality in order to foster our relationship and to protect it from distortions. Just as society has established certain rules and expectations to foster our marital, familial, and professional relationships and to prevent them from being distorted or misused, so, too, did Christ establish His Church whose rules and doctrine foster our personal relationship with Him and prevent it from distortions or misuse. We will look more closely at the role the Church plays in faith in Chapter 6.

Faith and Belief: Defining Terms

Thus far we have used the word *faith* in a generic sense to mean the relationship of trust that exists between a person and his interlocutor. We have also used faith in a religious sense as the relationship of trust that exists between believers and God. We will now begin to define faith in the religious sense, as well as other words associated with it, more precisely.

Let us begin first with the verb "to believe," which has two senses. First, it means to accept a claim or testimony as true, such as, "I believe the Gospel that John wrote," or, "I believe that God exists." Synonyms for this sense of the verb include to accept and to think that something is true. Second, the verb "to believe" can be followed by "in" to express a relationship of trust between people, such as, "I believe in Jesus, my savior." Synonyms for this second sense include to entrust and to commit. "To believe" translates the Latin verb *credere*, which is also used in these two senses, and is the source of our English word "creed." Pope Francis explains how these two senses of "to believe" intersect in Jesus: "We 'believe' Jesus when we accept his word, his testimony, because he is truthful. We 'believe in' Jesus when we personally welcome him into our lives and journey towards him, clinging to him in love and following his footsteps along the way."[6]

Related to this verb is the noun "belief," which is not entirely synonymous with faith. A belief is a conviction, something that is held to be true, such as, "The beliefs of Catholics are expressed in the Nicene Creed," or, "The parishioners shared the belief that the festival would be well attended." Beliefs may be true, but they can also be false, such as, "The belief that the moon was made of green cheese circulated widely among the kindergarteners." Beliefs are true or false depending on whether they conform to objective reality, to what is real outside the mind. We affirm beliefs about God are true when they conform to what reason and revelation say about Him. Hence we can say that the beliefs expressed in the Nicene Creed are true because they reflect the reality of what God has revealed about Himself in salvation history. Conversely, we know that a belief confessing four persons in one God is false because it contradicts the reality of revelation.

"Faith," which translates the Greek *pistis* and the Latin *fides* (the latter is the source of the English word fidelity), is deeper than belief. Cardinal Henri de Lubac memorably explains the difference between the two.

> [Faith] is something completely different from a simple conviction. It is an essentially personal act which, if rightly understood, involves the depths of one's being. It gives a definite orientation to one's entire being.... In addition, if faith, like many other beliefs, is based on testimony, this testimony

is of a unique kind; it is God's testimony.... Finally, faith is essentially a response: the response, which cannot be divided, to the Word of God who reveals and who, in revealing, reveals himself. By an ordinary belief, we believe something about a man; by faith, we believe something about God...we believe *in* God. Our faith is a response to his call.[7]

De Lubac presents three points of contrast. First, while a belief is merely a conviction held in the mind, faith reaches beyond the mind into the human heart; it is for this reason that faith in God provides meaning for our lives and opens us to a personal relationship with Him. This personal relationship is critical in distinguishing belief from faith: the former consists of ideas and objects, but the latter finds its genesis in a person, God. Second, belief rests on the authority of fallible human beings; faith rests upon the authority of God, who, because of His nature, "can neither deceive nor be deceived."[8] Faith, therefore, is certain, and, in the words of the *Catechism of the Catholic Church*, "it is more certain than all human knowledge because it is founded on the very word of God who cannot lie."[9] We will return to the issue of the certainty of faith later. Third, whereas human beings are capable of generating their own beliefs, faith is initiated by God; faith is our response to God who calls us first. Faith, then, is a gift that God freely grants to human beings of His own volition.

At this point we can formulate a preliminary definition of faith; a final definition awaits an examination of faith within the ministry of Christ and the Scriptures. For now, we know that faith has two dimensions that mutually presuppose and complement one another. First, faith is rooted in the conviction that God exists. This includes the acceptance of everything we know about God through the reasoning we saw in the last chapter: His properties; His triune nature; His incarnation, atonement, and resurrection; His Church and His word as revealed in Sacred Scripture and Sacred Tradition. This is the objective dimension of faith, and this is how faith is understood in such phrases as "the profession of faith" or "keep the faith." Second, faith is the personal relationship that exists between God and the believer, a relationship begun by God, built on the reciprocal trust of the believer, and destined to last forever. This relationship is lived out as a friendship with Jesus Christ, God made man. This is the personal or subjective dimension of faith. The exact way these two dimensions interact will become clearer when we see the dynamism of faith as revealed in salvation history.

Faith in the Bible: God Calls His Children

The Roman Canon of the Mass calls Abraham "our father in faith," for he is the parent of all who believe in God. At the age of 75, Abram, as he was then known, received God's revelation of Himself, seemingly from nowhere: "Now the Lord said to Abram, 'Go from your country and your kindred and your father's house to the land that I will show you. And I will make of you a great nation, and I will bless you, and make your name great, so that you will be a blessing.'... So Abram went, as the Lord had told him" (Gen. 12:1–2, 4).

Of His own volition God called Abram and presented him with a tremendous, even outrageous, command: in his advanced age he was asked to leave everything he knew—his home, family, and land—and go to some unknown place that God would show him at some undisclosed point. The sacred author of Genesis gives no insight into Abram's thoughts on receiving God's call. He must have been absolutely thunderstruck. Whether he hesitated initially or was terrified, we do not know; we only know that he decided to trust God completely: having accepted God on His own authority,

Abram left everything and went as God had commanded. This exchange began the relationship between God and Abram that lasted the rest of his life and into eternity. Since Abram believed, God "reckoned it to him as righteousness" (Gen. 15:6). With the benefit of several millennia of hindsight, we know that God indeed fulfilled His promise to his first disciple.

We have in this story the archetype of the relationship that is faith: God calls, inviting us to a relationship with Him, and we respond to Him. Like Abram's, our response is free and not coerced: no person or power compelled him to accept God's invitation. Hence through Abram, faith, as Pope Francis teaches, "takes on a personal aspect.... Faith is our response to a word which engages us personally, to a 'Thou' who calls us by name."[10] In responding to God, who is greater than we are, we submit to Him and His will; like Abram, we obey on account of our faith.[11] In addition to bringing us into communion with Him, throughout salvation history God's call has included a specific prescription for the individual recipient: for Abram, it was to found a new nation; for Moses, to lead God's people out of slavery; for Peter, to be the rock and leader of Christ's people; for St. Francis of Assisi, to rebuild God's Church; and so on for each believer, no matter how grand or seemingly insignificant the task. Further, this relationship requires a radical and complete transformation of our lives: Abram had to leave behind everything he knew in order to enter into the union that God desired for him. Finally, we learn that whatever God calls us to is greater than anything we have or can do on our own.

After God announced His covenant with Abraham—changing his name, giving him a son, and establishing him as the founder of many nations—He put Abraham's faith to the test by asking him to sacrifice his son Isaac. Again the sacred author provides no insight into Abraham's presumably heavy and confused heart as he climbed Mount Moriah. We see only Abraham's actions, the outward expression of his tested, and perhaps troubled, yet unbroken faith. In choosing not to withhold from God his son, his greatest and most avidly sought treasure, Abraham powerfully shows us that God, who gives us *everything* good, asks us to be willing to give *everything* back to Him, even our very lives and, as in Abraham's case, the lives of those dearest to us. God wants to be the first and foremost priority in each of our lives—which is only fitting, since He is both the source and the goal of each of our lives.

This thinking is foreign to our contemporaries who have unwittingly imbibed secularity's doctrine of individualism, which holds that a person must be able to do as he pleases and keep his life for his own purposes in order to be truly happy. Abraham proves the utter selfishness of the modern ethos: God commissioned him to prove that God cannot be outdone in generosity when we freely accept Him and submit to His will. Not only did God fulfill His promise to Abraham, He foreshadowed on Mount Moriah how He would reveal the full depth of His love for us as well as His steadfast commitment to His relationship to us: He chose not to withhold His own Son in an act of sacrifice to redeem us from the prison of sin.

With the incarnation the God whom Abraham could not see became visible in Jesus Christ. When Jesus healed the sick, the two dimensions of faith, objective and subjective, intertwined. The needy sought Jesus, either for themselves or on behalf of others, because they believed that He had the power to help them. In seeking Him they simultaneously entrusted themselves and their conditions to Him. Jesus acknowledged their trust in Him, such as when He addressed the woman with the hemorrhage who touched His garment: "Daughter, your faith has made you well; go in peace, and be healed of your disease" (Mark 5:34).

The woman's determination to reach Jesus was her expression of faith. In other instances, Jesus sought a verbal confession of faith in Him before He healed anyone, such as with the two blind men in Galilee.

> And as Jesus passed on from there, two blind men followed him, crying aloud, "Have mercy on us, Son of David." When he entered the house, the blind men came to him; and Jesus said to them, "Do you believe that I am able to do this?" They said to him, "Yes, Lord." Then he touched their eyes, saying, "According to your faith let it be done to you." And their eyes were opened. (Matt. 9:27–30)

Having found Jesus, a relationship was established between the three: by their persistence and by their cry for help, the blind men clearly believed *in* Him. Jesus, by asking them about His powers, was seeking whether they also believed *that* He was of God, for only a man of God could perform such a powerful deed. Hence both dimensions of faith, objective and subjective, were present together in their faith relationship.

The union of the two dimensions was even more explicit when Jesus sought a confession of faith from another blind man after Jesus restored his sight in Jerusalem: "'Do you believe in the Son of man?' He answered, 'And who is he, sir, that I may believe in him?' Jesus said to him, 'You have seen him, and it is he who speaks to you.' He said, 'Lord, I believe'; and he worshiped him" (John 9:35–38). For the Jews only God can be worshiped, and worship is the ultimate way in which human beings relate to God. By acting in such a way, the man revealed that he knew who Jesus was.

It is also noteworthy that in the healing of the two blind men, as with the woman with the hemorrhage, Jesus credits their faith—not Himself or His power—with causing their healing. Through these miracles Jesus demonstrates that faith is the most powerful and animating factor in our lives because it brings us into union with Him and His majesty. As Jesus Himself explained at the Last Supper, "[H]e who believes in me will also do the works that I do; and greater works that these will he do, because I go to the Father. Whatever you ask in my name, I will do it" (John 14:12–13).

Conversely, when Jesus's authority is denied and faith in Him is lacking, His power cannot be manifested: when He returned to Nazareth, He "did not do many mighty works there, because of their unbelief" (Matt. 13:58). The same happened with Peter when he saw Jesus walking toward his boat on the Sea of Galilee (Matt. 14:28–31). At first, the awestruck and elated fisherman expressed his faith in Jesus: "Lord, if it is you, bid me to come to you on the water." With this confession Jesus granted Peter the power to walk on the water. "[B]ut when he saw the wind, he was afraid, and beginning to sink he cried out, 'Lord, save me.'" As Jesus pulled him out of the water, he rebuked Peter, whose vanishing trust caused Jesus' power to vanish within him: "O you of little faith, why did you doubt?" Jesus rebuked His disciples in a similar manner when He explained why they did not have the power to cast out a demon on their own: "Because of your little faith. For truly, I say to you, if you have faith as a grain of mustard seed, you will say to this mountain, 'Move from here to there,' and it will move; and nothing will be impossible to you" (Matt. 17:20).

From these exchanges, Jesus reveals that faith—personal trust in Him—is an inestimable necessity for His disciples. During His ministry Jesus pointed explicitly to His miracles as reasons to believe in Him: "If I am not doing the works of my father, then do not believe me; but if I do them, even though you do not believe me, believe the works, that you may know and understand that the Father is in me and I am in the Father" (John 10:37–38). After his resurrection Jesus began to prepare His future disciples to have faith in Him even if He would no longer be visible on earth. His rebuke of the apostle Thomas, who refused to believe that Jesus had risen from the dead, helped make this transition: "You have believed because you have seen me. Blessed are those who have not seen and yet believe" (John 20:29).

Thomas was not at the tomb at the moment of the resurrection; the news of the awesome event was conveyed to him by his fellow apostles. But Thomas refused to believe their testimony. Jesus later appeared specifically to Thomas to remind him—and us through him—that faith in Jesus now hinges on the testimony of the apostles, of those who have seen Him risen. To this day we proudly proclaim that our faith is apostolic, meaning it is rooted in the testimony of the apostles who knew Jesus best and saw Him after the resurrection. To believe, as the philosopher Josef Pieper teaches, is "to participate in the knowledge of a knower."[12] When we confess our faith in Christ, we do so not just through the apostles, but with them, for what we know and believe about Christ is the same as what they knew and believed.

St. Paul explains that in the apostolic era, which began on Pentecost Sunday and will continue through the end of time, "faith comes from what is heard, and what is heard comes by the preaching of Christ" (Rom. 10:17). In order for us to believe *in* Christ to form a relationship with Him, we must first receive knowledge *about* Him through the testimony of others. Hence in the New Testament after Christ's ascension, faith is used in both the personal, subjective sense as well as in the objective sense. St. Paul writes to the Ephesians that "I have heard of your faith *in* the Lord," for in Him "we have boldness and confidence of access through our faith *in* Him" (1:15, 3:12, emphasis added). At the same time Paul also uses faith in the objective sense when he writes, quoting others' reports about him, that he "is now preaching *the* faith he once tried to destroy" (Gal. 1:23, emphasis added).

The Acts of the Apostles also uses faith in these two senses. When Peter explains how he healed a lame man, he points to personal faith: "His name, by faith in his name, made this man strong whom you see and know; and the faith which is through Jesus has given the man this perfect health in the presence of you all" (3:16). When St. Luke, the author of Acts, reports on the progress of the nascent Church, he uses faith in the objective sense: "the number of the disciples multiplied greatly in Jerusalem, and great many of the [Jewish] priests were obedient to the faith" (6:7). Similarly, St. Luke reports later that throughout the region, by the preaching of Paul, Silas, and Timothy, "the churches were strengthened in the faith, and they increased in numbers daily" (16:5).

As with the use of faith in the Gospels, in the time of the nascent Church both senses of faith are inherently tied. The objective sense of faith here is what the apostles preached: that Jesus of Nazareth died for our sins and rose from the dead, and we ought to repent and believe in Him. This basic proclamation of belief, called the *kerygma*, had as its goal to open its hearers to a personal relationship of faith with Jesus, to believe in Him. In the decades and centuries after Jesus' ascension, believers began to reflect more deeply on the person of Jesus and the experience of salvation as expressed in the *kerygma*: Who must Jesus be in order to rise from the dead and save us from sin? In time, and often as a result of controversies, the Church's understanding of Jesus deepened and developed through theology, which is the rational exploration and study of everything pertaining to God. The Church realized gradually that Jesus is fully equal and consubstantial with God the Father and the Holy Spirit; and that He, fully God, was born of the Virgin Mary and became fully man, like us in all things except sin. These facts about Jesus have been formulated in a series of creeds, statements of belief, the most famous being the Nicene Creed recited during Mass each Sunday, and they are nothing more than an expansion of the first *kerygma* preached on Easter Sunday: "The Lord has risen indeed, and has appeared to Simon!" (Luke 24:34).

Hence the Church's creeds, which have been further detailed over the centuries in Church doctrine and in the *Catechism of the Catholic Church*, provide a succinct formulation of objective faith, of what we believe—and must necessarily believe—when we enter into a personal relationship of faith with Jesus. To believe in Jesus is also to accept Him as He is, which is how He is described in the creeds and teachings of the Church. In other words, at the source of all the creeds, theologies, and doctrines of the Church is the person Jesus Christ and what He did and taught, and this source is as living and fresh today as it was 2,000 years ago.

Because the creeds are founded on Christ, the unity of faith comes from Him as well. With St. Paul we confess "one Lord, one faith, one baptism, one God and Father of us all" (Eph. 4:5–6). Warring denominations with differing interpretations of the creeds were not the intention of Jesus when he prayed to the Father that "they may be one even as we are one, I in them and you in me, that they may become perfectly one, so that the world may know that you have sent me and have loved them even as you have loved me" (John 17:23). Because Christ entrusted His infallible word to be passed on by fallible human beings, too often the world has not been able to know Christ because of the sins of His followers. Faith, sadly, does not inoculate us against temptation. Yet we have the guarantee from Christ that although those who profess His name may sin, the creed that they profess and that the Catholic

Church teaches is that of Christ Himself, who sent the Holy Spirit to "guide you into all the truth" (John 16:13).

Faith as Assent and as Virtue

Belief in God requires two concurrent actions: the acceptance of God and the formation of a relationship with Him. These actions correspond with the two dimensions of faith: objective faith, which requires us to receive God and the truths about Him, and thereby to submit to His power over us; and subjective or personal faith, by which we form a personal relationship with God. We have also seen that faith is a gift from God that a person receives by hearing the testimony of another. The testimony received is the person, teachings, and deeds of Jesus Christ, which are expressed in the creeds of the Church. The creeds are the formal manner of teaching and of passing on the reality of God, of Christ, and of salvation, and they help facilitate believers' personal relationship with God. This brings us to two further points about faith, both intimately related to the acts of acceptance and of forming a relationship, that will help us formulate a complete definition of faith.

The acceptance of God and the truths about Him is done with the intellect. Hence we can say that believers assent to—that is, accept as true—the facts about God as expressed in the creeds and in the teachings of the Church. Naturally, in accepting facts about God, we accept God Himself, since everything we know about Him stems from who He is. Pope St. Pius X instructs that faith "is the genuine assent of the intellect to a truth that is received from outside by hearing. In this assent, given on the authority of an all-truthful God, we hold to be true what has been said, attested to, and revealed by the personal God, our Creator and Lord."[13] We assent to the truth about Christ, and at the same time we assent to Him who is "the way, and the truth, and the life" (John 14:6).

Since assent is an act of acceptance, the intellect must be moved by a person's will to assent to the truths of faith. Hence faith is not merely knowledge: it is not the absorption and retention of facts and information acquired by studying.[14] Rather, faith is the willful acceptance of God and the truths handed on about Him. The key to belief, explains Josef Pieper, is volition: "the believer believes because he *wants* to believe."[15] As the intellect identifies what it hears as true, it is the will, the desire of the hearer, that recognizes this truth as a good to be desired and obtained. Hence faith, as de Lubac teaches, is an act of the whole person since it involves the mind and the will. To be a person of faith consists not in simply knowing facts about God, but in accepting knowledge that is constitutive of a person's whole being.

Because of the role of the will in assenting to faith, believers may feel emotions concomitant with their relationship with God, or they may not feel any reactions at all. Since the act of assent primarily involves the intellect, the feelings believers have, or do not have, toward God are secondary and not essential to the relationship of faith, although they may have an impact on it. We will explore the role of emotion and experience within the life of faith in Chapter 8. Ultimately, it is the continued assent of the intellect that adheres to God and sustains our relationship with Him through time.

Because of the primacy of the intellect, faith is also a virtue, that is, a disposition or habit of doing good repeatedly. A virtue, according to St. Thomas Aquinas, is an "operative habit," meaning its power is ordered to performing an action.[16] In particular, faith is an intellectual virtue, a habitual disposition of the mind that enables us to deepen and develop our relationship with God over the course of our whole lives. When we pray, fast, and perform acts of charity, we carry out acts of faith that flow from the virtue that so disposes us. By these actions our faith further grows and develops. Hence we can pray to Jesus with the apostles: "Increase our faith!" (Luke 17:5). Unlike the moral virtues such as fortitude and justice, faith is not acquired by a believer's own power. Rather, faith is infused—literally "poured into" us—through the sacrament of baptism, which bestows the grace of faith. We will consider the exact role of baptism and grace in the life of faith in the next chapter.

We can now present a formal definition of faith that will guide our further exploration of it within our contemporary secular context. Faith is the personal relationship of trust that exists between human beings and the invisible God, who invites us to accept Him and His word with freedom and generosity. This relationship is manifested in a friendship with Jesus Christ, the Son of God. As a virtue faith is sustained over time through our continued assent to God and the truth about Him, on account of the grace communicated by God to us, and through our continued responses to Him. Like a coin, faith has two sides yet remains one thing: objective faith refers to what we believe and assent to, and subjective faith refers to the believer's relationship with God. This formal definition unpacks the implications of the compact definition of faith presented in the Letter to the Hebrews: "faith is the assurance of things hoped for, the conviction of things not seen" (11:1).

Rejecting Faith

We have seen that faith is initiated freely by God who invites our free response. Since we are free to accept God's invitation, we are also free to reject it. As we saw in Chapter 3, the evidence for believing in God is convincing, but it does not coerce the mind into acceptance in the manner of a mathematical equation. Rather, since the will has to move the intellect to assent to God and the truths about Him, the person has to want to believe in God and want to accept the evidence for faith. It is therefore possible to reject the testimony of believers and, consequently, to reject God Himself and the truth about Him. Even many who saw Jesus and His miracles refused to believe in Him.

The Gospels seem to have as many accounts of people who believed in Jesus as of those who rejected Him. When Jesus returned to Nazareth to teach in the synagogue, the people there "took offense at him" because they could not account for how He obtained "this wisdom and these mighty works" (Matt. 13:55–57). When Jesus called Himself the bread of life and taught about the Eucharist, some of his disciples, recognizing the implications, hesitated: "This is a hard saying; who can listen to it?" (John 6:60). After Jesus confronted their misgivings and reaffirmed His teaching, "many of his disciples drew back and no longer walked with him" (John 6:66). Pharisees and legal scholars attempted multiple times to trap Jesus on issues concerning Jewish law. In Jerusalem the chief priests, scribes, and elders—men whose education and religious training should have made them the first ones to accept Jesus—maliciously confronted Jesus and later ordered His arrest.

Because believers' faith rests in an invisible God, they, from time to time, ask God for signs to confirm or convince them in their belief. Jesus' contemporaries actually saw His miraculous deeds and heard His words, yet still some did not believe. They refused to believe *that* He was the Messiah and therefore they would not believe *in* Him, nor would they entrust themselves to Him as disciples. Jesus' deeds and words, then and now, have to be accepted or rejected by each listener:

> Some of the people said, "This is really the prophet." Others said, "This is the Christ." But some said, "Is the Christ to

come from Galilee? Has not the Scripture said that Christ is descended from David, and comes from Bethlehem, the village where David was?" So there was division among the people over him. Some of them wanted to arrest him. (John 7:40–44)

Jesus Himself foretold the discord that would follow because of Him: "Do you think that I have come to give peace on earth? No, I tell you, but rather division; for henceforth in one house there will be five divided, three against two and two against three" (Luke 12:51–52). Jesus has brought division not because He wanted to cause disorder, but because the unprecedented and unfathomable nature of His person, deeds, and message demanded—and still demands from us—a response to Him. He knew that some would accept His invitation to them, and others would reject it: "Did I not choose you, the Twelve, and one of you is a devil?" (John 6:70).

Human beings are "hardwired" to use their freedom to commit themselves to someone or to something. Some human beings, who choose to reject or neglect God's invitation, commit themselves instead to money, to power, to pleasure, or to particular ideologies that range in merit, from scientific naturalism and secularism to humanitarianism and volunteerism. These people seek, often unwittingly, to find their salvation, in the sense of being saved from their difficulties in this life, in these things, ideas, or causes. Jesus chastised the Jewish leaders of His day for seeking salvation elsewhere rather than in Him: "You search the Scriptures, because you think that in them you have eternal life; and it is they that bear witness to me; yet you refuse to come to me that you may have life" (John 5:39–40). Today we can insert any number of contemporary fascinations in place of "Scriptures"—obsessions with health, technology, drugs, sex, money, fame—and Jesus' indictment can be applied equally to human beings today: we all seek eternal life, and so much of what is good and true in the world bears witness to Christ, yet some of us still refuse to accept Him.

It is possible for human beings who have rejected God to become so consumed by their own selves and their chosen gods that nothing can convince them to change their minds. The parable of the rich man and the beggar Lazarus is instructive in this regard (Luke 16:19–31). The rich man, who in this life "was clothed in purple and fine linen and who feasted sumptuously every day," found himself, upon dying, "in Hades, being in torment." From Hades across "a great chasm" that cannot be crossed, the rich man cries out for help from Abraham, next to whom Lazarus now reclines in comfort. When his plea is denied, the rich man begs Abraham to send Lazarus to his brothers "so that he may warn them, lest they also come to this place of torment." A sobering exchange then follows between them:

> But Abraham said, "They have Moses and the prophets; let them hear them." And he said, "No, father Abraham; but if someone goes to them from the dead, they will repent." He said to him, "If they do not hear Moses and the prophets, neither will they be convinced if someone should rise from the dead."

From the time of Abraham through today, the situation remains the same: God offers us numerous opportunities to repent, to turn away from sin and live according to His will. He has given us numerous signs of His existence in the world, He has spoken through Moses and His prophets, and He has invited us with internal promptings to receive Him. Many have accepted these signs and the God who has offered them. Yet there are just as many who have hesitated: some remain open to God but refuse to commit their lives fully to Him and to His way of life, while others have chosen not to believe at all.

In one last effort to convince the world, God sent His Son who manifested His divinity by rising from the dead. But if we refuse to accept the existence of God, if we refuse to accept the teachings of Jesus Christ and His Church, if we become so convinced of our own righteousness and independence from a higher power, then not even the resurrection of Christ from the dead or a personal manifestation of God will convince us otherwise.

Since Christ first began His ministry, there have been efforts to discredit Him or minimize His importance. His contemporaries called Him a blasphemer and an agent of Beelzebub. Today, some reduce Him to merely a great moral teacher who exhorts us to love each other, but makes no demands upon us; others perceive Him as a social and political reformer of the distant past who is nothing more than an ancient curiosity now. Like Lazarus ignoring the warnings of Moses and the prophets, truncated visions of Jesus ignore the miracles He performed in order to manifest His most important teaching to the world: that God is love, and He is God's Son who has come to reconcile us to His Father. A large number of apostles and New Testament writers were eventually killed for their steadfast belief in this truth. If Jesus Christ is really the Son of God, then He, as our creator and redeemer, has a claim over us. In order to receive Him into our lives, we have to accept His power over us. The history of the rejection of Christ, from His first persecutors to those who reject Him today, is one of men and women who, for whatever reasons, have preferred to follow their own desires rather than to accept the life-giving plan that He offers and to unite their desires to His. And it is one of the great mysteries of God that He respects our choice.

The choice to believe invites us to consider how faith's different facets impact our spiritual and personal lives. We will begin with the act of faith itself: how God calls us, and how exactly we respond to Him.

❧ CHAPTER 5

Living the Catholic Faith

Faith begins when God invites us to enter into a relationship with Him. But how does He call us? Since faith comes from hearing, God calls us through other people who serve as His messengers to us. These messengers can speak to us through personal conversations, books, and visual media; they speak above all through the Church's Magisterium, or teaching office, through Sacred Scripture and Sacred Tradition. For most Catholics, the first messengers are their parents, who present their children as infants for baptism in the Church to allow for the gift of faith to be received. Children then grow in their faith as they age through the testimony and instruction that they hear from family members, priests, teachers, catechists, and fellow parishioners. Catholics refer to this combination of testimony and instruction as children's faith formation because it shapes their relationship with God. Faith formation can vary widely from child to child, for, as we saw in Chapter 1, the environment in which children live directly affects their disposition toward faith.

The witness of other believers who pass on and teach the faith is indispensable to God's plan of salvation. There is a second element present and necessary in God's call to us. It is just as essential as the testimony of others, and prior to it, yet it is invisible and cannot be detected directly. When God calls us He provides an aid through the Holy Spirit that enables us to respond positively to Him. This aid we call *grace*, which is a free, supernatural, and unmerited gift from God for the benefit of our souls. Grace is imperceptible and immaterial, yet it can be conceived of, by analogy, as a beam of light sent by God to us in order to assist us in choosing Him and to keep us in relation with Him. God sends us His grace, which moves our will to accept what we hear about Him from other people. In other words, grace is efficacious, or effective, because it enables us to assent to God and His truth. In a certain sense, grace is similar to electricity: we cannot see grace, but we know it is present by its effects; just as we know electricity flows when our televisions and computers are functioning.[1] Grace is the help that we need to choose God's will just as electricity is the help our televisions need to work; only by reflecting on the work in front of us can we see either one present. But even with its presence in our souls, grace does not compel our action: we remain free to accept God's call with its attendant grace, or to reject it, but we are only able to accept because of the grace that moves us first.

Grace is the spark that enables human beings to respond to God in Sacred Scripture. When Peter confessed for the first time that Jesus was "the Christ, the Son of the living God," Jesus proclaimed that "flesh and blood has not revealed this to you, but my Father who is in heaven" (Matt. 16:16–17). God gave Peter the grace to realize that Jesus was the Messiah; Peter did not do so by his own power. The same God-prompted realization occurred when Paul travelled to Macedonia. Among a group of women listening to Paul was Lydia, for whom "the Lord opened her heart to listen to what was said by Paul" (Acts 16:14). It was God acting first who enabled her to receive Paul's message and assent to his teaching. Hence Paul was right to identify God's grace as the crucial ingredient in human action: "I planted, Apollos watered, but God gave the growth. So neither he who plants nor he who waters is anything, but only God who gives the growth" (1 Cor. 3:6–7).

The mysterious and dynamic interplay between God's grace and human freedom has been, and continues to be, misinterpreted in ways that can be severely damaging to a person's faith. There are two extremes that wrongly overemphasize either grace or freedom at the expense of the other. One error is Pelagianism, named for a fifth-century heretic, which holds that human beings are capable of choosing God and doing good actions solely under their own power and without the aid of grace. We find this attitude today when some, be they Nones or fallen away Catholics, assert that they do not need the Church, her teachings, or the sacraments, nor does it matter what they believe, in order to achieve salvation: all that matters, they claim, is that they be a good person. Since this position minimizes the role that belief in God has in a person's life, it follows that its holders assume, wittingly or not, that they are capable of being good and doing good strictly of their own power, a position clearly at odds with revelation. This overdependence on oneself undermines faith since it minimizes the role that God, the initiator and sustainer of grace in the faith relationship, plays in our lives.

The other extreme is Jansenism, named for a sixteenth-century heretic, which in part denies the capacity of free will to choose good or evil: those who choose good are predestined by God through a grace that cannot be resisted, while those who choose evil do so because they have been deliberately deprived of grace by God. This error persists today in people who think that their sins are too grave to be forgiven by God, or that they have wandered too far to be taken back by Him. This erroneous belief is particularly dangerous because it can cause believers to reject faith and turn away from God completely in the wrongful assumption that God has turned away from them.

Both manifestations of Pelagianism and Jansenism are incorrect because they fail to balance grace and freedom. As the late Father John Hardon, S.J., explained, "Grace without freedom would make us pawns of a blind Fate, and freedom without grace would erase the supernatural order and remove God from the providential care of His own creatures."[2] St. Augustine famously articulated the essence of the wondrous interplay between grace and freedom: "God created us without us: but he did not will to save us without us."[3] God gives us the gift of life and the gift of Himself, but the gifts are rendered useless if we do not strive to use them in our daily lives.

Baptism: The Sacrament of Faith

God communicates his grace with human beings continually and in many diverse ways. Theologians, seeking to articulate in intelligible terms how God relates to us, have classified grace according to how it works on our souls in different circumstances. The grace that God provides to stir the soul to respond to Him in a particular situation is called *actual grace*. Actual grace helps all human beings to perform works of charity or other works for which we ask God's help. It also can stir the soul of a nonbeliever toward faith, toward a permanent relationship with God and a type of grace that is sustained over time. To receive this grace, the adult person must desire to be baptized.

When Peter preached about the risen Christ for the first time on the day of Pentecost, his listeners "were cut to the heart" (Acts 2:37) by what he said. As with Lydia in Macedonia, actual grace opened their hearts, and they believed what they heard. And like the sick who encountered Jesus, these listeners desired to entrust themselves to the Christ whom Peter preached. They therefore asked what they should do. Peter replied, "Repent, and be baptized every one of you in the name of Jesus Christ for the forgiveness of your sins; and you shall receive the gift of the Holy Spirit" (Acts 2:38). In this brief instruction from Peter we see how baptism is the sacrament of faith.[4]

Baptism serves two purposes: the forgiveness of sins and the bestowal of the Holy Spirit. Both were the goals of Jesus' mission on earth, so the waters of baptism are the physical means whereby the salvation Christ won for us is applied directly to our souls. Since faith in Christ is a personal commitment, assent to His teaching is, as we have seen, more than an intellectual position. This commitment requires work on our part so that the relationship of faith may be maintained. The first act required upon our assent to His teachings is repentance, the rejection of sin in our lives and the petition for forgiveness. By Christ's own command, the sacrament of baptism, through the pouring of water together with the prayer of the Church's minister, confers grace that remits recipients' sins and the punishment due for them. By virtue of our baptism in Christ, we become "a new creation," for "the old has passed away, behold, the new has come" (2 Cor. 5:17).

Along with forgiving sins, baptism also bestows the gift of the Holy Spirit, meaning that God takes up residence in our souls through the Spirit. This fact, which is taught in catechism classes but is rarely comprehended in its full depth, is entirely astounding: not only did God once dwell among us as a man, He now dwells *within us*. As St. Paul writes, "your body is a temple of the Holy Spirit within you, which you have from God" (1 Cor. 6:19). God cares for each of us so much that he deigns to imbue us with His very self. This awesome reality—in the real sense of the word: awe-inspiring—boggles the imagination in its conveyance of the unique importance that humanity has to God. And it also confirms on the level of faith the philosophical reasoning expounded in Chapter 3: infinite Being itself does not ignore even the tiniest aspects of His creation. He is present to and effusing His life into all of it.

The grace of baptism is the bestowal of the Holy Spirit, who comes to dwell in the soul of the baptized. Theologians refer to this grace by two names, *sanctifying* or *habitual*, as the names signify what the grace does for us. This grace is sanctifying because it makes us holy, that is, pleasing to and worthy of God. God uses baptism as His means of adopting us into His family, the Church, which includes all the baptized here on earth and in Heaven. The grace of baptism is habitual because it inhabits our souls for an extended period of time. It establishes us in a sustained relationship with God that disposes us to perform actions to further this relationship. This is why faith is a virtue, a habitual state infused with the waters of baptism that serves as the basis for our acts of belief.

Here we see how baptism is the sacrament of faith: it is the very source of a real and lasting union with God. The faith of would-be adult converts, called *catechumens*, preparing for baptism is qualitatively different from their faith after baptism. Before the sacrament the act of faith that brings catechumens into the Church is prompted by actual grace, a temporary benefit from God. Baptism changes these catechumens forever because it infuses the Holy Spirit into their souls. The relationship of faith, therefore, is a direct and sustained union between the baptized and God. Actual grace continues to assist the baptized in performing particular actions, such as when we pray for help with a certain situation, but they are helped from within God's loving embrace rather than outside of it. With faith baptism also infuses the complementary and mutually enriching virtues of hope and charity: the former is the result of faith and the latter is faith's animating principle. Like faith, the infused virtues of hope and charity are far greater than mere human hope and charity because they have God as both their source and their end. Where hope and charity are lacking, faith is rendered lifeless and stale.

The difference between being baptized and not, therefore, is akin to the difference between being a citizen and a foreign tourist. A tourist can be helped with the aid of a phrasebook and map to navigate the land, but he clearly stands apart from the natives and from the country itself with his different language and cultural habits. The tourist also lacks some privileges that would make him at home in this land. As a visitor, his stay in that country is limited and he cannot participate in the public life of the nation. The citizen, by contrast, is at home in his land: he speaks the language, knows the customs, exercises the right to vote, receives the full benefits of citizenship, and has a permanent place as a member of that nation. Whereas the unbaptized, like tourists, receive small benefits in the form of actual grace from God while still remaining outside the fullness of God's love and care, the baptized are permanent citizens of the Kingdom of God, and have been given the supernatural gifts of faith, hope, and charity to help them participate fully in this Kingdom. They are permanent citizens because baptism imparts an indelible character or seal on the human soul that forever marks it for God, even if the person commits the most heinous of sins.

The experience of adult converts reveals the power of God to change a person's life irrevocably. Most Catholics, however, are baptized and given the gift of faith at infancy. These are often called "cradle Catholics" in popular parlance. Infant baptism, as the *Catechism of the Catholic Church* explains, underscores the "sheer gratuitousness of the grace of salvation."[5] Infants do not ask to be baptized, yet they receive faith as a free gift directly from God through the intermediating will of their parents and godparents. Further, infant baptism shows that God's call is not just reserved for the powerful or the righteous, but for the weakest and smallest among us.

For infants as for adults, baptism both remits sin and imparts faith. Infants, not possessing the burden of personal sin, are freed from original sin, the sin of Adam and Eve that is passed down to all human beings. (Adults, when baptized, are freed from both original sin and personal sin simultaneously.) Because of original sin, we are born deprived of God's original grace that was present at the dawn of creation. This deprivation has left human beings in a weakened state that is marred by an irregular attraction, unintended by God, toward sin. This irregular desire is called concupiscence, and it inclines us toward the seven deadly sins: gluttony, anger, pride, sloth, avarice, lust, and envy. Baptism remits original sin by filling us with sanctifying grace to unify us with God and to help us overcome concupiscence, which remains with us even after baptism.

Original sin is not a trivial matter that we can dismiss as a relic of a bygone era. St. Paul writes adamantly that "sin came into the world through one man and death through sin, and so death spread to all men" (Rom. 5:12). Sin was not—and is not—caused by God; it is human beings who have brought sin into the world by the misuse of the freedom God gave them. By virtue of our shared humanity, all people are interconnected in God's plan for the world; in fact, it is through our shared humanity that we all can call Jesus Christ our brother. Hence we all, even the cutest newborn baby among us, are born under the shadow of death wrought by our first parents and inclined toward deadly sin. Concupiscence is such a manifest reality in all of our lives that Chesterton was right to quip that original sin "is the only part of Christian theology which can really be proved."[6]

Modernity has rejected the existence of sin. Rather than understanding sin as a personal problem that is combatted by God's grace and mercy, it has deemed sin a psychological problem treatable with therapy. If sin is a pathology, then it should not exist at all: we should have no need for God or a savior. It is no wonder, then, that certain human beings, looking to rid themselves of obligations to God and prohibitions set by Him, have tried to make sin disappear. Times have indeed changed since Jesus walked the earth, but even with millennia of social and technical advancement human nature has remained stubbornly constant in its inclination to sin—to committing the exact same sins, over and over again. No amount of technical progress or psychological circumlocution can disguise the fact that we need God's grace through baptism to resist our sinful tendencies and instead perform salutary acts, that is, acts beneficial for our salvation. Because of this, we have a grave obligation to children that we remove them from the shadow of death into the light of God through baptism as soon as they are born.

The shadow of death is a reality for fragile newborns, even in the First World, where medical technology has rendered infant deaths very unlikely. With this fear removed, many parents in recent decades have developed the custom of delaying children's baptisms for several months after birth. Further, a statement[7] by a council of theologians that cast doubt on "limbo," the postulated place for unbaptized infants outside the realm of Heaven, also seemed to lessen the need to hurry to the baptismal font. But in reality, as we will see in Chapter 6, we do not know the judgment of God or the fate of souls after they depart this life. While, as the *Catechism* states, we "can only entrust [children who have died without baptism] to the mercy of God" through the virtue of hope,"[8] we ought to leave nothing to chance when it comes to our children and their salvation. Thus the *Catechism* continues that it is "all the more urgent" to have children baptized, which assures them—and us—of their salvation.

Through the waters of baptism infants, like adults, are given the Holy Spirit and infused with the virtue of faith, although they are incapable of confessing belief. As Cardinal Dulles explained, infants who are baptized "depend on the faith of the Church, which is expressed by the sponsors at baptism."[9] That is, because faith has an objective dimension, which is the faith that constitutes and is taught by the Church, infants can receive the virtue of faith when their parents and godparents exercise their own personal faith by choosing to have them baptized. Newly baptized infants, therefore, possess faith as a habit, a potency dwelling within their souls that, through the assistance of others, grows into personal faith gradually over time. If parents and godparents do not provide that assistance, growth in faith may be stunted.

Two related questions are often posed concerning—or challenging—the practice of infant baptism: Would it be more meaningful for children to grow and then allow them to choose baptism for themselves? And why should children who did not choose baptism be bound by it? Both questions, however innocently they may be asked, are products of the radical individualism described in Chapter 2, and they betray a more fundamental issue for the modern mind: that the individual alone—and not some outside force such as baptism, the Church, or parents—sets the parameters for one's life. Hence to answer these questions, we first have to reset the questioner's approach away from the hidden assumption that the individual is his own god to the Catholic understanding that life is a gift from God; in fact, we are the custodians of this gift whose goal and fulfillment is realized in living out the will of its creator.

From the Catholic perspective of life, these questions are now much more easily answered. Children find meaning once they find the truth, and the truth of God's creation of human life makes baptism the most desired gift a human being can obtain, for it brings us into direct union with God. Just as human beings do not need to experience illness to appreciate the gift of health, children do not need to choose baptism for themselves to benefit spiritually from its fruits. Likewise, to be bound by the call of baptism is to be placed in the loving and providential care of God. To reject this call, for any reason or any circumstance, is to enclose oneself within the prison of one's own desires.

Unlike adult converts, who begin with actual grace and then receive sanctifying grace to transform their lives, infants begin with sanctifying grace and then foster that grace through personal acts of faith as they age. The common factor, sanctifying grace, is the necessary ingredient for salvation—receiving the fruits of Christ's redemption in our souls. As St. Peter puts it, baptism "now saves you, not as a removal of dirt from the body but as an appeal to God for a clear conscience, through the resurrection of Jesus Christ" (1 Pt. 3:21).

Salvation and the Need for Baptism

This leads to a perennially challenging question: Must a person be baptized and have faith in Christ in order to be saved? On the one hand, Jesus Himself said that "unless one is born of water and the Spirit, he cannot enter the kingdom of God" (John 3:5). Before He died He told the apostles that "the Father himself loves you, because you have loved me and have believed that I came from the Father" (John 16:27). Before ascending into Heaven the risen Jesus declared, "He who believes and is baptized will be saved; but he who does not believe will be condemned" (Mark 16:16). The Letter to the Hebrews adds that "without faith it is impossible to please [God]" (11:6). On the other hand, we know that "God desires all men to be saved and to come to the knowledge of the truth" (1 Tim. 2:4).

Since more people throughout the world die unbaptized than baptized, how can we reconcile these two truths of faith—the necessity of baptism for salvation and God's universal will of salvation? Through Sacred Scripture we know clearly that God desires human beings to come to Him through baptism. For this reason, the Church, which teaches only what she has received from Christ and no more, "does not know of any means other than Baptism that assures entry into eternal beatitude."[10] Yet anyone who has never heard the Gospel and has never had the opportunity to be baptized, provided that he "seeks the truth and does the will of God in accordance with his understanding of it, can be saved. It may be supposed that such persons would have *desired baptism explicitly* if they had known its necessity."[11]

All human beings, regardless of their religion, nationality, or circumstance, receive a sufficient amount of grace to be saved. God actively desires our salvation; it is incumbent upon us to respond to Him. At the same time, however, it is undeniable that God gives more grace to some than to others. St. Paul explains that "grace was given to each of us according to the measure of Christ's gift" (Eph. 4:7), to which St. Thomas Aquinas adds that "what is given in measure, is not given to all equally. Hence all have not an equal grace."[12] This may strike us as unfair of God, but the varying quantity of supernatural grace conferred on each person mirrors the varying range of natural gifts each person has received. In the natural order, there are an immense range of personalities and abilities among people: some are intellectual geniuses, quick witted and funny, and physically attractive; others are sickly, have physical ailments and intellectual processing difficulties. In the same way there is a range of grace received among people in the supernatural order: some are inclined to prayer, to service of others, and to moral living; others struggle daily to relate to God and to keep His commandments

The parable of the talents (Matt. 25:14–30) provides an insight into God's diffusion of His grace. The owner of a property entrusted three of his servants with five, two, and one talent, respectively. (One talent, a monetary sum, was worth more than fifteen years of wages.) Then, after a long absence, the owner summoned the three servants to settle their accounts with him. The ones who received five and two talents had each doubled their master's money. The second servant, although his total money was far less than that of the first, heard the same commendation as the first servant from the owner: "Well done, good and faithful servant; you have been faithful over a little, I will set you over much; enter the joy of your master." But the third servant, fearing his master's wrath if he were to lose the money, had buried his single talent and returned it to him in full at the reckoning. The master reprimanded him for not using his money, claiming that he at least "ought to have invested my money with the bankers, and at my coming I should have received what was my own with interest." The master then ordered this servant's talent seized from him and given to the one with ten, and he ordered the servant cast "into the outer darkness, where there will be weeping and gnashing of teeth."

Grace, we learn analogously from this parable, is given to each person as God sees fit. God expects us not only to use the grace, however much we receive, that He gives us for good, but also to grow in it by responding to its promptings. God will then reward us if we use what He gave us to the best of our respective abilities. But should we squander His grace, He will expel us from His presence.

It follows that to be a baptized Catholic is to receive five talents, that is, to receive a substantial grace that bears fruit in this life and leads to salvation in the next. Like exceptional natural abilities in athletics, the arts, academics, personality, and so much more, grace is God's gift that He bestows upon those whom He chooses, not because He is a capricious tyrant, but because He has created an infinitude of situations to show His love is capable of transcending all things. Grace and the Catholic faith are not something earned, so Catholics should not swell with pride for being part of God's "elect" over the rest of humanity. Rather the gift of faith should fill us with humble gratitude and a resolve to use this gift the best we possibly can. As Christ warns, "Every one to whom much is given, of him will much be required" (Luke 12:48). In this vein, the Second Vatican Council strongly cautions Catholics who, like the servant with the one talent, squander the special grace God has given: "If they fail moreover to respond to [God's] grace in thought, word and deed, not only shall they not be saved but they will be the more severely judged."[13] If there is any scourge afflicting cradle Catholics in today's world, it is taking their God-given faith for granted.

It also follows that because there are different levels of grace in this life there are also different degrees of rewards in Heaven.[14] This is fitting since grace of any magnitude still must be freely accepted by its recipients, as it is possible to reject any amount of God's offering to us. Our decision to accept grace comes down to how much we are willing to trust God, and we show our trust by giving more and more of our lives into His care. The greatest saints have certainly received grace in abundance, but they also trusted in God in a radical way that defies ordinary human expectation, such as St. Francis giving away all his belongings and begging daily for food, or St. Teresa of Calcutta leaving the security of an established religious order to found a new congregation of sisters dedicated to working in the slums of India. The example *par excellence* is the Blessed Virgin Mary, who, unlike all other human beings, was conceived "full of grace" (Luke 1:28), and with this grace she willingly entrusted herself to the awesome mission God had created for her: "Behold, I am the handmaid of the Lord; let it be done to me according to your word" (Luke 1:38). Because of their heroic trust in God, these saints receive an even greater reward. "For to everyone who has will more be given, and he will have in abundance" (Matt. 25:29).

Most people do not receive such a tremendous call from God or have the courage for such heroic and self-sacrificing work. Yet we, too, as the Second Vatican Council declares, are called to holiness.[15] This means we are called to cooperate with whatever grace God gives us in our tasks in life: resisting sin; serving God through worship, prayer, and sacrifice; loving our neighbors; performing our daily labor; providing for our families; and working for the salvation of our souls and those of our fellow human beings. Our successes in these endeavors will be commensurate with the degree to which we place our trust in God. And the more we do for God, the more His grace will abound in us.

Because of this, an increase in grace in this life can increase the reward, and the chances of receiving this reward in the first place, in the next life. This leads us to a further conclusion: by bringing the gift of baptism and the Catholic faith to those who do not have it, we can increase the opportunities for grace—and salvation—in the lives of others. Since faith comes by hearing, God has chosen to tie the workings of His grace, at least in part, to human action. It is incumbent upon us who have received the gift of faith to bring this gift to others, just as Christ commanded: "Go into all the world and preach the gospel to the whole creation" (Mark 16:15). The salvation of our friends, neighbors, and fellow human beings very much depends on our willingness to share the faith with them.

Hence from the very beginning until the end of time, Christ sends missionaries to spread His grace and salvation, a task referred to as evangelization, or preaching the Gospel. For many centuries, countless Catholic missionaries have given their lives while evangelizing regions of the world where the name of Christ had yet to be voiced. These martyrs valued the salvation of others as more important than their own lives, and they knew these people needed Christ in order to be saved. Some parts of the world still have not heard of Christ; in other parts it is illegal to mention His divine name at all. In addition, the wave of secularity sweeping the western world has caused many to misunderstand or to forget entirely who Christ is and what He means for us; to these people a second evangelization—the *new evangelization*, as St. John Paul called it—must be undertaken. Because of the challenge of secularity, believers no longer have to travel great distances to be missionaries: neighbors and local affiliations have become our new missions.

Immediately after the Second Vatican Council the Church's centuries-long practice of organized missionary activity to faraway lands collapsed due to a mistaken understanding of sufficient grace. It was wrongly thought that because God gives peoples who have never heard the Gospel sufficient grace to be saved, they did not need baptism or Christ; they could be saved in a Pelagian manner of doing good on their own initiative according to the sufficient grace they have received. This mistaken notion misconstrued two tenets of faith.

First, it undervalued the necessity of baptism and faith in Christ as the keys to salvation so far as God has revealed them to us in this life. As the *Catechism* explains, "God has bound salvation to the sacrament of Baptism, but he himself is not bound by the sacraments."[16] For this reason we ought to presume that, unless we successfully evangelize those who have yet to believe, they will have greater difficulty being saved because they do not have the direct, personal relationship with God that comes with baptism.

Second, it mistook "sufficient grace" for "guaranteed grace," assuming that the unbaptized have a free pass to Heaven. To the contrary, St. Paul reminds even believers to "work out your salvation with fear and trembling" (Phil. 2:12), since none of us, even the holiest of saints, lives knowing that we are guaranteed salvation. Like faith, salvation is a free gift that is not merited. We ought to seek continually as much of God's grace as possible while simultaneously availing ourselves to His mercy, for it is possible for any of us to squander whatever quantity of grace we have received. For this reason, we must continue to evangelize so that those who have not heard of Christ may eventually come to receive the healing remedy of sanctifying grace to further their respective journeys to salvation. Or, as St. Francis Xavier, one of the original members of the Society of Jesus in the sixteenth century and one of the Church's most famous missionaries, put it in the negative when writing from Japan to St. Ignatius of Loyola about those who refuse the call to serve as missionaries: "What a tragedy: how many souls are being shut out of heaven and falling into hell, thanks to you!"[17]

Talk of salvation makes us uncomfortable today in a secular world given to pluralism and relativism. Secularity has conditioned us to see all religions as equally useless since none can be better than another. Nonbelievers especially bristle about this issue, both because they do not think there is anything that we need to be saved from, and because they doubt the power of religion to supply authentic benefits to our lives. Even among believers, salvation is difficult to consider because so much of it lies beyond our power and comprehension. We worry for our own souls, and at the same time we naturally wonder about the fate of our family and friends who do not believe or choose not to believe—and neither gives us comfort.

This returns us to the central tenet of faith: trust in God. The God who chose to call us to Himself is the driving force and senior partner in our relationship. He promises to provide everything for us, including salvation; our only task is to trust Him, to follow His lead, to place our lives into His hands willingly. So much of His divine plan we will never know in this life, especially in the realm of salvation. Hence the "hard cases"—questions about who exactly will be saved and who will be condemned given this or that circumstance—are best left to God rather than to us. We must trust Him and the plan that He revealed in Christ, even when it is difficult for us to do so. This is the true test of faith.

Living Faith: Living the Faith in the Sacraments

To this point we have considered faith in its many facets: God's initial call to us through His grace and through the testimony of others; our free acceptance of God and assent to His revelation; the formation of a lasting relationship with Him that is established through baptism. Now we will consider how exactly baptized teenagers and adults live out their faith over the course of their lives.

We were created by God and for God. Hence for Catholics, all actions, whether of faith, religious practice, work, or leisure, are done for God's glory. Since God has endowed us with everything we have, we show our gratitude to Him by acting according to our best potential, in conscious homage to Him who has provided our abilities in the first place. In this understanding, we can glorify God through activities ranging from athletics to the performing arts, as well as through our performance of daily tasks and chores. Even an activity as simple as being present to and enjoying a moment with family and friends can glorify God. As St. John Paul explains, expanding a famous line from St. Irenaeus of Lyons, "The glory of God is man fully alive with the life of God. The glory of God is the holiness of each person and of the whole Church."[18]

We glorify God whenever we act in accordance with His will. Whenever we pray the prayer that Jesus taught us, we ask God that "thy will be done, on earth as it is in Heaven." God's will for all human beings includes obedience to the precepts of His Church and to His natural moral law that is discernible through reason and taught by the Church. In addition, Catholics believe that God has an individual plan—a vocation—for each of our lives. Whether we are married, single, or called to the religious life as priest, brother, or sister, we obey God's will when we faithfully carry out the tasks of our particular state in life.

In our individualist secular world, obedience to God sounds like an oppressive remnant of a feudal society based on heartless commands and unfeeling responses. In reality, as Archbishop Charles J. Chaput explains, obedience to God's will is "actually a submission to God's love and mercy."[19] Because of this fact, contrary to the expectations of the world, when we willingly submit to God's will, we, like Mary at the Annunciation, find ourselves most truly free and happy.

At the heart of Catholic living is performing individual acts of faith that flow from the infused virtue of faith given at baptism. An act of faith is any response to God who calls us: a prayer offered, a decision made, an action completed that has God as its end and purpose. As Henri de Lubac explains, "in this act [of faith] which involves his total being, the believer replies with an undivided response to the God who reveals himself to him by manifesting to him his plan of salvation."[20] Every such act shows that a believer's faith is alive and vibrant.

As children baptized in their earliest days grow, the faith they have received begins to manifest itself in particular actions: they say prayers and perform acts of piety on their own initiative based upon their prior imitation of and instruction from family members. Beginning at the age of reason, approximately age eight, when human beings can discern right and wrong under their own power, we take full responsibility for our own faith and our relationship with God that lasts for the rest of our lives. This relationship of faith is never supposed to be stagnant, but always developing and growing throughout our lives.

Baptism fills us with sanctifying grace by bringing the Holy Spirit into our souls. But baptism is not the only source of sanctifying grace: Christ in His wisdom established six other sacraments whereby we come into direct contact—and the closest contact possible in this life—with God. Under the physical signs of bread and wine, oil, and the laying on of hands, or under the expressed signs of matrimonial consent and the confession of sins, together with the prayer of the Church, the other six sacraments also confer sanctifying grace on our souls. Like the grace imparted at baptism, each of the other sacraments provides grace that makes us holy, and that aids us in performing specific functions that correspond with the stages of life.[21] Confirmation strengths us to witness publicly for the faith as we reach the age of reason; the Eucharist transforms our relationship with God into a foretaste of Heaven; reconciliation frees us from sin after we have fallen; matrimony and holy orders provide grace to live our respective vocations over the long journey of life; and anointing of the sick confers a particular grace to facilitate our final journey back to God.

Each time we receive these sacraments, particularly reconciliation and the Eucharist, our relationship of faith is deepened and strengthened by a new gift from God. Through the sacraments,

God gives us more of His grace so we can give more of ourselves back to Him. This is the same with any human relationship, be it social, familial, or marital: as time passes the mutual give and take of the parties involved allows the relationship to strengthen and the trust that each has in the other to grow.

It is through the sacrament of the holy Eucharist, above all, that we grow in faith. Unlike the other six sacraments, where the physical matter transmits grace under its own state, the bread and wine of the Eucharist are completely and forever transformed into Jesus Christ, whose body, blood, soul, and divinity we receive under the appearance of bread and wine each time we approach to receive the sacrament during Mass. The Eucharist brings us into a real and living communion with Jesus Christ, and through Him, the entire Trinity.

Each time we receive the Eucharist, we make an explicit act of faith: to the priest who declares to us that the tiny bread he holds is the body of Christ, we respond, "Amen," meaning, "I do believe." And it does take faith to believe in the Eucharist, to trust that Christ is really present under the appearance of bread. There is no empirical proof or way to test the bread to see if Christ is present. For centuries through to our own day, when only six in ten Catholics believe in the real presence of Christ in the Eucharist,[22] doubts and denials about the Eucharist have been widespread. To believe in the Eucharist is a true test of faith, of trusting that what Christ has told us—that He remains with us in a real, rather than nebulous or idealistic, way, and that the Eucharist "is my body... is my blood"—is true, and true not on the level of mere symbols, but of reality.

When a priest prays the words of consecration over the bread and wine, there is no attendant theophany or thunderous sign to make the elements transform into the body and blood of Christ.

Nothing visible happens to the bread and wine. There is only silence, or perhaps a ringing of bells. God asks us to trust that what He has said through His priest has happened. Faith comes by hearing, so, as the Church sings in the famous hymn of St. Thomas Aquinas, we believe in the Eucharist not because of sight, touch, or taste, but only because we hear and accept the testimony of Christ Himself: "I believe whatever the Son of God has said: nothing is more true than His word of Truth."[23]

Whereas baptism is the source of faith, the Eucharist is faith's lifeblood. The Eucharist is "the source and summit of the Christian life"[24] because it is the ultimate font of grace: it brings about a real union with Christ Himself, the source of all grace; and in doing so it points us to the goal of faith: eternal and unmediated communion with God forever. The Eucharist nourishes faith the way that food nourishes the body: it helps it grow and remain strong among the challenges and threats of life. To receive this nourishment, Catholics must attend Mass each Sunday so that they come into direct contact with the goal of faith: Christ crucified and risen, whose once and for all sacrifice is re-presented at each Mass to allow us to receive directly the salvation He won for us.

The Eucharist is also called the sacrament of charity because it is born in the love of Christ who gave Himself up for us. We know that "God is love" (1 John 4:16), so through faith we are joined to Him, and to all those who believe, in love. Therefore it is incumbent upon all believers to "love one another; for love is of God, and he who loves is born of God and knows God" (1 John 4:7). Christ instructed His apostles that "all men will know that you are my disciples, if you have love for one another" (John 13:35). Since faith and love have the same source, they mutually reinforce each other: acts of charity become, as Benedict XVI teaches, "a consequence deriving from [believers'] faith, a faith which becomes active through love."[25] By performing acts of charity pleasing to God, our relationship with Him is enhanced and strengthened, particularly when love of God serves as the primary motive for our love of neighbor.

It is through the Eucharist, above all, that faith takes the form of a personal friendship with Jesus Christ, who deigns to come to us, His creatures, in a form easily ignored and manipulated. By presenting Himself to us in this vulnerable way, He invites us, like a true friend, to share our own vulnerabilities with Him. Because Christ remains really present in the Eucharist until it is consumed, we can spend time with Him in person, just as we do with other friends, as He reposes in the tabernacle of every church building or as He rests exposed on the altar for Eucharistic adoration. As we kneel before Christ in the Eucharist, our act of worship, which is the supreme action of faith, becomes simultaneously an act of friendship, as we express our love for Him and receive His in return.

Worship, which is the supreme act of love and devotion that can be offered by a human being, "is to acknowledge [God] as God, as the Creator and Savior, the Lord and Master of everything that exists, as infinite and merciful Love."[26] We owe worship to God in justice, for He is both our creator and redeemer, and our lives are His free gift to us. We find the model of worship in Mary's *Magnificat* prayer, a profound expression of gratitude and humility before the generosity of God: "My soul magnifies the Lord, and my spirit rejoices in God my savior.... [F]or he who is mighty has done great things for me, and holy is his name" (Luke 1:46–47, 49).

Worship is the ultimate act of freedom because it requires the willful submission of ourselves to another; and God, unlike any other earthly master, is unique because He responds to our free act of humility by elevating us to be His children and friends. And whereas Mary provides worship's model, the holy sacrifice of the

Mass provides worship's ultimate expression. The greatest gift we can offer to God is the self-sacrifice of Christ on the cross that is relived in an unbloody manner at every Mass. This is why our attendance at Mass is required each week: we must unite ourselves in the ultimate offering to God if we wish to receive back God's ultimate gift: salvation.

Prayer, too, is a simple yet indispensable exercise of faith that develops and strengthens our relationship of trust with God. St. Theresa of Avila calls prayer "an act of such special friendship"[27] with God, and it is: With every prayer uttered from the heart, be it a simple sentence expressing love for God or asking for His help, a formal prayer of the Church such as the Our Father or the rosary, or an extended conversation with God in our own hearts, we develop our friendship with Christ. Every prayer is a sign that our faith is alive, as prayer puts to action the potent, habitual grace we have received from baptism. And every prayer brings us a step closer to God who is the end and goal of our journey in life.

Benedict XVI explains how friendship with God, fostered by prayer, not only bears fruit for our souls after death, but it also makes us better human beings in this life.

> God wants your friendship. And once you enter into friendship with God, everything in your life begins to change. As you come to know him better, you find you want to reflect something of his infinite goodness in your own life. You are attracted to the practice of virtue. You begin to see greed and selfishness and all the other sins for what they really are, destructive and dangerous tendencies that cause deep suffering and do great damage, and you want to avoid falling into that trap yourselves. You begin to feel compassion for people in difficulties and you are eager to do something to

help them. You want to come to the aid of the poor and the hungry, you want to comfort the sorrowful, you want to be kind and generous. And once these things begin to matter to you, you are well on the way to becoming saints.[28]

Eternal Life: The Goal of Faith

The fictional exchange between Christ and two children that begins the *Baltimore Catechism* succinctly encapsulates what faith does for us: "Who made us?" "God made you." "What for?" "To know Him, to love Him, and to serve Him in this world, and to be happy with Him forever in heaven."[29]

These four tasks listed by Christ are intrinsically united by faith, which joins us to God so that we may know, love, and serve Him in a relationship that, as mentioned in the previous chapter, does not end with death, but continues eternally in Heaven. After death our relationship with God is transformed as the trust we have in the invisible God in this life yields to a direct and unmediated encounter with Him that has no end. This encounter is called the beatific vision, which is not an action of physical sight but of knowledge: in Heaven we finally and truly *know* God. Thus St. Thomas Aquinas explains faith as "a foretaste of knowledge that will make us blessed in the future."[30] Faith prepares us for the future, and what responsible human being is not concerned for the future?

Yet today we are not comfortable talking about Heaven. For one, secularity, with ubiquitous material items that compete for our attention, has us so consumed with the present world that a still invisible world to come does not seem desirable. Benedict XVI captures this sentiment well: "Perhaps many people reject the faith today simply because they do not find the prospect of eternal life attractive. What they desire is not eternal life at all, but this present life, for which faith in eternal life seems something of an impediment."[31] In addition, in order to think of Heaven, we are forced to confront our own death, a fact so repugnant to our nature that we are quick to redirect our thoughts elsewhere. And when we do bring ourselves to consider Heaven, we know so little about it that contemplation of it is extremely difficult.

Even in the Church there seems to be a reluctance to talk about Heaven, save at funerals. In recent years attempts to bring wayward Catholics into the Church, and to keep the current ones in, often have focused on the worldly benefits that faith and religious worship bring. There is nothing necessarily wrong with this approach, as faith does generate worldly benefits; but not to emphasize the next life is to contribute further to Heaven's gradual disappearance from the Catholic mindset. The proper perspective is expressed in the Church's Code of Canon Law, which states that "the salvation of souls, which must always be the supreme law in the Church, is to be kept before one's eyes."[32]

In order to complete our understanding of faith, we have to keep eternal life with God in full view, for that is the reason for faith in the first place. Christ told the Pharisees that "I came that they may have life, and have it abundantly" (John 10:10). Our relationship with God cannot, therefore, terminate with death, for the abundance of grace that Christ's redemption gives us has conquered death's sting. For believers, death is not the end, but a new beginning, a new form of our lives as they continue united with the Trinity forever.

The whole prospect of Heaven may seem farfetched or even ridiculous to some people, and many religions have their own accounts of life after death. Christ spoke about it, but He was rather scarce on specifics. He told His apostles, as we saw earlier, that "this is eternal life, that they know you, the only true God, and Jesus Christ whom you have sent" (John 17:3). He also told them

that "[i]n my Father's house there are many rooms; if it were not
so, would I have told you that I go and prepare a place for you?"
(John 14:3). In the parable of the sheep and the goats about the last
judgment, those who performed acts of charity for their neighbor
heard these words from the Son of Man: "Come, O blessed of my
Father, and inherit the kingdom prepared for you from the foundation of the world" (Matt. 25:34). Jesus analogously compared
this kingdom to a wedding feast (Matt. 22:2–14, 25:10), but He
elaborated no further. In writing about eternal life and the return
of Christ, St. John admitted that "it does not yet appear what we
shall be, but we know that when he appears we shall be like him,
for we shall see him as he is" (1 John 3:2). St. Paul, for his part,
simply acknowledged that in this life explicit knowledge of Heaven
is beyond our grasp: "What no eye has seen, nor ear heard, nor the
heart of man conceived, what God has prepared for those who love
him" (1 Cor. 2:9).

As with the Eucharist, we are left to trust Christ's testimony
that Heaven is real, and that the Father will prepare a place for
those whom He finds worthy. The lack of details on Heaven itself is
a further point of authenticity: it is not postulated as a release from
the doldrums of earth, nor is it the saturation of every carnal desire
for pleasure. Rather, as Benedict XVI instructs, Heaven is "something more like the supreme moment of satisfaction, in which
totality embraces us and we embrace totality—this we can only
attempt. It would be like plunging into the ocean of infinite love, a
moment in which time—the before and after—no longer exists."[33]

This conjecture posits a fitting end to the relationship of faith:
if God is all in all, is Being itself, then we will find our ultimate
fulfillment when we are united to Him.

❧ CHAPTER 6

Faith and the Church

The personal intimacy that faith creates between the individual believer and God is nourished by a prior community of believers in whom God's revelation and the testimony of Jesus Christ reside. This community of believers is the people of God, and they do not exist on their own: this collective people shares in a real spiritual union with the Triune God who is Father, Son, and Spirit. To use St. Paul's analogy, the people of God comprise the body of Christ, who, as the redeemer and lord of this people, is the head of the body. All believers, therefore, are called to be united to and directed by Christ as the parts of the human body are united to and directed by the head.

The members of this body, this people, are not incorporated solely by their own volition, as they would join a club, a gym, a team, a political party, or any other secular organization. Rather, they become members by the prior invitation of God and by the witness of prior members who pass on the gift of faith through the sacrament of baptism. These members, then, are those who are called out from the world by God into a new life in union with Him. Together they comprise the *ecclesia*, the assembly of those called out by God, which is translated in English as "church."

Around the world are myriad church buildings where believers go to worship God. These buildings are the visible manifestation of the diffusion of God's people throughout the earth in fulfillment of Christ's mandate to preach His Gospel to the whole world. Yet regardless of where and how many they are, the people of God remain one people, for they all share the same objective faith and they are all part of the one body of Christ. Thus, even with the multitude of parish churches and dioceses that exist in the world, we refer to "the Church" as a single entity, and by "the Church" we mean the Catholic Church.

The Catholic Church is one of the most criticized and maligned organizations in the world. She is constantly the subject of misunderstandings, protests, and calumnies in public discourse and in the media. Even believers can have misgivings about the Church for a host of reasons: misconceptions about her teachings, frustrations at her workings, confusion over her functions, and scandal from the sins of her clergy and members. Yet the Church is essential to faith in all its aspects, including objective and subjective faith, for she is the indispensable means whereby we approach God. To assent to this reality, we first have to understand what the Church is—and what she is not.

The Church is not a business or corporation, either in terms of mission or of governance. All businesses are founded by finite human beings with the mission of generating a monetary profit. In general, the energy and resources of any given business are directed to achieving this end. A governance is established to help achieve this mission, and individuals decide to join the business to help achieve the end and to receive back some of the profit in the form of pay. If the goal is not attained, then changes are made to the business itself, to its governance, or to its employees in the form of terminating unproductive workers. Prolonged failure to meet the goal causes the company to go out of business.

The Church is a very different type of organization. First, her founder is not any ordinary man, but the Son of God. Christ founded the Church as the living home for His teachings, His laws, and His authority, which He passed on to His apostles: He promised to guide her and remain with her "always, to the close of the age" (Matt. 28:20). As the divine founder and director, Christ Himself guarantees her fidelity to the mission he gave her: to bring all human beings into union with Him, first in this life and continuing into eternity. The Church, therefore, is not an end in herself, but a means to the end that is Christ.[1] The Church functions as the means to Christ by handing on His teachings, by showing how we ought to live in a manner pleasing to Him, and by sanctifying us with divine grace. This last task is done chiefly through the sacraments, the visible means of conveying God's invisible grace, which are efficacious only because they flow from Christ's body, just as His blood and water flowed from His pierced side on the cross. In a very real way, then, the Church serves as a warehouse of grace since she is connected to grace's very source and head. Just as an arm or leg has no power to operate apart from the body, so the sacraments have no ability or authority to dispense grace apart from the Church.

Unlike profit margins, the mission of salvation is not easily quantified because there is no natural way to measure invisible and supernatural grace. Yet evidence of grace in a soul can be discerned through a person's commitment to performing acts of faith and charity. Unlike a business that can run out of capital and be forced to close, the Church will never run out of grace or go out of business because Christ promised that "the powers of death shall not prevail against it" (Matt. 16:18). And unlike a business that may terminate unproductive workers, the Church will never terminate her relationship with any of her members: she will always receive even the most wayward Catholics, the most notorious sinners, and her most ferocious critics into her ranks. It is, after all, for these that the Church exists, as we will consider below.

The Church's governance was created by Christ to facilitate her mission of sanctification and salvation. Following the structure of Israel's twelve tribes, Christ chose twelve apostles to govern the Church, with one, Peter, serving as both the leader and the guarantor of unity among them. Since the goal of their governance was to ensure the sanctification of all who would follow Him, at the Last Supper Christ also made the apostles priests, men who sanctify their people by administering grace through the sacraments. Just as Christ handed on His authority to His successors the apostles, so did the apostles hand on their authority to their successors the bishops, who as overseers (from the Greek *episcopoi*) guide God's people with the assistance of priests, with whom the bishops share some of their authority. All acts of governance in the Church are intended to facilitate the ultimate goal of salvation.

The Church, then, is an institution both divine and human, invisible and visible. She has a divine founder, she has been given divine guidance, and she has a divine end. She is at the same time made up of human beings who, weakened by concupiscence, commit sin, make bad judgments, and obscure the presence of grace. The interrelationship between the divine and human elements of the Church, like that of grace and freedom, is a mystery whose resolution lies not with the human intellect, but with God. This why Pope Pius XII expanded St. Paul's analogy by calling the Church the Mystical Body of Christ: we see His body in the Church's human members, but her real connection to Christ the head occurs in the divine realm beyond our full comprehension.[2]

In the opinion of many, however, especially of those hostile to the Church, it is only the human element of the Church that counts; and with the prevalence of sin among her members, it is all too easy to dismiss the Church as hypocritical or even farcical. And in no area is she more derided than in governance. Many take issue with how the Church conducts herself as an institution, such as her ownership of property and other goods; they take issue with her teachings, especially those concerning human morality, a matter we will consider below; and they take issue with the governors themselves, who as older men and fellow sinners can be perceived as out of touch, incompetent, or, as it has been made known recently, complicit in covering up horrible crimes. These difficulties are certainly understandable, but they are not completely fair since they do not consider the Church in her totality as what she really is—the extension of the incarnation in time. We will now consider each of these issues in light of the true essence of the Church and her critical role as the mediator of faith.

The Church's Unholy Holiness

Each Sunday we stand to profess our belief in "one, holy, catholic, and apostolic Church." These four adjectives are called the four marks of the Church because they distinguish her very essence, that is, they describe how the Church has been constituted by God. The four marks are not goals that the Church hopes to realize some day: they are divine gifts to be lived by her members. We have already seen that the Church is *one* because Christ willed to draw all people collectively to Himself; she is *catholic*, meaning universal, because her message is intended for all people, regardless of nationality; she is *apostolic* because she is founded, in the words of German theologian Karl Adam, "upon the uninterrupted communication by imposition of hands of that commission which the apostles received from Christ."[3] And the Church is *holy* because she has been created and consecrated by God to bear His people through this life and back to Him in the next.

The Second Vatican Council, using St. Paul's image of the Church as the bride of Christ, expresses how exactly the Church has been made holy: "Christ, the Son of God, who with the Father and the Spirit is praised as uniquely holy, loved the Church as His bride, delivering Himself up for her. He did this that He might sanctify her. He united her to Himself as His own body and brought [her] to perfection by the gift of the Holy Spirit for God's glory."[4] Because of the infinite power of Christ's redemption, the Church is "indefectibly holy,"[5] meaning her holiness will never fail or cease—if she did fail, then the "powers of death" would have prevailed over her, a situation that Christ explicitly prohibited. And because of the Church's lofty consecration, "in the Church, every-one whether belonging to the hierarchy, or being cared for by it, is called to holiness," which "must be manifested in the fruits of grace which the Spirit produces in the faithful."[6]

This description of the Church is admittedly foreign to the experience of many Catholics and non-Catholics alike, although it is no less true on this account. All too often our perspective on the Church is marred by the poor decisions and wrongful conduct of her bishops, clergy, and members, with the scandal concerning the abuse of minors by priests and its subsequent cover-up by bishops being a particularly devastating blow to faith in the Church. How can the Church be holy and her members act in such a manifestly unholy manner?

Joseph Ratzinger calls this tension the "unholy holiness of the Church."[7] The Church in her essence is most certainly holy, that is, consecrated for God: her grace and sacraments, her teachings and laws, her apostolic structure and fidelity of her members all are gifts directly from God, the source of all holiness and the end for whom the Church was founded. These gifts were not intended to be enclosed in an unapproachable sphere of holiness, however.[8]

They are to be directed by the Church to all human beings to help them struggle against concupiscence and complete their journey back to God. The journey is rarely a straight line of ascent, but one of many trials and errors, triumphs and setbacks. In the struggle of her members the Church continues the mission of Christ: "Those who are well have no need of a physician, but those who are sick; I have not come to call the righteous, but sinners to repentance" (Luke 5:31–32).

This remark of Jesus was His response to the Pharisees who criticized Him for associating with sinners, a term which referred not to all human beings who fall short at one time or another, but to those leading a life of manifest public sin. The Pharisees prided themselves on maintaining ritual cleanliness, which included maintaining their distance from such sinners. Jesus could not be a holy man of God, they assumed with pride, since He was making himself unclean by associating with sinners. In evaluating Jesus, the Pharisees were right, but for the wrong reasons; St. Paul, once a Pharisee himself, points out the correct reason: "For our sake [God] made him to be sin who knew no sin, so that in him we might become the righteousness of God" (2 Cor. 5:21). Ratzinger explains what this important line of Scripture means for holiness and the Church.

[Christ] has drawn sin to himself, made it his lot, and so revealed what true "holiness" is: not separation, but union; not judgment, but redeeming love. Is the Church not simply the continuation of God's deliberate plunge into human wretchedness; is she not simply the continuation of Jesus' habit of sitting at table with sinners, of his mingling with the misery of sin to the point where he actually seems to sink under its weight? Is there not revealed in the unholy holiness of the Church, as opposed to man's expectation of purity, God's true holiness, which is love, love that does not keep its distance in a sort of aristocratic, untouchable purity but mixes with the dirt of the world, in order thus to overcome it? Can, therefore, the holiness of the Church be anything else but the bearing with one another that comes, of course, from the fact that all of us are borne up by Christ?[9]

Certainly, believers can become their own worst enemy when, despite their allegiance to Christ and His Church, they acquiesce to temptation: they become a scandal, a stumbling block, in the literal sense of the word, to believers and nonbelievers, and we can scarcely blame the latter for not accepting Christ when His messengers act in so unbecoming a manner.[10] But we also must remember that the members of the Church do not become perfect by virtue of their baptism—they make no such claim, nor does the Church promise instant sanctity upon incorporation. Believers themselves maintain an unholy holiness: they are sinners weighed down by concupiscence yet given grace to combat temptation and make their journey back to God. This is not an excuse for sinful actions by believers: it is the reality of Jesus' own ministry being played out in time. The expectation placed upon believers by critics, that they be pure and wholly without sin, is akin to the Pharisees' demands for Jesus' cleanliness—believers and Christ Himself are expected to act on their terms, not on God's. Ratzinger has identified the real source of this type of criticism.

At bottom there is always hidden pride at work when criticism of the Church adopts that tone of rancorous bitterness which today is already beginning to become a fashionable habit. Unfortunately it is accompanied only too often by a spiritual emptiness in which the specific nature of the Church as a whole is no longer seen, in which she is only regarded as a political instrument whose organization is felt to be pitiable or brutal, as if the real function of the Church did not lie beyond organization in the comfort of the Word and of the sacraments that she provides in good and bad days alike.[11]

We see this spiritual emptiness on the pages of the books by the New Atheists like Richard Dawkins who deride the Church and the Catholic faith for a host of issues without seriously engaging the real function of the Church and her teachings. The sins of the Church's members are horrific, but we cannot forget that the heroic acts of faith and charity by other believers are just as real, and they are the true fruits of membership in the Church. The divine element of the Church is just as real as the human, and it is more powerful. As Henri de Lubac summarizes,

> men may be lacking in the Holy Spirit, but the Holy Spirit will never be lacking to the Church. In virtue of her witness and sovereign powers, she will always be the Sacrament of Christ and make him really and truly present to us. She will always reflect his glory, through the best of her children. Even when she shows signs of weariness, germination is in progress toward a new spring, and in spite of all the obstacles we heap up, the saints will spring up once more.[12]

The holiness of the Church includes the holiness of her constitution, which rests upon another frequent target of critics today: the hierarchy, which consists of the bishops who govern the Church in union with the pope, who is the bishop of Rome and successor of St. Peter. The Second Vatican Council teaches that bishops by divine institution have succeeded to the place of the apostles, as shepherds of the Church, and he who hears them, hears Christ, and he who rejects them, rejects Christ and Him who sent Christ. In the bishops, therefore, for whom priests are assistants, Our Lord Jesus Christ, the Supreme High Priest, is present in the midst of those who believe. For sitting at the right hand of God the Father, He is not absent from the gathering of His high priests, but above all through their excellent service He is preaching the word of God to all nations, and constantly administering the sacraments of faith to those who believe, by their paternal functioning.[13]

Again in this teaching we see the tension between the Church's divine and human elements, between the holiness of her hierarchical governance as willed by Christ and the humanity of the finite men charged with executing Christ's commands. There is hardly a person, Catholic or not, who has not looked askance at a bishop for some seemingly poor decision made or incorrect action done. The Church's hierarchy receives added scrutiny in a cultural climate that perceives all authoritarian structures as antithetical to individual freedom. In addition, this same modern sentiment drives those who want to change the hierarchical structure of the Church in some way, be it to allow women to be ordained so that they may receive greater authority in the Church, or to divest the pope and bishops of some authority and spread it in the hands of standing councils or lay people. A change in hierarchical structure or a reduction of episcopal authority, it is thought, will help the real holiness of the Church again appear from beneath the weight of official trappings, bureaucracies created around the bishops, and countless regulations. Many Protestant communities have formed under this mantle, calling themselves "nondenominational" or focused on "just Jesus."

To reject or reduce the hierarchy in its essential nature and structure is actually to undermine the Church's holiness and the presence of grace within her. The bishops in union with the pope guarantee the unity of the Church throughout the world, for all profess the same teachings coming directly from Christ Himself in unbroken succession. Ratzinger identifies Sacred Scripture and the Eucharist as the lifeblood of the Church since together they enkindle her unity; at the same time the "episcopal organization appears in the background as a means to this unity."[14] The hierarchy authenticates that the Scriptures are those of the Church and not alien documents. It also authenticates that the Eucharist is truly the body and blood of Christ since the authority to confect it comes in unbroken succession from the apostles at the Last Supper. In other words, the Church's greatest treasures that bring about the sanctification of humanity—her teachings and her sacraments— depend upon her episcopal governance, which serves the goal of sanctification by ensuring our certainty of receiving God's grace. To change the nature of the hierarchy, be it by reducing the power of the pope, by ordaining women, or by diffusing episcopal authority into the hands of the laity, is to act contrary to the will of Christ Himself in constituting His Church.[15] Groups who desire to focus on "just Jesus" must of necessity make room for the Church He founded and the offices He established to continue His work of salvation in the world if they want to meet Him in the first place.

Hence, as the Second Vatican Council explains, to hear the pope and the bishops preach the teachings of the Church or to receive the sacraments from their consecrated hands is to hear Christ Himself and to receive His grace directly from Him. This does not mean that ideas bishops express about politics or policy, or decisions they make about parishes, schools, finances, and personnel come from Christ, nor are these ideas and decisions guaranteed to be correct. We are permitted to disagree with them on these issues and to express our opinions to them with charity. In the history of the Church, a few bishops have even taught heresy, which is an incorrect belief that distorts the teachings of the Church, or have broken away from the Church in acts of defiance. Yet the abuse of power by some bishops does not negate the authority of the episcopal office. When they teach what Christ has taught, they speak for Him. Should a bishop teach something contrary to what Christ has taught, then he is in error, and the faithful not only are not obliged to heed the teaching, but they may admonish him, just as St. Paul did to St. Peter (Gal. 2:11).[16]

The powers of their office also do not prevent bishops from committing sins. Popes, bishops, and priests are consecrated by God and for God, yet they still remain, like all human beings, sinners in constant need of God's grace even as they carry out their office. Bishops and priests, too, possess an unholy holiness. The Church, as the Body of Christ, does not consist solely of the hierarchy even as it remains essential to her structure: for Christ the head transcends the limits of His body's ministers, through whom He has chosen to work. For this reason we are not dependent upon the personal sanctity of the pope, bishops, or anyone else to receive God's grace. Karl Adam explains that when bishops and priests perform the sacraments, the "effective cause of grace is exclusively Christ Himself, who proclaims and effects His gracious will through signs determined by Himself."[17]

St. Paul writes that "this is the will of God, your sanctification" (1 Thess. 4:3). Expanding on this, the Second Vatican Council adds that all human beings, regardless of nationality or social status, are called to holiness, to be made perfect in and for God. For believers being sanctified, that is, becoming holy, is a process that begins with baptism and continues over an entire lifetime. Yet the goal of sanctification is not fully completed in this life: it awaits and requires a final purgation of all our remaining imperfections after death before we can emerge fully sanctified, worthy to stand in the direct presence of God forever.

The Church, since she is Christ's Body, already shares in the holiness of God along with the multitude of her members who have been admitted to Heaven, even while she journeys to Him, as a pilgrim, in this life along with all her sinful members here on earth. Here again we see the interplay between the Church's divine and human elements: she is simultaneously the community of those in Heaven who have been sanctified fully by Christ's redemption and of those on earth whom she is currently sanctifying. Henri de Lubac beautifully encapsulates this mysterious unity of divine and human, the sanctified and the sanctifying:

> It is one and the same Church that is to see God face to face, bathed in his glory, and yet is our actual Church, living and progressing laboriously in our world, militant and on pilgrimage, humiliated daily in a hundred different ways.... We ought, indeed, to love that very element in the Church which is transitory—but we ought to love it as the one and only means, the indispensable organ, the providential instrument, and at the same time as the pledge, the passing image, the promise of the communion to come.[18]

The Church: Mediator of Faith

As mentioned earlier, the Church, the people of God united as the Body of Christ, is a community of believers—the faithful who trust in Christ. It is in these believers that faith in the objective sense resides. God's revelation and Christ's teaching are not fossilized objects that exist in the earth waiting to be discovered, like dinosaur bones or fallen meteors.[19] God's Word is alive, and it is so not only because God Himself is alive, but also because it resides in the hearts and minds of living human beings, with its authenticity guaranteed by the pope and the bishops who have their authority from Christ. It is from this living community's collective experience of God's revelation, which the Church calls Tradition, that Sacred Scripture was born: the words recorded by the divinely inspired writers have captured these momentous and salvific events, preserving them for all time. But the words of Scripture themselves would lose their effect without the living community of the Church in which they can be read, interpreted, and revered.

It is into this living community's faith that we are baptized, whether as infants or as adults. This is the objective faith expressed in the creed. As we have seen, to accept God's invitation to enter into relationship with Him is to accept God and everything He has revealed about Himself, including how He has saved us in Christ and how He wants us to live in His Church. This act of acceptance necessarily makes us part of the Church since she puts us into direct union with God. In Karl Adam's summary, "Christ the Lord, as the Head of His members, never works on the individual believer in dissociation from His Body, but always in and through it."[20]

The individual believer becomes part of something far greater upon becoming a member of the Church. This fact in no way minimizes either the importance of the individual as a person or her role within the Church. In freedom each individual decides whether or not to accept God's invitation to a personal relationship, an invitation which comes through the Church. The individual, in becoming part of the Body, freely accepts Christ as well as His Church, including the teachings and rules she proposes to foster our relationship with Him. All believers share the same faith, but each individual believes with a different fervency according to the grace each person receives and to the effort that each one commits to the relationship. Each individual may also be drawn to different aspects of the Church's patrimony: one may be attracted by the Church's commitment to charitable works, others to prayer, others to doctrine, others to the moral life she proposes. Such attractions, unique for each Church member, may lead to a believer's participation in apostolic works ranging from teaching, to taking care of the sick, elderly, or poor, to participating in prayer groups like the Legion of Mary or in community groups like the Knights of Columbus.

These individual ways in which we live out the one true faith the Church proposes reflect the genuine plurality within the Church that we discussed in Chapter 2. "Catholic" means "universal," not "uniform"; even as we all share the same objective faith, no two personal relationships with God are the same. So many of the great works and events of Church history were born in the fervency and uniqueness of one individual's relationship with God: St. Joan of Arc's leadership of a French army in battle helped save her country from invasion; St. Ignatius of Loyola's foundation of the Society of Jesus in 1540 has grown into an enormous, and enormously influential, congregation of priests and educators spread throughout the world; St. Elizabeth Ann Seton's establishment of the first parochial school in America produced a model of education that for two hundred years has been duplicated in every state; and St. Patrick's determined preaching of the faith in Ireland sparked the conversion of an entire population. More recently, New York Police Department Detective Steven McDonald's public forgiveness of the man who shot him, and thereby caused his permanent paralysis from the neck down, inspired the largest city in the U.S. with a message of love, prayer, and forgiveness for three decades until his death in 2017. These are just a few examples of how one individual has made a colossal and lasting difference within the life of the

Church and of the world. The one faith inspired them to use their unique talents to bring about unique works for God's glory and the benefit of the whole Church.

The Church, then, is the mediator of faith. Protestants often criticize this fact by quoting St. Paul: "there is one mediator between God and men, the man Jesus Christ, who gave himself as a ransom for all" (1 Tim. 2:5–6). The Church has always taught exactly what Paul has written. By His sacrificial death on the cross, the relationship between God and human beings that had been broken by Adam and Eve was forever restored. Christ mediated between God and humans in a manner analogous to a mediator who restores the lost harmony between two differing sides.

The Church in no way impedes the relationship between God the Father, Jesus Christ, and human beings. Rather, the Church allows the relationship to happen in the first place. There can be no faith in Christ without the Church to pass faith on. Otherwise, information about Christ would be just that—information, a dead letter that is no different from facts about other religious founders or historical persons. As a community of believers united to the living Christ, the Church makes faith a living relationship between Christ and the members incorporated into His Body. The Church's mediation, then, is not akin to an arbitrator but to a conduit or electrical wire: she puts believers into direct contact with the power-supply plant who is Christ. The structure of conduits and wires is essential for ensuring the transmission of power from the supply source to individual homes. If there are no wires running into a house, or if the members of a household intentionally disconnect the wires, they cannot receive any power. In the same way, if we are not connected to the Church, we are not connected to Christ. We cannot have Christ as our mediator before God the Father if we are not joined to Christ's Body in the first place.[21]

As the Body of Christ, the Church brings us into direct communion with Christ her head. This calls to mind the Eucharist, the sacrament of the body and blood of Christ. The Eucharist and the Church are intimately related: as St. John Paul explains, "the Eucharist builds the Church and the Church makes the Eucharist."[22] The Eucharist builds the Church by forming a real unity of believers incorporated into Christ's Body, for through our reception of the Eucharist we fulfill one of Christ's commands at the Last Supper: "Abide in me, and I in you" (John 15:4). St. John Paul elaborates on this further: "Our union with Christ, which is a gift and grace for each of us, makes it possible for us, in him, to share in the unity of his body which is the Church."[23] Because of this unity we are able to call the Eucharist the sacrament of holy communion. At the same time, the Church makes the Eucharist through the power of sacramental grace given to her by Christ and deputized to bishops and priests through the power of ordination. Each time a bishop or priest celebrates Mass, he carries out Christ's command to "do this in memory of me." He transforms the bread and wine into the body and blood of Christ not by his own power as a human being but by the power of Christ acting through the Church. This reality is often expressed with the Latin phrase *in persona Christi Capitis*, meaning that the bishop or priest acts in the person of Christ, head of the Church, when at the altar. In this intimate union of the Church and the Eucharist we also see the necessity of the priesthood in the life of the Church: through the priest's sacred power Christ becomes truly present in our midst so that we can enter into a real union with Him.

The Eucharist, then, "creates communion and fosters communion,"[24] writes St. John Paul. "The sacrament is an expression of this bond of communion both in its *invisible* dimension, which, in Christ and through the working of the Holy Spirit, unites us to the Father and among ourselves, and in its *visible* dimension, which entails communion in the teaching of the apostles, in the sacraments and in the Church's hierarchical order."[25] These two dimensions of communion follow from accepting the gift of faith and are indispensable to faith. They are akin to the bond of marriage: there is the visible communion that exists in the public declaration of marriage before the Church and before the government, recorded in the marriage license and publicly signified by the wearing of rings; and there is the invisible communion that is the love between the spouses. Both aspects are essential: without the visible communion of an authentic marriage, the couple may have a loving relationship, but they are not married and lack its attendant privileges; without the invisible communion of love, the couple's marriage lacks vitality.

To receive the Eucharist at Mass is to consummate one's faith in God because the sacrament puts us in the closest possible union with Him in this life. Since believers encounter Christ and receive Him in the Eucharist only in and through the Church, they must maintain both visible and invisible communion with the Church. That is, they must be practicing members of the Catholic Church and they must be in the state of grace, which means their relationship with God is not impeded by mortal sin, in order to receive.

The bonds of visible and invisible communion are of tremendous importance: they both safeguard the majesty of the Eucharist and ensure the authenticity of our own relationship to God. To receive the Eucharist with one or both of these bonds missing is to undermine the deep expression of faith and of divine intimacy that comes with allowing Christ the Lord to come under our roof in holy communion. Thus the Church insists that its norms concerning the reception of the Eucharist be observed; by them she does not intend to "exclude" anyone, in the sense of making people feel marginalized, as detractors often allege. Rather, through them she brings about a deeper, more authentic inclusion into the life of Christ by safeguarding our relationship with Him. This relationship then fortifies us to reach out to those who are not in communion with the Church and to invite them in.

Faith and the Teachings of the Church

The holiness of the Church includes not only her hierarchical structure, but also her teachings and laws. These are holy because they come from God. Yet today these teachings and laws are the subject of much misunderstanding and criticism, even among Catholics. Some see the core elements of the Church's testimony, such as the incarnation of the Son of God, His birth by the virgin Mary, His resurrection from the dead, and His real presence in the Eucharist as too fanciful to be believed in a world governed by reason and science. Others criticize and even ridicule her moral teachings, particularly those pertaining to human sexuality, as outdated or irrelevant in a culture where moral truth has been undermined by relativism.

These criticisms of and challenges to the Church's teachings are almost always present in any reporting about Catholicism done by public media outlets, and they have sadly become part of the prevailing narrative about the Church after the Second Vatican Council—a narrative that even Catholics have unwittingly absorbed. From these negative forces many Catholics have been led to believe that they can determine on their own which teachings of the Church they ought to believe, which teachings they want to believe, and which teachings they prefer to ignore. This phenomenon has been dubbed *cafeteria Catholicism*, and it is a symptom of our secular culture that exalts individual freedom at the expense of both institutional authority and of a universal moral law that is binding for all human beings.

Everything we have said about the Church so far should make the problems with cafeteria Catholicism manifestly clear. We join the Church not solely by our own choice but by God's prior invitation. If we come to the Church on God's terms, it cannot be the case that how we act once we join God's Church is suddenly determined on our own terms. This is especially true given what the Church is: if she is the Body of Christ, the extension of the incarnation in time, then the heart of her teachings emanates directly from God. To reject the formal teachings of Christ's Body is to reject Christ himself, the Head of the Body. Because all these teachings are part of the same Body and they come from the same divine source, they have an intrinsic unity that binds all of them together, from the truths about God to the truths about the moral life.

When St. Paul compared the Church to the Body of Christ, he mentioned teaching as one of her functions to which some are called. The part of the Church charged with teaching is called the Magisterium, which consists of the pope and the bishops in communion with him. Guided by the Holy Spirit, whom Christ promised to the apostles to "guide you into all the truth.... [F]or he will take what is mine and declare it to you" (John 16:13–14), the Magisterium interprets and teaches without error the teachings of Christ. The Second Vatican Council succinctly presents the mission of the Magisterium and its four essential actions:

> [T]he task of authentically interpreting the word of God, whether written or handed on, has been entrusted exclusively to the living teaching office of the Church, whose authority is exercised in the name of Jesus Christ. This teaching office is not above the word of God, but serves it, *teaching* only what has been handed on, *listening* to it devoutly, *guarding*

it scrupulously and *explaining* it faithfully in accord with a divine commission and with the help of the Holy Spirit.[26]

The Magisterium does not invent new teachings for the Church. It merely announces what the Church has received from Christ and clarifies particular teachings in the wake of challenges or difficulties raised about them. These teachings include everything from the Nicene Creed that we profess each Sunday to the bodily assumption of Mary into Heaven. The Magisterium interprets with the authority of Christ the words of Sacred Scripture and the lived Sacred Tradition of the Church for the benefit of the faithful. These interpretations make up the teachings, or doctrine, of the Church. The most important components of the Church's doctrine are her dogmas, which are statements of the Church's experience of God's revelation that can be taught and handed on to others; that is, they are teachable formulations of real events that have occurred in salvation history. These real events form the substance of objective faith.

By analogy, we can understand dogmas as the carefully written cooking recipes that present in instructional form the results of real meals cooked in a kitchen. Every article stated in the Nicene Creed, for example, is a dogma of faith. Some dogmas are clear from our experience of salvation as transmitted in Sacred Tradition and Sacred Scripture, such as the incarnation of the Son of God. Other dogmas express sacred realities that are not formulated in as many words in Sacred Scripture, with the teaching on God's triune nature being one example: that God is a Trinity of three co-equal and co-eternal persons, Father, Son, and Holy Spirit, who equally possess the same divine nature is the dogmatic and teachable formulation of the Church's experience of God and her understanding of Jesus' own teachings about His Father and about the

Holy Spirit. The word *Trinity* is not present in Sacred Scripture; the word has been designated by the Church as ideal for conveying the triune reality of God that she has experienced and has recorded in Sacred Scripture.

Dogmas, therefore, express the very essence of faith: faith is trust in God, and we can have this trust precisely because the dogmas show us how God loves us and why He is eminently worthy of our trust. Hence the *Catechism* speaks of "an organic connection between our spiritual life and the dogmas. Dogmas are lights along the path of faith; they illuminate it and make it secure. Conversely, if our life is upright, our intellect and heart will be open to welcome the light shed by the dogmas of faith."[27]

Dogma cannot and should not be falsely criticized as an obstacle to charity or religious practice, for dogma properly received should be an impetus for them both.[28] Christian charity is not to be confused with mere humanitarianism: the good deeds done by believers are ultimately for God, who, in creating the world for our good and in creating our fellow human beings in His image, bids us to love our neighbor as an expression of our love for Him. We help those in need both to alleviate their human sufferings and to point them to God through our actions. Dogma and charity are complementary realities, just as Jesus was both a teacher and a healer.

As mentioned, the Magisterium's formal declarations are guided and protected by the Holy Spirit. This divine gift allows the Church herself, and the pope as the head of the Church, to teach infallibly, that is, without error, on matters of faith and morals; the former comprise the events of salvation and the teachings that logically result from these events, and the latter are the ways we are to live according to God's law. The Church's gift of infallibility is all too often misunderstood, but in fact this gift makes logical sense.

If the Church is Christ's Body, and if her leaders are guided by the Holy Spirit when they teach according to Christ's promise, then it follows that Christ the Head of the Church would guarantee that His Body teach what is true about Him. The mirror of history supports our belief in infallibility: despite the moral failures and sins committed by Church leaders over the centuries, whenever controversies have arisen over doctrine—whether these concerned the full divinity and humanity of Christ, the real presence of Christ in the Eucharist, or the role of the sacraments in salvation—the Church has always managed to articulate her teaching according to the totality of what exactly God has revealed to us. Because of the gift of infallibility, we can be certain that what the Church teaches about God is true.

It is helpful to clarify three common points of confusion concerning infallibility. First, the content of what is infallibly taught is limited to revelation, that is, to the events of Sacred Scripture and Sacred Tradition. When the pope and the Church formally declare a teaching infallible, they declare that this teaching has been revealed directly by God; in other words, the teaching is of divine origin, not human origin. Dogmas can be proclaimed by the pope teaching *ex cathedra*, that is, from the chair of St. Peter, when he purposefully and solemnly declares that a particular doctrine has been revealed by God, or by a solemn declaration of an ecumenical council of all the world's bishops in union with the pope; the Nicene Creed is one example of the latter. To believe dogmas is to believe the word of God Himself. The aforementioned use of the word *Trinity* to explain the nature of God is a prime example of this: we know that God is triune only because He has revealed Himself as such, and we see this fact throughout Sacred Scripture. The Church's decision to use *Trinity* to explain God's nature was the fruit of several centuries of serious reflection on how God can be one and three simultaneously, and, ultimately, the declaration of the Trinity as dogma was made with the guidance of the Holy Spirit.

Second, the infallibly taught dogmas of the Church are the essence of what we believe as Catholics. To enter into a personal relationship with God is to believe all the dogmas taught by the Church because they express in human terms who God is and how He has related to us in salvation history. Since God is one, the dogmas collectively form one body of teaching about Him. In addition to the contents of the Nicene Creed, other dogmas include the creation of the first man and woman by God, the foundation of the Church by Christ, the existence of original sin, the direct transmission of God's grace through the seven sacraments founded by Christ, the real presence of Christ in the Eucharist, the ability of the pope to teach infallibly on matters of faith and morals, and the immaculate conception and bodily assumption of the Blessed Virgin Mary.[29] Because these dogmas collectively teach us about God, if a person withholds his belief from one, he is refraining from trusting in God.

Third, the other teachings of the Church that are not formally defined as infallible are not to be ignored, discarded, or trivialized. All other teachings are derived from the font of revelation. Some of these teachings are part of the perennial teachings of the Church, such as teachings of general morality and human sexuality, and are therefore considered infallible, as will be seen below. Other teachings are uniquely intended to advise the faithful on contemporary matters that pertain to politics, economics, or social policy. These latter teachings are not statements of faith, and therefore are not matters for belief and not infallible; rather, they are to be respectfully received by the faithful, as they are intended to guide our consciences for making practical decisions worthy of the God who made us.[30] For example, Catholics do not "believe in" (in the sense of a revelation from God) that workers have a right to a just wage. Rather, this principle is to be accepted by believers since it derives from the Church's reflection on the doctrine of creation, which is revealed by God in Sacred Scripture and taught infallibly by the Church, as we saw in Chapter 2. The Church does not and will not teach what the exact dollar amount of a just wage is, since that varies according to many temporal circumstances and is the subject of proper juridical authorities, not the Church.

It is the former type of teachings—those perennially taught concerning general morality and human sexuality—that have been the center of so much backlash in recent decades by Catholics and non-Catholics alike. Although these moral teachings have not been solemnly defined by the pope or by a council, they are considered infallible teachings of the Magisterium, that is, they are teachings without error, because of their intimate logical and historical connection to God's revelation.[31] Hence these teachings can never be changed or reversed to mean the opposite of what they say: to contradict them would be to contradict God's own revelation, which the Church does not have the power to do.

For example, the three teachings regarding human sexuality that receive the most attention today—the reservation of sexual union to married couples only, the prohibition of homosexual acts, and the prohibition of artificial contraception—all follow directly from what God has revealed about creation, marriage, and family life. The *Catechism* explains in detail how each of these three teachings corresponds intimately to the revelation contained in the Bible, to the natural moral law created by God, to the nature of marriage as elevated to a sacrament by Christ Himself, to the inherent dignity of each individual person, and to the complete gift of self that each spouse is to give to one another.[32]

These teachings are also not matters for belief since they do not concern supernatural acts of God; they are to be firmly held, that is, to be accepted as true because of the Holy Spirit's guidance of the Church in teachings on faith and morals. But we hold them in faith, that is, we trust that living according to these moral teachings brings happiness to God, and by necessary extension, brings peace of mind to ourselves.[33]

As we said earlier, the Church does not exist as an end in herself, but as a means to the end who is Christ. She does not seek to thwart personal human happiness, but to enable it in this fallen world by teaching what God desires for us. Just as the Church's sacraments function as conduits of God's grace, her teachings function as conduits of Christ's own teachings. None of us saw Christ walk the earth two thousand years ago or heard his voice directly with our own ears; yet the Church's teachings, which are nothing other than the testimony of Christ handed on by apostolic witnesses, put us at the feet of Christ, as if we were watching Him act and listening to Him teach as He lived in Palestine. Christ declares that "Heaven and earth will pass away, but my words will not pass away" (Matt. 24:35). His word is preserved and kept alive by the Church for all those who are willing to listen.

Pope St. John XXIII calls the Church our "mother and teacher" because "to her was entrusted by her holy Founder the twofold task of giving life to her children and of teaching them and guiding them—both as individuals and as nations—with maternal care."[34] Tragically, the Church is perceived by too many today not as a nurturing mother who teaches her children what is best for their lives, but as a stifling drill sergeant who demands obedience to burdensome commands. Admittedly, given the repeated failures of her members and leaders, it is often more difficult to trust the Church that we can see rather than the invisible God whom we cannot see. Nevertheless, Christ, who knew Peter would deny Him three times yet still entrusted the Church's leadership to him, asks us to trust the Church that He founded and that He will never abandon, no matter how turbulent the situation surrounding her may seem. Individual bishops and priests may do horrible things, but the teachings of Christ preserved by the Church cannot be corrupted by even the most corrupt hierarch.

To trust Christ is to trust His Church. We can study and investigate the complete doctrine of the Church to establish intellectual satisfaction that what we are asked by the Church to believe and to hold are correct. But even before we do this, we know through faith, through the personal guarantee of Christ, that the Church's teachings are true and according to His will, even if our intellects cannot see this initially. The Head will not forsake His Body. The fact that the Church has survived for two thousand years amidst heinous scandals involving her leaders and bitter infighting among her members while countless peoples, nations, and empires—all ostensibly more powerful than a Church without guns or battalions—have come and gone may well be God's way of showing us that He is indeed with the Church always, to the close of the age.

The Church and Other Religions

The fullness of truth resides in the Roman Catholic Church as a gift from God.[35] It is not the case that the Church has a monopoly on truth, or that truth is something we possess due to our own merits. The truth is given to the Church by God to bring all human beings to Him—"you will know the truth, and the truth will make you free." (John 8:32). Benedict XVI cautions that "we cannot say 'I have the truth', but the truth has us, it touches us. And we try to let ourselves be guided by this touch.... [W]e are 'co-workers of the truth.' One can work with the truth, because the truth is a person."[36] Jesus Christ, "the way, and the truth, and the life," has touched all believers and guides them through His Church, the vessel of His truth. The Church offers Christ Himself, and everything that He taught—the fullness of His truth—to the world, not as a bludgeon, but as life-giving water for all those who thirst. This truth is to be received with humility and gratitude.

This insistence on the necessity of seeking and living the truth, combined with the perennial teaching that the Church "is necessary for salvation,"[37] is sorely at odds with a secular world beholden to a pluralism that denies the existence of universal truth. On the one hand, today there are many sincere religious believers who think that all religions provide an equally valid path to God. For them, religions are an expression of relativism: what someone wants to be true for herself is true. On the other hand, some deem religion a false diversion that is futile and the cause of chronic problems in the world due to endless infighting between religious sects. If not serving as a means to obtaining truth, religion is reduced either to sentimentality or to factionalism.

Catholics cannot allow these challenges to lead them into the paralyzing state of self-doubt that undermines the very core of the faith relationship between the believer and God. Neither challenge—that everything is true or that nothing is true—fits with human experience, which affirms the existence of a reality that has standards for our behavior and that produces outcomes that are good, indifferent, or bad. This is how we can measure the truth of morality and religion: "you will know them by their fruits" (Matt. 7:16). If we could not find truth in morality and religion, we could not, for example, call the Holocaust or slavery evils in themselves: they would be wrong or right according to one's opinion. Furthermore, human beings across all cultures throughout human history have agreed that malefactors should be punished, children should be reared, and the killing of innocents should be forbidden, even as there are differences in the details that derive from each of these general precepts. We have a natural, spontaneous reaction to certain moral and immoral actions which point us to an underlying moral law that governs these actions. Our joy when we help someone succeed, our horror when we see someone suffer, and our sorrow when someone dies are the responses of our internal moral compass whose magnetic north is the truth of the natural moral law that all human beings infer by the use of reason. These responses precede and transcend the particular norms of cultures, epochs, and societies.

Human experience and our internal moral compass can also help evaluate the truth or falsity of certain religious claims. For example, any religious teachings that command adherents to harm another innocent person deliberately cannot be true, since they require something that is contrary to the natural moral law, and, by extension, to what is good for human beings. In the same way, religious teachings that contradict confirmed scientific or logical truths must be rejected as false teachings: as Benedict XVI affirms, "not to act in accordance with reason is contrary to God's nature."[38] Any teaching or act of religion, therefore, that contradicts reason is false because it is contrary to God Himself. On the other hand, a religious teaching that obligates acts of charity and love of neighbor can be judged as true because they are in accordance with the natural moral law and with what is good for humanity. At the most basic level, then, there is truth in religion, in what it professes and in what it demands of its adherents. And this truth exists even if religion's detractors wish to deny it or ignore it.

Many religions of the world include positive elements that are true since they are in accord with the natural moral law, and some religions have more positive elements than others. For example, a religion that teaches love of neighbor but denies the existence of the one God has a positive element; but, on the whole, it is deficient, because denying the truth of God's existence can lead its adherents further away from truth. By contrast, Judaism and Christianity both teach love of neighbor and the existence of the one God. Since both of these teachings are in accord with the natural law, we can judge them as containing more truths than other religions that do not share both of these teachings.

Beyond basic morality and the existence of God, determining the truth of Judaism and the different branches of Christianity becomes more difficult since these religions are all based upon God's self-revelation that cannot be crossed-checked by some outside reference. Yet we can still use reason to consider the content of revelation, an action which is also part of the process of accepting God's invitation of faith. We have already made the case for the divinity of Christ, the Son of God, a truth Judaism does not accept. We cannot prove Jesus' divinity empirically; we allow our reason to conclude that, based on the evidence that Jesus Himself presented to us and has been passed down by His apostles, it is reasonable to have faith, to trust, that Jesus is God. If He is not God, then detractors have to present a compelling case as to His identity that takes into account all the evidence—His teachings, behavior, miracles, and resurrection. Perhaps, if Jesus was not God, he was a liar or a lunatic, as C. S. Lewis famously postulated.[39] Perhaps He was just an itinerant preacher, a liberal, reforming rabbi, or a political revolutionary.[40] Perhaps Jesus was mistaken in His own identity, a man who thought He was God.[41] Perhaps His divine status was invented by His followers.[42] Yet these theories, based on a careful examination of the New Testament as well as non-Christian ancient sources, prove nothing definitive about Jesus. In fact, these theories are really acts of faith by their respective originators and adherents, just as certain scientific assumptions about the universe are really acts of faith by the scientists who make them. In the end, it is the Church's act of faith in Jesus as the Son of God that is the most plausible theory because it takes into account the entire witness of the New Testament.

Divisions between Catholics, Eastern Orthodox Christians, and Protestants vary in degree and quantity, although there are certainly more shared beliefs than not: the incarnation of the Son of God and the redemption wrought by Him, the necessity of baptism, the truth of Sacred Scripture, and the existence of Heaven and Hell are but a few. Surely these beliefs direct their adherents toward the truth who is God. But these branches of Christianity all lack certain elements of Catholic teaching, teaching that has developed organically, through the guidance of the Holy Spirit, over the centuries as we have reflected more deeply on the events of salvation. The use of *Trinity* to describe God's nature is one example of this development.

When comparing Catholicism with Eastern Orthodox Christians and Protestants, Father Thomas Kocik explains that these groups that have broken from the Catholic Church "all have one thing in common: a strong attachment to one theme or one portion of Christian revelation, which they have never learned to balance and integrate with the rest."[43] Protestants rejected Catholic teaching on salvation, on the sacraments, and Tradition, while Eastern Orthodoxy rejected the primacy of the pope over other bishops; and in doing so, to compensate for these rejected teachings, they disproportionately embraced particular aspects of Christianity over others, be they justification by faith alone, *sola Scriptura*, or the equal sharing of episcopal authority without the juridical primacy of the bishop of Rome.

By rejecting certain teachings of the Church, these Christian groups have deprived themselves of essential aspects of the life of grace as designed by God. As Kocik concludes, "fragmentary Christianity, especially where it rests on the principles of private judgment in matters of faith and morals, cannot be relied upon for the truth that makes us free. The only sure foundation of Christian hope is the entire Christian revelation—the fullness of truth" found in the Catholic Church.[44] The act of switching from one Christian religion to the next illustrates this concept of the fullness of truth: when Protestants or Orthodox Christians become Catholic, they believe more about God and His workings than they did previously.[45] Conversely, should Catholics fall away from the Church and participate with other Christian groups, they reject some of their previously held beliefs—they believe less than what they did as Catholics.

Divisions among Christians have been caused not just by pride, but by a loss of faith. Each division has manifold origins, including in many cases the bad behavior of Catholic popes, bishops, and lay faithful, but there is also the reality that those who deliberately broke from the Catholic Church over doctrine ceased to trust Christ and His promise to guide the Church. The inter-Christian wars that have occurred over the centuries and that receive the continual scorn of secular critics have not been caused by Christian teaching, but by believers who, weakened by concupiscence like everyone else, trust their own finite judgment rather than trust in God. The divisions in Christianity that still remain do so not because there is no truth or no right answer, but because within the lives of believers faith has been compromised by pride on all sides. Of course, since every Christian is a sinner, conflicts inevitably occur, even between fellow Catholics. Yet because of the guaranteed guidance of the Holy Spirit, we can still trust the official teaching of the Catholic Church, "which is the Church of the living God, the pillar and bulwark of truth" (1 Tim. 3:15).

❧ CHAPTER 7

Faith, Certitude, Doubt, and Conscience

The nature of faith creates a paradox: We cannot see and quantify all the evidence for God, but we know that objective faith, the substance of what we believe, is true because of the authority of God who reveals them. God and His revelation to us are the source and content of objective faith; we know, therefore, that faith is certain because of the perfection of its revealer. There is no need for believers to shrink from this fact: if God is who we know Him to be, then faith is objectively certain. By contrast, other forms of rational human knowledge are less certain because they depend on human reason, with its finite capacities, for their source and content.[1]

In one sense, then, the authority of God should be sufficient to provide believers with confidence in their faith. As St. Paul told the Thessalonians, "[W]hen you received the word of God which you heard from us, you accepted it not as the word of men but as what it really is, the word of God" (1 Thess. 2:13). God is the cause of faith, the substance of faith, and the end of faith. But at the same time, human beings can and do encounter difficulties as they live out the subjective dimension of faith in their own individual experiences. God, after all, infinitely exceeds the capacity of human understanding and lies beyond the realm of empirical verification. How can we be sure, therefore, in terms of our personal relationship with God, that what we believe is true?

If this disparity between God and man did not exist, then faith would not be needed: we would instead be compelled to *know* that God exists in the same manner that we are compelled to know that two plus two equals four. Belief in God would then be replaced by direct knowledge of Him, a situation which would remove freedom and trust from the relationship between humans and God. But since this disparity is real, it is quite possible for genuine believers to profess sincerely the Nicene Creed, the objective dimension of faith, while still feeling unsettled on a personal level concerning whether they, deep down, feel in their heart what they profess with their lips. In examining such issues, we pass from objective certainty, which pertains to the real content of revelation itself, to subjective certitude, which pertains to "the firmness of the believer's internal assent."[2]

Subjective or individual certitude is of critical importance in understanding the nature of faith, for it helps us understand how we relate to God on a human level. In its nature certitude is similar to the term we use for prosecutors proving their case in a court of law: the judge and jury must be led to believe that the accused is guilty "beyond a reasonable doubt." Yet certitude is stronger than this legal standard, which sets a negative norm as its low bar; certitude aims for congruence between the truth of an objective fact or proposition and an individual person. Blessed John Henry Newman cautions that "if we cannot establish certitude, then truth cannot be known."[3] The skeptical and relativistic mindset that drives contemporary secularity denies both that objective truth exists and that the individual can know it. If this is the case, then the most authentically human expression of moral certitude—the statement, "I love you"—is an empty and meaningless set of words. Relativism not only eschews truth and certitude, but also the most basic elements of what it means to be human.

Newman defines certitude as the "deliberate assent given expressly after reasoning."[4] For Newman, three conditions must be met to establish certitude: certitude follows from careful investigation; it is accompanied by a sense of intellectual satisfaction; and it is a commitment that is irreversible. If any of these elements are lacking, then we are left with a rash judgment, a prejudice, an inference, or a personal conviction, none of which are equated with objective truth. Certitude, then, is not a starting point or sudden choice, but the end result that follows from careful deliberation. Since certitude depends on the reasoning of the human mind, the act of assent is inherently personal. It is the subjective complement to objective truth. The discernment of a vocation to the Catholic priesthood is one such example: a man deeply considers the signs given to him by God as well as his own personal desires, together with consultation from members of the Church. To assent to the vocation by choosing to become a priest, he expresses his certitude that the call from God is real; no one else can come to that decision for him. If he possesses real certitude, then he will experience personal consolation that he has made the correct decision, and he will remain a priest forever.

Newman argues that certitude is indefectible, meaning we cannot be mistaken in it since it brings about "the termination of all doubt or fear about its truth."[5] Any perceived certitude that is abandoned or disproved was never, in fact, a certitude. There is no internal test to prove a certitude true rather than false; instead, there is a negative test: certitude must withstand all challenges that are put to it from without. Newman gives the example of those who saw Christ die, and then saw Him alive again days later. The astonishment of seeing Him alive did not destroy the certitude they had of His death. They *knew* that His death was a real, true event; seeing Him alive did not and could not change their assent. At the same time, this astonishment at the prospect of a dead man coming back to life, coupled with the threat of death for telling others about this event, did not destroy their certitude that they saw Him alive and risen.

When believers possess certitude of faith, they know in their hearts that the objective faith that they profess in the Nicene Creed is true *for them*. Some believers may be at a loss, for example, how to respond to a particular criticism of faith by an unbeliever, or what to make of a scientific discovery about the origins of life that seems to challenge their faith. They may even be upset by these experiences and begin to question their beliefs. Nevertheless, they make the conscious decision to remain steadfast in their relationships with God: their assent to God and the truths about Him is irrevocable. Although they may feel unsettled in their belief from time to time, by an act of their will they remain convinced that what they believe is true.

By contrast, those who have changed their religion over the course of their lives, or those who have ceased to practice their faith, never possessed certitude of it. Their personal relationships of faith might have included strong feelings of belief and duty to God at one point or another; but those relationships lacked the firm, deliberate, and lasting assent that comprises authentic certitude. Firm assent that leads to certitude is akin to building one's house of religious faith on rock: this assent endures through rains, floods, and winds. Without firm assent a believer builds his house on sand: it may be beautiful and a source of joy and peace for a time, but eventually the weather will cause its ruin, "and great was the fall of it" (Matthew 7:27). Put another way, "Faith must be firm assent, or it is not really faith."[6] For Catholics, firm assent must be made to the entire content of the Nicene Creed as well as all of the dogma taught infallibly by the Church's Magisterium.[7]

Newman helps us understand the firm assent that brings certitude:

> Assents may and do change; certitudes endure. This is why religion demands more than assent to its truth; it requires certitude, or at least an assent which is convertible into certitude on demand. Without certitude in religious faith there may be much decency of profession and of observance, but there can be no habit of prayer, no directness of devotion, no intercourse with the unseen, no generosity of self-sacrifice. Certitude then is essential to the Christian; and if he is to persevere to the end, his certitude must include in it a principle of persistence.[8]

Persistence in certitude does not necessarily mean that a believer's personal relationship with God will always be perfect—difficulties and doubts may beset us. In this regard, the model of firm assent and perseverance may well be the apostle Peter, who possessed the certitude of Jesus Christ's divinity. Yet, when under duress, Peter denied that he even knew Jesus. His denial was not a rejection of his certitude of faith: it was an act of selfishness in which his love for Jesus was momentarily eclipsed by his fear. When he came to his senses, Peter realized the wrong he had done, sought God's forgiveness, and then, chastened but strengthened by his experience, he resumed his relationship with Him. Like Peter, our own loyalty to Christ is often tested by our own fears and impetuosity. Like Peter, our faith can be renewed by seeking God's forgiveness and confessing our love for Him.

We opened this chapter noting a paradox within the nature of faith: it is certain, yet beyond the realm of empirical verification. How can we establish subjective certitude if we cannot fully investigate the reality to which we assent? Although there are good reasons to assent to God, the lack of definitive, empirical evidence leaves faith, by its very nature, open to challenge and doubt.[9] If challenge and doubt were not possible for believers, faith would not require trust and commitment. Dulles illuminates the inner workings of faith: "If the evidence of credibility were not strong enough to preclude doubt, a firm assent could not be reasonable; but if it did preclude doubt, the assent would be necessary rather than free.... We can at any time envision how, having freely come to faith, we could freely cease to believe. In other words, we can see that faith is faith."[10]

In the absence of definitive evidence, we are able to assent firmly to God and possess certitude about Him because of the aid of divine grace. As Dulles explains, in "the supernatural assent of faith, the will, freely submitting to the attraction of grace, gives special force to the assent following upon practical judgment to believe."[11] Grace, then, allows the assent of faith to coexist "with the realization that faith is a risk and that it hovers over an abyss of nonevidence."[12] Grace can be resisted, and it never forces the will to comply. Hence religious certitude follows from an act of freedom: we can only assent by willing to do so. Grace makes assent possible by strengthening our resolve to choose God. Yet even with the help of grace, we should not pretend that the assent of faith is easy or automatic. If it were, everyone would believe.

For Catholics baptized in infancy, the assent of faith does not necessarily happen in a single moment. Baptism provides the grace we need as we grow and learn about the faith through the help of our parents, families, teachers, fellow parishioners, and, above all, through our attendance at Mass each week. The assent of children, who intuitively trust what they learn, becomes firm as they ask questions about the faith and learn the import it has for them as individuals. This process may take many years and continue into adolescence and adulthood. Conversely, when baptized infants are not taught the faith by their parents or brought to Mass regularly, firm assent becomes much more difficult. Such children are thus deprived of the primary nourishment of the grace received at baptism. Without the certitude of faith, these young Catholics lack the virtue of perseverance, and therefore they are far more likely to cease practicing their faith when they become adults.

When adults convert to Catholicism from another religion, they accept the teachings of the Church as a condition for baptism. If their acceptance is genuine, the grace of baptism makes their assent firm and fosters certitude. When we see recent converts who are energetic and excited to practice their new faith, their zeal is animated by the certitude they possess. By contrast, should an adult convert for strictly social reasons, he would lack certitude in his faith, and, consequently, his religious practice may well be wanting. In addition to converts from other religions, the term "revert" has been coined in recent decades for adult Catholics who spent years away from the Church and from their practice of the faith, only to return to the Church with their assent to faith made firm at long last.

As mentioned above, because faith brings us into a relationship with God whom we cannot see, it is normal for believers to feel unsettled from time to time, or to have questions arise about some of their beliefs. This unsettled feeling brings us to consider another aspect of faith: its obscurity. Faith is "obscure," meaning "dark, dim, or lacking light," in that it points to truths whose full reality lies beyond our comprehension, in the "dark shadow" of human unknowing.[13] When we are in a loving relationship, we naturally desire to see our beloved. In the loving relationship of faith, by contrast, we cannot see God, our beloved. He remains beyond the limits of human sight; and even if we were to see Him, His grandeur far exceeds what our finite intellects can comprehend. In this life, St. Paul teaches, "we see in a mirror dimly;" only in Heaven, when we see God "face to face," will we understand fully the faith that we now believe (1 Cor. 13:12). And so we often long for that face to face encounter with God now in this life: we want Him to manifest Himself to confirm our belief, to remove potential dangers, to save us from trying situations.

This desire to see God creates a state which Josef Pieper calls "mental unrest" for the believer: we constantly long for a deeper encounter with God.[14] This leads to a tension that exists within the life of faith. On the one hand, we have already seen that faith is certain because it is revealed by God Himself. When, with God's grace, we assent to the truths of faith with individual certitude, our minds rest confidently with God. On the other hand, since the ultimate realities of faith reside beyond our comprehension and sight, we are not completely settled in our knowledge of God; we experience mental unrest since we cannot see what we long to see. This unrest is similar to other human experiences: the excitement we may feel just before the arrival of a guest or an old friend; the eagerness we feel just before returning home to our family after a business trip; the longing that parents feel for their children away in a distant place. In all of these instances, love is present and strong in the relationship, yet there exists a dissatisfaction at the separation that exists between persons. Such is the nature of our relationship with God.

For St. John of the Cross, this inherent tension between the certitude and the obscurity of faith, between God's grace and our mental unrest, exists because in faith we "believe truths revealed by God Himself, which transcend all natural light, and exceed all human understanding, beyond all proportion."[15] John compares the experience of the believer to a man born blind receiving a description of colors: since the man "has never seen such colors or anything like them by which he may judge them, only their names would remain with him; for these he would be able to comprehend through the ear, but not their forms or figures, since he has never seen them."[16]

Faith, as we noted earlier, comes to us by hearing the testimony of others, a testimony that we cannot verify for ourselves. The blind man has a choice: He can accept the fact that color exists based on what he has heard, although he does not have an experience of it; or he can reject the description on the grounds that his interlocutor is trying to deceive him, or that the idea of color is too farfetched to be real. The religious believer is free to make the same choice: to accept or reject the testimony of God that he has heard. In accepting the testimony, the believer realizes that, like the blind man, he will have only a limited experience of what he hears for the rest of his life. Yet the limited experience that the believer has of God in this life does not negate the reality of his or her experience.

St. John of the Cross reiterates the insight of the prophet Isaiah when it comes to the tension of faith's certainty and obscurity: If you will not believe, you will not understand.[17] This does not mean that we believe uncritically without regard for logic or reason: this is fideism, which is a heresy condemned by the Church. Rather, because God so exceeds our comprehension, if we do not first trust that He exists, we will not be able to understand Him or His revelation, insofar as we are capable. Put positively, understanding follows from belief. This is a reason why the Church has so many external critics: without belief, without faith, so many of the Church's teachings do not seem to make sense. It is only with faith that we understand how God's revelation and the Church's teachings fit together in the symphony that is God's plan for the world.

To believe before understanding is not to put the cart before the horse, as if God somehow has to prove Himself to us before we will believe in Him. It is instead the opening of one's heart to God and the promises that He offers, and these promises can only be received when we are docile to God's grace. Before Paul healed the man crippled from birth at Lystra, he noted that the man "had faith to be made well" (Acts 14:9). That is, he had the seeds of faith in his heart; intellectual understanding about the intricacies of God's law and revelation follow after this initial willingness. Similarly, when a young girl sets out for her first piano lesson, she knows nothing about how exactly the piano works or how she is to play it; yet she has faith that she will be able to make music after receiving the proper instruction. If she were not willing to learn and she did not trust her potential to play, she would never learn to play in the first place. And so a willing heart is more prepared to trust Him who cannot be seen than an unwilling heart, as the Pharisees who challenged Jesus demonstrated so clearly.

The obscurity of faith does not undermine faith's certitude. These two properties of faith coexist in a natural, healthy tension, in a manner akin to a successful physics experiment that raises as many questions as it solves: the genesis of new questions does not undermine the answers to the previous questions. We saw earlier that St. Paul defined faith as "the assurance of things hoped for, the conviction of things not seen" (Heb. 11:1). Responding to this statement, St. John of the Cross notes that "although the understanding may be firmly and certainly consenting to [the things not seen], they are not things that are revealed to the understanding, since, if they were revealed to it, there would be no faith. So faith, although it brings certainty to the understanding, brings it not clearness, but obscurity."[18] There are good reasons to trust what we believe, yet the fact remains that the full reality of faith lies beyond what our minds can know in this life. Hence the act of faith also requires courage to accept what transcends our human limitations.

Difficulties and Doubts

Two ingredients are necessary to sustain the life of faith: God's grace and the conscious decision of the believer to remain steadfast in his relationship with God. Since God never ceases to pour His grace upon those who desire it, difficulties occur in the life of faith on the human, subjective side of faith. As St. Thomas Aquinas acknowledged, the nature of faith, with its trust in an unseen God and with the mind of the believer in a state of unrest, leaves open the possibility of doubt.[19] Some devout Catholics experience difficulties and doubts about particular beliefs or about God's existence entirely. Such experiences can be fleeting or they can last for years. Difficulties and doubts are not necessarily par for the course of every believer; yet they are still the real experiences of many, and a person is not blameworthy or "less" Catholic for having such experiences.

A believer's faith can be challenged from without, either by skeptical attacks on faith, by scandals caused by believers, or by the experience of evil or trauma. A believer's faith can weaken and even erode from within if he ceases to practice his faith by not attending Mass, frequenting the sacraments, and praying; or if he allows the external challenges to his beliefs to undermine his assent to faith without trying to combat them by seeking answers from books, from the saints, or from fellow believers. All of these experiences can create difficulties within the life of faith that can lead to further doubts and uncertainties. While such experiences are to be expected within the life of faith, they can, if unchecked, weaken or even destroy the subjective faith of believers.

Before proceeding we must define the terms "difficulty" and "doubt" within the context of religious belief. A difficulty is a challenge or obstacle to belief that is not readily understood. Today's secular world has no shortage of difficulties to present to the believer. A news item, criticism, or calumny over issues ranging from the authority of the Church herself and her hierarchy, to the authenticity of Sacred Scripture, to the existence of God in an age of science, to the Church's teachings on marriage and family can all prompt sudden discomfort and questions within the minds of believers. In addition to these contemporary items, other more perennial events can raise difficulties for our faith, such as when we ask God whether we should marry a certain person or take the unexpected job transfer to another state. The greatest difficulties of all are usually born in hardship, such as when we ask God why He allowed a certain suffering or death to occur.

A believer contends with a given difficulty within the context of his personal relationship with God and seeks God's help to overcome it. The encounter between the angel Gabriel and the Blessed Virgin Mary is the best example of meeting and overcoming a difficulty in faith (Luke 1:26–38). When greeted by the angel as "full of grace," Mary "was greatly troubled at the saying, and considered in her mind what sort of greeting this might be." Upon hearing that she would conceive and bear a son who "will be great, and will be called the Son of the Most High," she asked a practical question that shows her considering her present circumstances: "How can this be, since I have no husband?" Gabriel's response, at root, asked her to put her particular worries aside and trust in God. There is no record of what Mary thought or of the emotions she felt. Any concerns she might have had she chose to return directly to God: "Behold, I am the handmaid of the Lord; let it be to me according to your word."

From Mary's encounter we learn two things about how we ought to encounter difficulties that arise within the life of faith. First, we should bring whatever spiritual, moral, or personal difficulties we have to God in prayer, and ask Him for help, for understanding, and for strength in meeting them. In other words, we must meet these difficulties within the context of our relationship with God rather than outside of it; difficulties presented to us must be re-presented by us to God. There is never a reason to hide the difficulties we have in living our faith from God, as if He would somehow condemn us for not being perfect in our belief. On the contrary, the nature of an authentic, loving relationship leaves space for discussing delicate issues with the beloved, and the relationship of faith is no exception. We may not be full of grace as Mary was, yet we know God will supply us with the grace we need to address our concerns within His loving embrace.

Second, after a period of prayer and wrestling with the difficulty, we ought to entrust it to God. Our act of trust can echo Mary's, or it can be that of the father who brought his possessed son to Jesus in searching of healing: "I believe; help my unbelief!" (Mark 9:24). This latter expression can be our own when we decide to trust the Magisterium of the Church and the authenticity of the Bible in the midst of some uncertainty in our minds; when we decide to live according to the Church's teachings on marriage and family life even if we are experiencing peer pressure and serious financial woes; or when we continue to practice our faith despite the sorrow we feel at the loss of a loved one or the anger we feel at the sins of bishops, priests, and other believers. Here again we see the freedom and courage needed for maintaining the relationship of faith, even when faced with real suffering. Overcoming difficulties within the life of faith can only be accomplished through a deliberate choice to remain faithful.

Doubts about the faith resound more deeply than do difficulties, since doubts challenge believers' trust in God, which is the very foundation of our life of faith. Newman famously made a distinction between difficulty and doubt: "Ten thousand difficulties do not make one doubt... difficulty and doubt are incommensurate. There of course may be difficulties in the evidence... A man may be annoyed that he cannot work out a mathematical problem, of which the answer is or is not given to him, without doubting that it admits of an answer, or that a certain particular answer is the true one."[20]

As a noun, "doubt" refers to "the (subjective) state of uncertainty with regard to the truth or reality of anything; undecidedness of belief or opinion."[21] We see doubt in this sense when we question God's existence, dispute the possibility of miracles, or hesitate about the reality of the incarnation and resurrection. It is also possible for difficulties that go unchecked to morph into doubts if the believer ceases to handle them within his relationship of faith with God.

As a verb, "to doubt" can be used in two senses. First, one can "be wavering or undecided in opinion or belief,"[22] such as when the apostles saw the risen Jesus in Galilee before the Ascension: "[W]hen they saw him they worshiped him; but some doubted" (Matt. 28:17). Doubt can also be used to express uncertainty, hesitation, or mistrust toward something in particular,[23] such as, "I doubt God's existence," or "I doubt that Jesus rose from the dead."

Doubt, as the opposite side of faith, is a necessary capacity of the human mind. It is a natural response to doubt information that we find unlikely to be true. Sacred Scripture contains many stories concerning how certain people have experienced religious doubt, both for good and for ill. Two biblical passages especially highlight doubt as it is lived and experienced today.

The first is the story of Naaman, commander of the Syrian army, who was encouraged by an Israeli slave to seek the king of Jerusalem to heal his leprosy (2 Kings 5:1–27). Upon news of Naaman's arrival, the prophet Elisha sent for him. When Naaman arrived at Elisha's house, the prophet sent him a message: "Go and wash in the Jordan seven times, and your flesh shall be restored, and you shall be clean." Naaman flew into a rage at the news, and shouted, "Behold, I thought that he would surely come out to me, and stand, and call on the name of the Lord his God, and wave his hand over the place, and cure the leper. Are not Abana and Pharpar, the rivers of Damascus, better than all the waters of Israel? Could I not wash in them and be clean?"

The reaction of Naaman is one not uncommon of believers at varying points in our lives of faith: we doubt God because He does not conform to our desires, or because He did not act according to how we think He should. Sometimes such doubts can arise from our own self-created expectations about how our lives should be, and our ensuing disappointment when things do not turn out as we wish. We wonder if God is really there if He has not acted as we wanted. Other times doubts may arise when God does not answer a prayer or petition according to our desires, such as when prayers for the recovery of a fatally ill family member seem to be ignored.

Such doubts are common, serious, and trying, and they can test the very core of our faith relationship with God. Sometimes these doubts can even harden into resentment and bitterness toward God, especially after the experience of a serious trauma or evil. We doubt His existence or His care for us. These doubts then tempt us to stop attending Mass and to stop praying.

A second biblical example of doubt is that of Thomas the apostle, who was not with the other disciples when Jesus appeared to them on the day of His resurrection (John 20:24–29). When the disciples told Thomas that they had seen the Lord, Thomas responded, "Unless I see in his hands the print of the nails, and place my finger in the mark of the nails, and place my hand in his side, I will not believe."

Thomas doubted that Jesus had risen because he wanted tangible proof to justify his belief. This form of doubt takes the desire of believers to see God, the mental unrest that is native to the life of faith, and subordinates it to the demands of empirical knowledge. To withhold religious belief until physical evidence is produced is an act counter to the nature of faith; rather than trust God, Thomas and those demanding physical proof express their distrust of Him. In doing so, they seek to make themselves—and not God—the initiator and guarantor of the faith relationship.

With religious doubt we again see the tremendous freedom inherent in the faith relationship. We have the freedom to respond to God's call, and we have the freedom to reject it. Experiences of doubt remind us that our relationship with God is not necessarily a walk on a flat, steady plain. The strength of our faith can fluctuate based both on our experiences and on the effort we put into it. Doubt brings the sobering reminder that we can be led away from God at any point in our lives.

How are we to respond to experiences of doubt, whether they be generated by our own lofty expectations or by our demand for proof from God? As the conclusions of the stories of Naaman and Thomas teach us, the best way to respond to doubt is to make a reciprocal act of faith.

In response to Naaman's incredulous rage, his servants said, "[I]f the prophet had commanded you to do some great thing, would you not have done it? How much rather, then, when he says to you, 'Wash, and be clean?'" Naaman then went and washed as the prophet had commanded, "and his flesh was restored like the flesh of a little child, and he was clean."

Naaman's servants remind us that we should not subordinate God's will to our expectations. In fact, God explained to the prophet Isaiah the problem of forcing Him to act according to human desires: "For my thoughts are not your thoughts, neither are your ways my ways... For as the heavens are higher than the earth, so are my ways higher than your ways and my thoughts than your thoughts" (Is. 55:8–9). We cannot pretend to understand God's whole plan for the world and for our lives, particularly when we face the reality of evil, a prospect we will consider later: we are inveterate seekers of explanations, but explanations are not always available. In addition, our fallen nature leads us to trust ourselves over others, particularly those with authority over us. It is all too easy, when faced with a trying situation, to reject God because we know that He may not desire for us what we desire for ourselves. Faith requires us to fight this tendency and entrust ourselves to God—to put our worries, our expectations, our fears, and our doubts into His hands. And, as Jesus told Peter, the more we surrender our lives to God, the more He will give to us in return: "[E]veryone who has left houses or brothers or sisters or father or mother or children or lands, for my name's sake, will receive a hundredfold, and inherit eternal life" (Matt. 19:29).

Eight days after His resurrection, Jesus again appeared to His disciples, but this time Thomas was with them. Jesus immediately sought Thomas and called him out for his doubts: "Put your finger here, and see my hands; and put out your hand, and place it in my side; do not be faithless, but believing." Thomas responded by confessing his now reassured faith: "My Lord and my God!" Even with this confession, Jesus rebuked Thomas, as we saw earlier, for his lack of faith, a rebuke that rings true for us today: "You have believed because you have seen me. Blessed are those who have not seen and yet believe."

Faith comes through hearing others and trusting their testimony of God's action in the world. It does not come through seeing or from physical evidence. Reading theological treaties can be helpful, but only to a point, in combating doubt. Although faith is reasonable, something more than reason is needed in order to believe. A deliberate and renewed act of trust in God—the very antithesis of doubt—is the most effective response because it strikes doubt at its very root. Through Thomas, Jesus teaches us that we overcome doubt by an act of the will: He will provide the grace to help us, but only we can make the choice to trust Him, despite any misgivings that we may feel. In the face of doubt, our most effective prayer may be a simple declaration: "Jesus, I trust in you."

Faith and Conscience

Conscience is one of the ways we become aware of God's existence. Newman spoke of conscience's twofold nature: the moral sense for judging proper action and the awareness of an authoritative monitor. Conscience is God's way of hardwiring us, His human creatures, to know Him. Hence the Second Vatican Council describes conscience as "the most secret core and sanctuary of a man. There he is alone with God, whose voice echoes in his depths."[24] When human beings hear God's voice, which is the call to faith, they hear and respond in conscience. Conscience, therefore, is both the awareness and inner ability to hear God's voice and to know the truth, as well as the moral judgment we make in response to Him. The *Catechism* calls this latter aspect of conscience "a judgment of reason whereby the human person recognizes the moral quality of a concrete act that he is going to perform, is in the process of performing, or has already completed."[25]

Each and every time we hear God calling us, we make a practical judgment in conscience to follow God's will or reject it. Throughout our lives we are constantly making such judgments: the judgment to attend Mass every time we go; the judgment to pray every time we do so; the judgment to follow God's will as expressed in the Ten Commandments, the teachings of the Church, and in His own personal dialogue with each of us are all acts of conscience. Conversely, every time we choose to disregard or disobey God's voice, we judge that our own will is more important than God's. The judgments we make for or against God indicate the quality of our relationship with Him: the more we choose Him, the healthier our faith.

The twofold nature of conscience also illustrates the inherent connection between belief in God and the moral life. On Mount Sinai, God revealed through Moses that worship and morality, that love of God and love of neighbor, are inseparable. Jesus himself made this connection clear when a rich young man asked Him, "Teacher, what good deed must I do, to have eternal life?" (Matt. 19:16ff) Jesus responded by linking good deeds with God, the essence and source of good: "Why do you ask me about what is good? One there is who is good." After stating the commandments, the young man realized that something more was being asked of him than just doing good deeds: "All these I have observed; what do I still lack?" Jesus replied, "If you would be perfect, go, sell what you possess and give to the poor, and you will have treasure in heaven; *and come, follow me.*"[26]

The performance of good actions should lead us to Jesus. Conscience enables us to choose both the good action as well as God Himself. Conscience also makes the connection between God and morality because it is oriented toward the truth of how we ought to live, and Jesus Christ is this truth. For this reason the

Second Vatican Council teaches that for those who have never heard the Gospel, whatever good they do or truth found among them prepares their hearts for receiving Christ.[27] And it is also for this reason that Jesus repeatedly emphasized that loving God and loving neighbor are two sides of the same coin: "Truly, I say to you, as you did it to the least of these my brethren, you did it to me" (Matt. 25:40).

Since the same conscience makes judgments about answering God's call and obeying the moral law in particular circumstances, we see that one cannot profess genuine belief in God while at the same time disregarding the Ten Commandments and other moral teachings of the Church. Conscience is not a power given to us to decide on our own what is right or wrong in a given circumstance. Rather, attuned by its nature to the truth of God's voice and God's law, conscience makes a practical judgment about how to act in a given situation based upon the natural law of God. St. John Paul II clarifies that

> whereas the natural law discloses the objective and universal demands of the moral good, conscience is the application of the law to a particular case; this application of the law thus becomes an inner dictate for the individual, a summons to do what is good in this particular situation. Conscience thus formulates moral obligation in the light of the natural law: it is the obligation to do what the individual, through the workings of his conscience, knows to be a good he is called to do here and now.[28]

Proper Formation of Conscience

As a practical judgment made by finite human beings, conscience "is not an infallible judge; it can make mistakes."[29] In order to minimize the possibility for mistakes, the Second Vatican Council underscores that in "the formation of their consciences, the Christian faithful ought carefully to attend to the sacred and certain doctrine of the Church. For the Church is, by the will of Christ, the teacher of the truth. It is her duty to give utterance to, and authoritatively to teach, that truth which is Christ Himself, and also to declare and confirm by her authority those principles of the moral order which have their origins in human nature itself."[30]

To this, St. John Paul adds that in teaching moral principles, the Church does not restrict individual freedom; she actually enhances freedom by allowing conscience to more closely hear the voice of God for which it was designed:

> The Magisterium does not bring to the Christian conscience truths which are extraneous to it; rather it brings to light the truths which it ought already to possess, developing them from the starting point of the primordial act of faith. The Church puts herself always and only at the service of conscience, helping it to avoid being tossed to and fro by every wind of doctrine proposed by human deceit, and helping it not to swerve from the truth about the good of man, but rather, especially in more difficult questions, to attain the truth with certainty and to abide in it.[31]

It follows that the individual conscience is not the supreme power in the universe; it functions as a servant of the law rather than its inventor. In St. John Paul's words, "the judgment of conscience does not establish the law; rather it bears witness to the authority of the natural law and of the practical reason with reference to the supreme good, whose attractiveness the human person perceives and whose commandments he accepts."[32]

It is wrong to use conscience as an excuse for disobeying God's commandments. Because the same conscience hears both God's call to faith and His moral law, we cannot pretend to love God but disregard His commandments. Nor can we decide on the grounds of conscience that an action that is contrary to the natural law and Church teachings is somehow permissible for us on an individual basis. Conscience, the same faculty hardwired to hear God's voice, does not have the authority to tell God what should be done.

When a person's conscience makes a judgment, he is bound to live by that judgment. In the case of morally good actions, the person deserves praise for making the correct judgment. But in the case of morally wrong actions, a person is not free from guilt because he acted in conscience. If this latter circumstance were the case, many horrific evils and crimes could be justified on appeal to conscience. Joseph Ratzinger carefully explains that the fault lies in the distinction between the judgment and the refusal to hear God's voice. The judgment does not justify either the refusal or the action itself if it is contrary to God's law.

> On this level, the level of judgment, it can be said that even the erroneous conscience binds.... No one may act against his convictions, as Saint Paul had already said (Rom. 14:23). But the fact that the conviction a person has come to certainly binds in the moment of acting, does not signify a canonization of subjectivity. It is never wrong to follow the convictions one has arrived at—in fact, one must do so. But it can very well be wrong to have come to such askew convictions in the first place... The guilt lies then in a different place, much deeper—not in the present act, not in the present judgment of conscience but in the neglect of my being which made

me deaf to the internal promptings of truth. For this reason, criminals of conviction like Hitler and Stalin are guilty.[33]

"If today you hear his voice, harden not your hearts" (Psalm 95:8).[34] When God speaks to us in conscience, we have the freedom and power to accept or reject His call. Each judgment we make depends on the firm assent of faith that we make with our intellect. Yet the heart, where we feel God's love in our relationship with Him, also plays a role in the life of faith. As Blaise Pascal famously writes, "the heart has its reasons which reason itself does not know."[35] To faith and feeling we now turn.

❧ CHAPTER 8

Faith, Experience, and Emotion

Since faith involves the commitment of the whole person, emotion and personal experience play an important role in the spiritual life. Sacred Scripture presents the complete spectrum of human sentiment: love and hate, joy and sorrow, hope and despair, courage and fear, gratitude and jealousy, trust and doubt. These are all part of the divine economy because they all bring us into contact with God. God created human beings for a unique relationship with Him; it is fitting, then, that every aspect of the human experience be incorporated into that relationship.

We saw in Chapter 3 that religious experience can bring a person to know that God exists. The experience alone, however, is not enough to inspire faith; during or after the experience, we have to make a firm assent with our intellect that God, in fact, was the cause of this experience and that He is worthy of our trust because of it. After all, it is possible to have a profound experience or to witness a miracle and still deny God's working of it, as was the case with Jesus' detractors who denied that He came from God (Matt. 12:24; John 10:33), with Richard Dawkins and the miracle at Fatima, and with countless others throughout history.

From this we learn that experience and emotion, as powerful

as they are, do not comprise the essence of religious faith; they are part of the life of faith, but not constitutive of faith. As we have seen, faith hinges on the assent of the intellect moved by the will. It is the intellect that accepts what comes from God and trusts in Him. Because faith is a personal act made with complete freedom, a person must choose with her will whether or not she wishes to believe. Experience and emotion have the power to influence what human beings choose or reject. Hence it is important for believers to integrate all their experiences and emotions properly within the broader context of their faith in order to develop further their relationship with God. Yet the presence or absence of emotions does not indicate that faith is present or absent.

The mantra "never let your emotions get the best of you" applies in all aspects of life, and the spiritual life is no exception. In everyday life, our intellect ought to control our emotions; the volatility of the latter can incite us to do things that we may regret later. Examples of this are manifold: anger is a natural human reaction, but unbridled anger can prompt us to sever relationships, to destroy property, or even to inflict harm on another person. In these instances the irate allows emotion, rather than intellect, to induce his will to choose these improper actions. By contrast, when a person makes a conscious decision to control his anger, he can then process the entire situation rationally and make an appropriate response: he could seek the aid of a third party, seek forgiveness if he offended, offer forgiveness if offended, or move on from the experience entirely. On occasion there can even be a righteous anger that leads to reform, such as the anger Jesus directed toward the moneychangers in the temple.

It is just as important for our intellect to maintain control over our emotions in the spiritual life. To be sure, feelings of happiness and joy can be a great spiritual benefit, and it is possible to learn from negative emotions such as pride, anger, or envy. But all of these have the potential to damage a believer's faith: joy that is not grounded in gratitude can lead one to forget God as the source of all good, while negative emotions can spark animosity toward God for not removing the cause of these feelings. Experiences, too, can have a tremendous impact on our faith for good or for ill: a positive encounter with God acting in the world can transform a person's spiritual life forever, while a negative experience of evil or trauma can cause a person to despise and even reject God completely.

Emotions and experiences must be understood under the umbrella of God's providence. Knowing that God is our loving father, we trust that whatever happens to us—for good or for ill—is according to His plan and for the benefit of our salvation, even if we do not understand the reasons why. This includes accepting suffering and death. No single emotion, experience, or event should make or break our faith. Rather, all emotions, experiences, and events comprise the encounters we have with God, who is faithful to us forever, and who often speaks to us through these occurrences. Our task is to ask God in prayer what He wishes to communicate to us through them, and then to respond accordingly.

Two further points about how we respond in faith to emotions and experiences are important. First, we should not pretend that steering the emotions is easy: some people will have more success than others, and different circumstances affect people in different ways. Since the emotions affect not only our souls but also our minds and our bodies, dealing with difficult emotions or experiences can involve more than spiritual counseling. Depression, for example, is real, and it can afflict even the firmest believers. There is nothing wrong with believers seeking help from their doctors as well as their pastors in order to overcome certain difficulties. Even when outside help is not required, it is not unusual for believers to struggle for years dealing with challenges they have experienced.

Second, we must remember that despite the severity of emotions and experiences, it is up to us to control them and not to be controlled by them. Psychologist and Holocaust survivor Viktor Frankl observed this reality in Nazi concentration camps. Although the prisoners suffered horrific physical and psychological tortures that were intended to destroy their spirits, "the sort of person the prisoner became was the result of an inner decision, and not the result of camp influences alone. Fundamentally, therefore, any man can, even under such circumstances, decide what shall become of him—mentally and spiritually."[1] Just as the assent of faith is made with the intellect guided by our free will, our reactions to experiences and emotions also depend on our free assent determined by the will.

Despite the fleeting nature of emotions and their proper place as ordered by the intellect, there have been throughout history many attempts to reduce religious faith to the sum total of human emotion and experience. One of the most prominent proponents of this theory is the nineteenth-century thinker Friedrich Schleiermacher, who writes that "faith in God" is "nothing but the certainty concerning *the feeling* of absolute dependence, as such, i.e. as conditioned by a Being placed outside of ourselves.... [F]aith is nothing other than *the incipient experience* of a satisfaction of that spiritual need by Christ."[2] Schleiermacher has been influential in attempting—and failing—to give Christianity an emotional basis that can survive the seeming imperatives of science. Feelings and experiences are fleeting: it is possible to have the feeling and experience Schleiermacher describes at one moment, and then lose that feeling the next. If faith is a real and lasting relationship with God, it must be based on more than feelings for it to endure.

Due to the power that emotions can have over us, many Church movements and programs over the centuries have appealed to human sentiment to induce belief. Such events range from small parish and school events, to music concerts, to Catholic summer camps, to the massive, world-wide World Youth Day celebrations that bring together millions of Catholics from across the globe. This approach can be effective—provided it develops the emotions produced into the genuine commitment of the faith relationship. To do so, participants in such movements and programs must also learn the nature of God and the content of His revelation, and then assent with their intellect to the truth of God that is the goal of religious sentiment. Leaving the participants with an emotional experience that does not include God's revelation taught by the Church is akin to giving a child dessert without having a nutritious dinner: the moment of joy will be brief, and soon real hunger follows that will not be satisfied. Believers need more than religious experiences to sustain their faith: for their faith to be strong they require "the unleavened bread of sincerity and truth" (1 Cor. 5:8) that is the substance of God and His revelation.

We also see the priority of assent over sentiment when we consider the nature of human love, and especially familial love. Love between a man and a woman is often sparked by intense feelings of mutual affection and passion. But true love is more than romantic sentiment, which, like any other feeling, is fleeting: true love depends on an act of the will to place the other before one's self. Only this mutual commitment will lead to a lasting marriage. Feelings and affections will come and go; love endures through all types of emotions so long as the will to serve the other remains. Over the course of a marriage, the full gamut of human emotions that the spouses experience can both enhance and debilitate their commitment to love, which is truly manifested through actions rather than feelings. Caring for an ill spouse, assisting the other with chores, and dealing patiently with the other's idiosyncrasies are just a few ways in which love is proved in deeds, even as personal feelings may be trending in the opposite direction.

The same can be said for the love between parents and children. A mother may be filled with tremendous emotion as she interacts with her infant or toddler child. But when the child wakes up crying in the middle of the night, it is not a love of happy feelings, but a love born in personal commitment to the child, that prompts the mother to spring from bed to soothe her. The same reality holds near the end of the mother's life, when her adult child now tends to her ailing mother's needs, not with feelings of mirth and excitement, but with devotion and tenderness, acts of real love born in a willing heart.

The love that God has for us, and that we have for Him in turn, is of the same nature. Our love for God can be born in a powerful religious experience, or it can develop slowly, without feeling or emotion, over the course of our lifetimes. The presence or lack of emotion does not necessarily correspond with our love for God, as Carmelite Father Gabriel of St. Mary Magdalen explains: "[T]he enkindling of love does not consist in the joy the soul may experience, but rather in the firm determination of the will to give itself entirely to God."[3] Only the determination of the will has enough force to help us "love the Lord your God with all your heart, and with all your soul, and with all your mind" (Matt. 22:37). This determination is made not once, but repeatedly, day after day for the course of our whole lifetimes. And it is made not necessarily with an iron will that acts in spite of all opposition, but with the whole self: body, mind, and soul. We love God as persons, not as faculties: our will expresses our personal commitment to the God who created us.

God, of course, is not subject to emotion and sentiments, yet His love is also marked by the firm commitment of His will toward us, despite our sins and our failed attempts to return our love to Him. God's love for each of us individually surpasses our understanding and is, therefore, easy for us to overlook: it is all too easy to fall into the trap of thinking, "God does not love me because I am like this," or, "God cannot love me because I did that." We must take the words of Sacred Scripture and the sacrifice of Christ on the cross as the definitive proof of His love—for each and every one of us. The Psalmist tells us that "great is his mercy towards us; and the faithfulness of the Lord endures for ever" (Ps. 117:2). The loving relationship that is faith is best expressed by the apostle John: "God is love, and he who abides in love, abides in God, and God abides in him" (1 John 4:16).

Emotion and Liturgy

The priority of assent over emotion is also seen in the Catholic choice of ritual in her worship of God. In a world driven by a disordered understanding of freedom and individualism, rituals such as the Mass and the sacraments are perceived as constricting, dull, and lacking in feeling. Some Catholics have even left the Church in order to participate in the livelier and more emotive worship services of certain Protestant communities. A ritual is a fixed and repeatable form of worship, and it is at the center of Catholicism because it reminds us that, when it comes to God and faith, "we ourselves do not manufacture but receive as a gift."[4] To be sure, no human-generated creation or expression of emotion can come close to the power and sublimity of the Catholic Mass, which is a gift received from Christ Himself for the specific purpose of supplying us with the most perfect way to honor God. Faith exists because God initiates a relationship with us; it is fitting, then, that God also initiated the form of worship He desires from us through the Eucharistic self-sacrifice of the Last Supper and on the cross offered by His Son. Human emotion is then born in awe and in humble gratitude at so great a gift.

The Mass, as well as the other liturgical traditions of the sacraments and the divine office, have grown directly from the ministry of Christ and His apostles. Specific forms and words have varied through the centuries, but, regardless of location and language, the essence of each liturgical celebration has remained constant, and each one brings us back to the very source of our faith. Hence Joseph Ratzinger explains that liturgical rites "elude control by any individual, local community, or regional Church. Unspontaneity is of their essence. In these rites I discover that something is approaching me here that I did not produce myself, that I am entering into something greater than myself, which ultimately derives from divine revelation."[5]

The decision to enter into Catholic liturgy illuminates both the role of sentiment in worship and the role of the individual worshiper within the Church. Romano Guardini teaches that prayer "is, without a doubt, 'a raising of the heart to God.' But the heart must be guided, supported, and purified by the mind…. Prayer is beneficial only when it rests on the bedrock of truth."[6] Just as assent takes priority over sentiment in the life of faith, worship and prayer, which are the ways we express and manifest our faith in God, follow the same order. This is not to say that sentiment does not have a place in the liturgy, for the "Church's worship is full of deep feeling, of emotion that is intense, and sometimes even vehement…. But as a rule it is controlled and subdued. The heart speaks powerfully, but thought at once takes the lead."[7] As the liturgy repeats most of the same words day after day, year after year, century after century, this subdued emotion strikes us in different ways, sometimes gently, and sometimes not at all. But it is not emotion that constitutes the liturgy: it is the action of God Himself, and our commitment to Him, rather than our feelings for Him, that comprise the heart of the liturgy.

Guardini adds that "liturgy is no mere commemoration of what once existed, but is living and real; it is the enduring life of Jesus Christ in us, and that of the believer in Christ, eternally God and Man."[8] In baptism Christ made us part of His Body, the Church, so through the liturgy we encounter the living God together, not as individual entities, but as individual members of the one Body.[9] The individual, continues Guardini, must desire to be part of this body, and being so requires an act of humility on his part: "he must lay self aside, and live with, and for, others, sacrificing to the community a proportion of his self-sufficiency and independence."[10] This act of self-sacrifice enables the individual to transcend his own limits in being part of something greater. And "in doing so he is not swallowed up by, and lost in, the majority; on the contrary, he becomes more independent, rich, and versatile"[11] because the believer comes into closer contact with the source of life itself on God's terms rather than his own. To pray as a member of the Church is to fulfill the promise of Jesus: "whoever exalts himself will be humbled, and whoever humbles himself will be exalted" (Matt. 23:12).

To be a strong and helpful member of the body of Christ, the individual must both participate in liturgical prayer by attending Mass each Sunday and pray privately on her own. Personal prayer is our free conversation with God, by which we live out and develop our relationship with Him. The Second Vatican Council teaches that personal prayer is nourished by liturgical prayer[12] because the latter directs the believer to the heart of the mystery of faith: Christ's passion, death, resurrection, and ascension, referred to collectively as the Paschal Mystery. The Church's treasury of prayers, including the Our Father, Hail Mary, and the many others we have learned by rote, also are important because they tie our personal prayer—our subjective faith—back to the objective faith of the Church. Hence, in addition to nourishing our faith, liturgical prayer prevents our prayer and our faith from collapsing in on ourselves. As Guardini candidly puts it, "[i]t is only truth—or dogma, to give it its other name—which can make prayer efficacious, and impregnate it with that austere, protective strength without which it degenerates into weakness.... Dogmatic thought brings release from the thralldom of individual caprice, and from the uncertainty and sluggishness which follow in the wake of emotion. It makes prayer intelligible, and causes it to rank as a potent factor in life."[13]

In practice, liturgical and ritual prayer carry the danger of becoming external actions empty of meaning. But we must also guard against the tendency to deem ritual empty simply because it is ritual. The presence or absence of feeling felt during these rituals is of secondary importance to our assent to their truth and to our decision to partake of them to the best of our abilities. The true joy and excitement of ritual lies not in our reaction to its performance, but in our understanding of what these rituals are and what they convey.

Spiritual Aridity

As important and powerful as emotions and religious sentiment can be, many believers do not experience either in their relationship with God. For months and even years at a time, believers may not feel any emotion at all during prayer or at Mass. This situation, which is common enough, is referred to as spiritual aridity or spiritual dryness. In the midst of spiritual aridity, it is as if the believer were alone in a quiet room waiting for a response of any kind, yet none is forthcoming. God seems absent to those experiencing aridity, and as a result, prayer can become difficult. The believer's subjective faith can suffer in this situation, as she wonders whether God still wants to remain in relationship with her.

Spiritual aridity is experienced even by the greatest saints who have given their entire lives to God and to prayer. St. Thérèse of Lisieux, known as the Little Flower, was a Carmelite nun who died in 1897 at the age of 24. Although she never left her monastery, which she entered at the unusual age of 15 due to her tenacious insistence that this was God's mission for her, St. Thérèse has become one of the most popular saints of our time. Many miracles have been attributed to her intercession. She has been declared Patron of the Missions because of her devotion to praying for others as well as a Doctor of the Church on account of her writings' contributions to Catholic learning. Even with her sincere and humble faith for which she has become so well known, St. Thérèse experienced spiritual aridity.

In her autobiography, St. Thérèse writes that during an Easter season in which "I was enjoying such a living faith, such a clear faith, that the thought of heaven made up all my happiness," God suddenly granted her a very different experience: "He permitted my soul to be invaded by the thickest darkness, and that the thought of heaven, up to then so sweet to me, be no longer anything but the cause of struggle and torment. This trial was to last not a few days or a few weeks, it was not to be extinguished until the hour set by God Himself and this hour has not yet come."[14]

Seeking an analogy to explain her situation, St. Thérèse compares the state of her soul to one born into a country covered in thick fog without having experienced "the joyful appearance of nature flooded and transformed by the brilliance of the sun."[15] For St. Thérèse, "the fog that surrounds me becomes more dense; it penetrates my soul and envelops it in such a way that it is impossible to discover within it the sweet image of my Fatherland; everything has disappeared! When I want to rest my heart fatigued by the darkness that surrounds it by the memory of the luminous country after which I aspire, my torment redoubles."[16]

Many believers of all times and circumstances can commiserate with St. Thérèse's experience. Sometimes it can seem to us that our faith relationship has become entirely one-sided as we feel abandoned by God: we call to Him, and we feel as if He is not responding. Our spiritual life then becomes more difficult as we do not find satisfaction in prayer; we can even be tempted to give up prayer entirely because we think it is not efficacious. And, as with any human relationship that becomes one-sided, strains of anger, jealousy, and blame can fester in our attitude towards God as a result of our aridity.

Addressing the sources of spiritual aridity can help us understand more deeply the nature of faith and of God's relationship to us. Father Gabriel of St. Mary Magdalen identifies three sources of aridity.[17] First, it can come from our own infidelity toward God if we become lax with our spiritual practices and in our relationship with Him: prayers not said, acts of charity omitted, temptations not avoided, sins committed and not confessed, decisions that swell our pride can all "ultimately reduce to lukewarmness a once fervent soul."[18] Although we may feel that God has abandoned us, it is really we who have abandoned Him by not living out our end of the faith relationship. In fact, we can know that we, and not God, are the cause of our aridity in this instance when we do not actively fear that we have lost God and when we are not urgently trying to find Him through increased spiritual devotion. In the situation of our own infidelity, the only way to drive out the aridity and restore vigor to our faith is to return more forcefully to the life of prayer, charity, and penance.

Second, aridity can spring from trials we experience in our daily living: illness, fatigue, difficulties at work or within the family can all subsume spiritual consolations within their oppressive shadows. To meet this challenge, believers must discern God's hand in these trials and understand that, for whatever the reason, He wills them for our spiritual growth.

Third, aridity can come from God Himself, who withdraws His consolations from us intentionally. God does this not to torment us, but to purify our love for Him: through this spiritual trial God teaches us that our love for Him ought to be based on Him alone, and not on what He can do for us. Further, the difficulties we experience in prayer help us grow in humility, for aridity reminds us that apart from God, we cannot do anything on our own.

In dealing with spiritual aridity, although we do not feel a desire to pray, we must nevertheless persevere in prayer out of duty to God. Aridity is God's way of teaching us that love of God, just like human love, ultimately depends on a commitment of the will, not on emotion or sentiment. "One who, in order to please God, perseveres in prayer although he finds no consolation in it, but rather repugnance, gives Him a beautiful proof of true love."[19] In fact, not only does the believer prove his love for God, he strengthens it by deepening his commitment to Him with each act of faith. Here again we have the example of St. Thérèse: "[God] knows well that while I do not have *the joy of faith*, I am trying to carry out its works at least. I believe I have made more acts of faith in this past year than all through my whole life."[20]

The duty to persevere in prayer and in faith regardless of how we feel is the unanimous experience of the saints. St. Peter of Alcantara, for one, writes, "It is not difficult to persevere in prayer when we find consolation in it, but there is great merit in doing so when sensible devotion is reduced to a minimum. Yet it is precisely then that prayer becomes more meritorious and humility is increased, as well as patience and perseverance."[21]

When we experience aridity in our own lives, St. Francis de Sales provides the following advice:

> I implore you not to be in the least troubled thereat, but sometimes open the door to vocal prayers: complain to our Lord, confess your unworthiness, ask him to come to your aid, kiss his image if you have it, say to him the words of Jacob: "I will not let thee go, Lord, except thou bless me."… At other times, take a book in your hand and read it with attention, until your spirit be awakened and restored within you; sometimes stir up your heart by some posture or movement of exterior devotion.[22]

These spiritual practices may well help rekindle the fire in our prayer. There is a chance, however, that the believer's aridity remains even amidst these practices. For this situation, St. Francis adds further counsel:

> But if after all this you obtain no consolation, be not troubled, however great your dryness may be, but continue to keep yourself in a devout attitude before your God. How many courtiers there are that go a hundred times a year into the prince's presence-chamber without the hope of speaking to him, but only to be seen by him and to pay their respects. So also…should we come to holy prayer, purely and simply to pay our respects and give proof of our fidelity. If it please the divine Majesty to speak to us and to converse with us by his holy inspirations and interior consolations, it will doubtless be a great honor for us, and a very delightful

pleasure; but if it please him not to show us this favor, leaving us there without so much as speaking to us, as though he saw us not and as though we were not in his presence, we must not, for all that, depart, but on the contrary, we must remain there before this sovereign Goodness, with a devout and peaceful mien; and then infallibly will he be pleased with our patience, and will take notice of our diligence and perseverance, so that another time when we come again before him, he will favor us, and will converse with us by his consolations, making us realize the sweetness of holy prayer.[23]

St. Francis's advice reminds us that the end goal of our prayer and our faith is not our own good or our own self-improvement, although these things certainly follow as a secondary result. The goal of prayer and faith is to praise and glorify God, who, because of His very nature as the all-powerful and all-loving creator, simply must be praised. Just as we cannot help but praise someone who has done something heroic, or thank someone who has benefited us, we cannot help but praise God because of who He is. To be in union with Him is the reason for our existence. Prayer and faith may become very difficult at times, yet we must persevere in their practice: We may not feel anything, but we can have confidence knowing that, by prayer and by faith, we take a step closer to Him who is the end of all things.

The Spiritual Life

Our relationship and interactions with God in faith comprise what is called the spiritual life. At the center of the spiritual life is the human soul, the animating principle of the body. We know that human beings are composed of body and soul from the book of Genesis: "The Lord God formed man of dust from the ground, and breathed into his nostrils the breath of life; and man became a living soul" (2:7). The soul is integral to the body yet, at the same time, it is distinct from it. As the *Catechism* explains, "it is because of its spiritual soul that the body made of matter becomes a living, human body; spirit and matter, in man, are not two natures united, but rather their union forms a single nature."[24] The soul together with the body makes us who we are as persons. There cannot be a disconnect between who we are in our bodies and who we think we are in our souls.

The soul is pure spirit: it is not made from material substance. Therefore, the soul is not produced by a person's parents, nor can it evolve, since evolution only concerns the transformation of physical matter. As a spiritual, immaterial substance, the soul can only come from God, who Himself is pure spirit. Further, since the soul is immaterial, it cannot break down or be destroyed: once created, it lives on without end.

Our souls separate from our bodies at death: the former go to Heaven, Purgatory, or Hell, while the latter decompose in the earth. This separation is temporary, however: we profess in the Nicene Creed that we "look forward to the resurrection of the dead," when at the end of time God, in a manner that exceeds our comprehension, will reunite our souls with our bodies, which will be made spiritual bodies akin to Christ's after His resurrection. The resurrection of the body is one of our most challenging beliefs— just as it was in St. Augustine's day 1,600 years ago.[25] Yet there is a certain logic to it: God created human beings for Himself, and then redeemed them by the blood of His Son, so they may live forever with Him. Our bodies are an essential part of who we are as human beings, and so they, too, will someday share in our eternal life with God. The resurrection of the body may be difficult for us to imagine, but we believe it nonetheless on account of our trust in God who revealed this fact to us.

The soul is a real entity. It is not the product of human brain activity, nor is it the convenient name we give to the sum total of our physical processes. The existence of the human soul explains why we can do what other animals cannot imagine: love, sacrifice, trust, hope, dream, serve, worship.

The soul is the part of us that is in union with God, and that receives grace from Him. Like the body, the soul must be exercised regularly for it to be healthy and strong; if it is not exercised regularly, the soul, like the body, becomes spiritually flabby and susceptible to atrophy. Just as the physical shape of the body depends on how well—or not—we nurture it with the proper food and exercise, the shape of the soul depends on how well—or not—we nurture it with its own particular forms of food and exercise.

The soul's food is the sacraments and its exercise is prayer, sacrifice, acts of virtue, and acts of charity. The frequency and effort with which we devote ourselves to these activities lead directly to the health of our spiritual lives. As mentioned earlier, the cornerstone of the spiritual life is the Mass, where Jesus' self-sacrifice on the cross is re-presented so that the infinite graces of this action can be applied directly to our souls. By receiving holy communion we bring our souls into the closest union possible with God in this life. It is not a coincidence that the Eucharist, the body and blood of Christ, retains the physical appearance of bread: just as bread nourishes the body, the Bread of Life nourishes the soul.

The body needs regular care to ensure its proper function; the soul, too, needs regular maintenance through frequent examinations of conscience and the confession of sins in the sacrament of reconciliation. Confession forces us to examine critically our relationship with God and find the ways we have failed Him. When we confess our sins to a priest, we not only receive God's forgiveness so we can renew our relationship with Him, but we also receive grace to overcome future temptations.

Regular exercise makes the body healthy and strong. Prayer, sacrifice, acts of virtue, and acts of charity are the primary means of exercising our soul and living out our relationship with God. The more we engage in each, the stronger grows our faith. And just as progress in physical health is marked by physical signs such as weight loss, muscle growth, and overall fitness, certain signs point to spiritual growth: a resolve to pray, a willing adherence to the commandments, willing sacrifices of things that are dear to us through fasting and acts of mortification, development in the practice of the moral and spiritual virtues, the performance of acts of charity, the avoidance of sins, and acts of penance in reparation for the sins we do commit. When engaged in these practices, we often (though not always) experience spiritual consolation, through which God assures us that we are on the right path.

It also happens that physical health can reach its optimal point: then maintenance of what has been established, rather than growth, becomes the goal. The same goes for the spiritual life: the actions that get the soul into spiritual shape are also the ones that maintain this shape. Neither the body nor the soul is guaranteed smooth sailing and unchecked positive progress once in shape: the former can succumb to illness or injury, and the latter can suffer from aridity or complacency. There are certainly times when we "don't feel like" exercising. But regardless of how we feel when exercising, our body is still reaping the physical benefits. The same goes for the spiritual life: there are times when we "don't feel like" praying, whether this be because we are tired, busy, or distracted by some other occupation. Nevertheless, the soul profits when we make the effort to pray despite our inertia. And not only does the soul profit, but God appreciates even more the efforts we make on His behalf when these efforts do not come easily for us.

In this analogy between exercising the body and the soul, however, there is a major difference. The body eventually reaches a peak of physical health beyond which it cannot go: to push further would cause injury. The soul, by contrast, can always be drawn more deeply into union with God in this life. In fact, St. Thomas Aquinas teaches that "the end of the spiritual life is that man be united to God…while all things pertaining to the spiritual life are ordained to this union."[26] This union begins and is sustained by God's grace, and it requires a willingness on our part to enter more deeply into the inner life of God. In the spiritual life, deeper union only comes at great personal cost to ourselves: as we draw closer and closer to God, He asks us to sacrifice more and more of ourselves to make this union possible. This is what Jesus meant when He said, "[W]hoever would save his life will lose it, and whoever loses his life for my sake will find it" (Matt. 16:25).

Union with God is a union of love. Since love consists of willing and free actions for the benefit of the beloved, the key to union with God is to conform our will with His.[27] We pray for this each time we recite the Lord's prayer: "Thy will be done, on earth as it is in Heaven." The more we can both forsake what is contrary to God's will and carry out what is in accord with it, the more we grow in love for God.

The "Dark Night of the Soul" and Union with God

In order to reach this deeper level of union with God, the soul must first be freed from all its earthly concerns and from all its imperfections. The process of purification of the soul that leads to this union has been termed "the dark night of the soul," named from a work by St. John of the Cross. In actuality, the Spanish mystic differentiates levels of purgation that comprise this "dark night," an intense deprivation of God's consolation, so acute that the believer feels as if he were alone in the darkness of night without any light, guide, or comfort. St. John reminds us that early on in the spiritual life "the soul, after it has been definitely converted to the service of God, is, as a rule, spiritually nurtured and caressed by God."[28]

Yet in the midst of this spiritual striving, certain problems can develop due to the believer's own weaknesses and imperfections: pride in what the believer has achieved in relation to God can cause him to denigrate the less fervent, to desire to be seen as pious by others, to become lax in restraining his will, to rationalize his faults and sins. Pride foments other problems rooted in the other deadly sins: avarice, sloth, anger, gluttony, envy, and lust. These problems can remain small, or, if unchecked, they can grow into bigger problems: each scenario will injure our faith to one degree or another.[29]

The dark night of the soul purges us first from our disordered attachments to the sensual world and, second, from spiritual imperfections caused by the seven deadly sins. St. John warns that "the first purgation or night is bitter and terrible to the sense" while "the second bears no comparison to it, for it is horrible and awful to the spirit."[30] Many will undergo the first night of the senses, but very few are strong enough to enter into the night of the spirit. The dark night forces us to realize our littleness and unworthiness before the infinite majesty of God. Because we are often deeply attached to the things of this world and to our own ego, the purification of sense and of spirit inflict genuine suffering: each requires radical self-renunciation and abandonment of all of one's concerns into God's hands.

Why is it that reaching this level of love for God is so costly? If God wants to be in a relationship with us, why must we suffer so much in order to maximize this relationship? Father Gabriel of St. Mary Magdalen explains that the reason has everything to do with the nature of love itself. Perfect love demands the complete and exclusive gift of self to another, without a divided heart. Perfect love demands equality between persons, and for us to be more like God, who is infinite perfection in Himself, He has to remove from us all imperfections. And "in the measure that He strips [the soul], He clothes it with Himself, with His own divine life."[31]

Finally, Father Gabriel continues, perfect love also leads to unity with the beloved. "[Love] desires complete fusion of hearts; and God, who infinitely loves the soul that sincerely seeks Him, desires nothing more than to unite it to Himself; therefore He purifies it of every stain that would impede perfect union with His infinite purity."[32] Our purification came at a horrific cost: the passion, crucifixion, and death of Jesus Christ. "And if it has cost Him, Innocence itself, so much, is it not just that we should suffer a little, too, we who are culpable, having so offended God, and having so many times, by our willfulness, put obstacles to the outpouring of His love in our souls?... Just as purifying sufferings are the work of God's love for us, so we want our acceptance of them to be the work, the proof, of our love for Him."[33] By emptying Himself, Christ became one with us; by emptying ourselves, we become one with Him.

To empty oneself of sin, pride, self-love, and of all the other obstacles that impede our union with God is extremely demanding. It is, at the same time, obtainable even for the least among us. It is usually done not in one Herculean action, but by small actions done with love and generosity. "[W]hoever gives to one of these little ones even a cup of cold water because he is a disciple, truly, I say to you, he shall not lose his reward" (Matt. 10:42). Each time we go out of our way to help someone in need, sacrifice something that we desire, and respond with patience—rather than anger—to a trying family member, we continue the act of purification and self-emptying whose goal is complete union with God.

We thus learn that faith and the spiritual life are not ultimately about how we feel in relation to God, but how closely we can enter into union with Him, a feat that comes about through our imitation of Christ's sacrifice for us. We know we are drawing closer to God not when we are overwhelmed by emotion, but when our hearts, deprived of consolation, long to be in accord with God's will. Then we can pray sincerely the *Suscipe* with St. Ignatius of Loyola: "Take, Lord, and receive all my liberty, my memory, my understanding, and my entire will—all that I have and call my own. You have given it all to me. To you, Lord, I return it. Everything is yours; do with it what you will. Give me only your love and your grace. That is enough for me."

❧ CHAPTER 9

Faith, Action, and Politics

Because of the formative and transformative power of the grace, faith shapes our actions and our entire way of life because "it comes," writes Henri de Lubac, "from the center of the personality, from the *heart*."[1] Our faith is manifested, and must be manifested, by the effect it has on our hearts: by our acts of charity and by our public profession. This latter action can take the form of verbal confession, the wearing of a crucifix or displaying of religious articles at home or at work, or simply doing what is required of believers in any given situation.

It is impossible, then, to claim to hold faith in private but to disregard that faith deliberately when acting in public, a position that has become common in our secular world, particularly among political figures. To claim this is self-contradictory, as it causes a divorce at the very center of a person, and "if a house is divided against itself, that house will not be able to stand" (Mark 3:25). Further, this claim disparages one's friendship with God, for it says that God and one's relationship to Him are of secondary importance. This position is not necessarily born out of malice but out of fear of losing the support of nonbelievers. Nevertheless, these claimants fall into the same error that trapped some Jewish authorities in

Jerusalem who believed in Jesus: "for fear of the Pharisees they did not confess [their belief]…for they loved the praise of men more than the praise of God" (John 12:42-43).

When we act contrary to God's law or choose something that is not part of His plan we sin. To sin is to squander the grace God has given us, to choose to do things our way as determined by our own finite intellects rather than according to God's way and with God's help. The presence of sanctifying grace can help us resist temptation, but it does not guarantee our resistance or force our choice: we retain free will to choose God or to ignore the grace we have received, and instead choose evil, just as Adam and Eve did and just as human beings have done ever since.

Sin is the greatest hindrance and poison to the relationship of faith because it is the choice of ourselves over God. Venial sins, or small sins, damage our relationship with God, while mortal sins, gravely wrong actions done freely and with full knowledge of their import, destroy our relationship with God. When a person falls into habitual sin, committing the same gravely wrong actions repeatedly for a period of months or even years, he lives like the Prodigal Son when he first set off from his father's estate: he lives as if He is dead to God, and as if God is dead to him. For this person faith, effectively, is dead and lost.

Dead or lost faith has become, sadly, the lot of far too many Catholics who have fallen away from the Church. Many faithful Catholics rightly worry about family members and friends who were baptized yet have ceased to practice their faith in varying degrees, which may range from outright rejection of faith, to the adoption of a different religion, to refraining from attending Mass, or to living in an irregular arrangement; and they have done so for varying reasons, which may range from the malicious effects of sin, poor catechesis, the scandal caused by the sins of clergy and believers, or the enticing allure of worldly pleasures. The good news is that all baptized persons who have fallen away can renew their faith and again experience sanctifying grace because of the permanent character, or seal, that was imparted to their souls at baptism. This character can never be destroyed or renounced; it forever marks the baptized as children of God. Sanctifying grace, which came with the character, can be revived and help restore the once lost faith relationship with God.

The dormant baptismal character is revived and lost grace is restored when believers repent of their sins—they acknowledge the wrong that they have done and their need for God's mercy—and receive God's forgiveness after confessing their sins to a priest in the sacrament of reconciliation. The grace of God's forgiveness serves as the medicine that makes the baptismal grace healthy again. There is no sin, no matter how grave or awful, that cannot be or will not be forgiven by God, who welcomes home all his prodigal children as soon as they admit to their wrongs and go to meet Him in the confessional, his tribunal of mercy.

If, however, we refuse to be reconciled with God, if we insist on remaining stubbornly wrapped in the selfish cocoon that sin generates around each one of us, if we refuse the grace of reconciliation that He offers us, then we risk eternal damnation. As unpleasant as it is to consider, and as much as the modern world has tried to pretend that it does not exist, Hell is real and we can go there if we die without sanctifying grace in our souls. To discount the existence of Hell is to dismiss the repeated—and sometimes harrowing—warnings of Jesus Himself that we will be punished if we fail to live up to the call He has given to us. We may tell ourselves that the loving God would not condemn anyone to Hell, that God will somehow have mercy on us no matter what we do or say. But it stands to reason that if we refuse to allow God into our lives on earth, and we want nothing to do with Him and refuse His will and His commandments while living, why should we be with Him after death? The cause of our damnation is not God's doing but our own, because we have rejected Him. With the freedom of choosing God comes the awesome responsibility of doing so, or suffering the consequences.

Although grace comes from the omnipotent God, in our daily living we often feel the tormenting pull of concupiscence and of worldly attractions far more strongly than we feel grace's gentle invitation. On the most benign level, this reality is lived out when in the midst of prayer or Mass we find our minds drawn away from God and toward the grocery list, the car left unlocked, or any other mundane thing, to say nothing of when we feel a temptation toward sin. Human beings are rational animals, and it is our constant task to restrain and direct the strong inclinations of our animal nature away from concupiscence and toward God by deliberate acts of our will. There is no denying that physical, tangible, and worldly things resonate with us more immediately than divine and invisible things.

Herein lies the genius of the seven sacraments of the Church: they are physical signs of the transmission of invisible grace, and they were established by Christ because He knew that our human nature needs and responds to physical realities. The sacraments confer grace to perfect or complete our nature wounded by sin, but this is a lifelong process filled with many fits and starts. Just as God spoke to Elijah not in the power of an earthquake or fire, but in a gentle whisper (1 Kings 19:9–18), so does grace work on our souls: not in the clamors of the body or the enticements of the world, but in the quiet depth of our hearts. Like Elijah, our challenge is to hone in on God's quiet voice and not allow the booming noises of the world to distract us from our journey to Him.

Faith and Politics

The union of faith and personal action leads directly to questions concerning the relationship between faith and our interaction with others in the broader political sphere. Politics refers to the public affairs of ruling authorities and government at all levels, and it is only possible because of the faculty of reason, by which human beings are able to consider, plan, and arrange a structured way of living together in harmony. Animals, although they live in common, cannot plan a community or establish rules for its governance because they lack the ability to reason. Since reason is the *sine qua non* of political existence, faith lends a support for politics just as it does for reason.

Pope Leo XIII teaches that, because of man's social instinct for living in common with others, there must exist within each community a governmental structure to ensure order. The source of this authority, therefore, lies "in nature, and has, consequently, God for its Author."[2] The task of government, and therefore politics, is to safeguard the common good of society.[3] The common good grows out of social conditions that help individuals, families, and groups reach their proper end, and it has three essential elements: respect for the person's God-given dignity, development of group and social well-being, and peaceful, secure existence.[4] To carry out the tasks of governing and of fostering the common good, rulers and citizens exercise the faculty of reason to discern and then employ the best possible laws and policies within their borders.

Because politics concerns the flourishing of human beings, faith has a natural role to play within politics. Just as faith purifies reason by directing it toward the truth, yet without impinging upon reason's internal prerogatives, so, too, does faith purify politics: it illuminates for the State the truths of humanity that should be protected, all while allowing the State to craft its own specific policies to protect and foster these truths. Faith helps politics keep its focus on its true purpose, but faith itself is not, and should not be, a political machine.

This vision for the relationship between faith and politics requires nuance and explanation, especially today, when we often hear that there is, or ought to be, a wall of separation between Church and State, and that religion should have no role in politics whatsoever. In this same fashion, secular detractors often seek to undermine faith-inspired policies or laws as impositions of an impending theocracy, a term that rings hostile to American ears. On the other end of the spectrum, it is possible for faith and religion to become so consumed by politics that they lose sight of their proper supernatural orientation.

Our faith relationship with God is constitutive of our very being since it points us to the meaning and purpose of our existence. Hence, as mentioned, it is impossible to separate our religious faith from our actions, both private and public: our adoptions as sons and daughters of God at baptism make us children of God forever, at all times and in all places. Our faith relationship has an essential moral component that bids us to adhere to God's commandments—those explicitly revealed in the Decalogue, known in the natural law, and preached in Jesus' new law of love—no matter the time, season, or location.

Not only, then, must we act in accordance with these commandments within our own lives, but we must also support public policies and laws that uphold them while opposing those that are contrary. St. John Paul teaches that "in the sense of serving persons and society, the lay faithful are never to relinquish their participation in public life, that is, in the many different economic, social, legislative, administrative and cultural areas, which are intended to promote organically and institutionally the common good."[5] Doing so "would include the promotion and defense of goods such as public order and peace, freedom and equality, respect for human life and for the environment, justice and solidarity."[6]

In a democratic republic such as the United States, we can work for these causes of the common good by voting for the candidates who promise to uphold laws consistent with God's commandments, by voicing our concerns to lawmakers about the importance of such laws, and by participating with others in groups dedicated to advancing these ends. Politics is a collaborative effort. Catholics have an important role to play in the public square because their faith offers a robust teaching on social issues, a teaching which has developed Jesus' command to love one's neighbor within the context of the public welfare. In addition, the Catholic faith also provides a healthy worldview through which Catholics can properly view humanity's practical problems within God's overall plan for creation. This includes the crucial reminder that human beings' most pressing needs are spiritual rather than material.

It is important to clarify that, within the public arena, the divine commandments we are obliged to support are harmonious with the moral norms that derive from the natural law, which is applicable to all human beings because it is discernible through reason and in accord with the truth of human nature. One need not be a Catholic to see the necessity of protecting all human life, from the unborn to the poor to the elderly to the handicapped— this is a precept of natural law. The same can be said for other precepts of the natural law: the duty to do good and avoid evil; the protection of personal property; the nature of marriage as a union between one man and one woman for the procreation and rearing of children.

From these general precepts, countless specific laws are then made by the competent ruling authorities according to temporal and circumstantial needs: laws prohibiting murder and theft, and laws promoting marriage and fostering the education of children, for example, all derive from the natural law, and these particular laws vary depending on the times and citizenry for which they are written. It is the task of politics to enact these laws for the benefit of the common good.

How these specific laws are written, debated, and promulgated is a very complex process, and there are a multitude of ways in which general natural law precepts can be made into practical legislation. In the cases of health care and taking care of the poor, for example, the natural law and the Church both remind us of the necessity of caring for the individual person; but how we do this is a matter for public debate. There may well be more than one way in which this goal can be met, and Catholics, like all citizens, are free to decide what practical means will be the most effective. So long as both the general goal and the specific means are just and in accord with the natural law, then Catholics can support whatever laws, candidates, and political parties they deem most appropriate. But when laws, candidates, or parties stand contrary to the natural law, Catholics must voice their opposition and withhold their support. "A well-formed Christian conscience does not permit one to vote for a political program or an individual law which contradicts the fundamental contents of faith and morals. The Christian faith is an integral unity, and thus it is incoherent to isolate some particular element to the detriment of the whole of Catholic doctrine."[7]

In recent decades secular critics have undermined the Catholic perspective—particular on issues pertaining to marriage, family life, and human sexuality—by intentionally ignoring its rational basis in the natural law. As Archbishop Chaput explains, these critics "reduce all [Catholic] moral convictions to an expression of subjective religious beliefs. And if they're purely religious beliefs, then—so the critics argue—they can't be rationally defended. And because they're rationally indefensible, they should be treated as a form of prejudice. Thus two thousand years of moral truth and religious principle become, by sleight of hand, a species of bias."[8]

The fact that moral norms which derive from the natural law happen to be affirmed by God's revelation is simply consistent with the common sense of Christianity. Divine revelation further solidifies our confidence in such naturally derived laws in the same manner that faith gives us confidence that reason is ordered to find and serve the truth. Hence one cannot argue, for example, that laws preventing abortion are invalid because they have religious roots. Instead, since these laws derive from the faculty of reason that is common to all humanity, they are applicable to all human beings regardless of a law's religious ties or of an individual's religious beliefs.

Contemporary secularity is exhibiting extreme prejudice against faith and religiously-rooted opinions. Intolerant of religious faith and its demands, secular critics have sought to silence the Church and religious believers who would bring their religiously formed views into the public square. Part of the secularist success in popular opinion stems from the denial of truth, particularly moral truth, and our ability to discern it through reason: without truth or the higher power of God to sanction moral norms, laws, public morality, and social mores become determined by the most powerful ruling faction.

So, in attempting to advance their own secular, and sometimes strictly anti-God, agenda, secularists claim that believers cannot "impose their beliefs" on others—all so that (with believers being marginalized) they can impose their own secular beliefs on everyone else, even those who reject contemporary secularism. This is all supremely hypocritical. It is also thoroughly misleading: public policy arguments informed by Christian religion do not demand that non-believers accept any supernatural beliefs or form a relationship with God: this would be a true imposition of belief. Rather, religious belief, supported by reason and the natural law, serves as a legitimate source and inspiration for arguments that pertain to public behavior and public policy. Historically, arguments that are simultaneously religiously inspired and rationally based are responsible for abolishing slavery and establishing civil rights in the United States. Surely no one today would claim that abolishing slavery or establishing civil rights was an unjust imposition of Christian religion on America.

In this regard, let us consider just one example: Dr. Martin Luther King, Jr.'s famous "Letter from Birmingham Jail," which draws directly from the natural law to show that racial segregation is unjust.

> How does one determine whether a law is just or unjust? A just law is a man-made code that squares with the moral law or the law of God. An unjust law is a code that is out of harmony with the moral law. To put it in the terms of St. Thomas Aquinas: An unjust law is a human law that is not rooted in eternal law and natural law. Any law that uplifts human personality is just. Any law that degrades human personality is unjust. All segregation statutes are unjust because segregation distorts the soul and damages the personality.[9]

By appealing to the natural law as the standard for determining the injustice of segregation, Dr. King makes his appeal applicable and understandable for all people. That God is nature's designer and the guarantor, so to speak, of natural law in no way undermines his argument, which is based primarily on reason. The fact that divine revelation also supports the same conclusion adds further force to his rational appeal.

The point to bear in mind is that all public policy arguments have grounding in prior principles, be they religious or secular. Opponents of certain policy arguments may not like these foundational principles, but not liking them is not justification for excluding them outright or dismissing them as illegitimate. When it comes to public policy, the content and current import is more important than the source; but if the source is strong and valid, the policy content has a greater chance of strength and validity in its own right. And since public policy seeks what is best for human beings in the temporal realm, we have all the more reason to consider approaches inspired by Christianity, which exists for "a single intention: that God's kingdom may come, and that the salvation of the whole human race may come to pass."[10]

The Relationship of Church and State

The formal relationship between the Church, be it the Catholic Church or other religious denominations, and the State extends the relationship between faith and politics onto an institutional level. The Catholic Church in particular has a long history of theological and philosophical reasoning as to how the Church and State ought to interact. Although some particular aspects of this relationship have fluctuated over the centuries, certain core principles have endured the test of time. They should also endure through our current secular age.

In the view of the life of faith, the State can only pass laws that concern faith's moral dimension. Truths revealed by God that have both a supernatural origin and a supernatural end, such as teachings on the divinity of Christ, the real presence of Christ in the Eucharist, or the immaculate conception of the Blessed Virgin

Mary, as important as they are, do not have any bearing on the tasks of government. We do not seek civil laws to coerce the spiritual life of individuals, such as requiring prayer, fasting, or attendance at church. Doing so would violate one of the essential elements of faith: that we respond to God freely by our own wills, not by the command of any other. Detractors of the Church mention the Inquisition as a government supported means of policing faith. In reality, the Inquisition was trying to prevent the spread of heresy and error among the faithful; it was not trying to force individuals to become personally pious.

At the same time, however, it is right and beneficial for the State to pass laws that provide a means of fostering religious faith and the moral life, since the exercise of these lies at the heart of human welfare and the common good. While the State cannot command church attendance, it can promote attendance by, for example, requiring stores to be closed on Sundays until a certain hour. The State has long promoted the moral life by limiting or prohibiting certain activities that can lead to vice, to destruction, or to reckless death—limitations on alcohol sales and gambling, and prohibitions of prostitution and drugs are just a few ways in which the State uses its power in the moral sphere for the promotion of the common good.

This is not to say, as Benedict XVI cautions, that the Church ought to control the State or that the Church ought to impose on all people a specifically Catholic worldview.[11] Stemming from Jesus' own teachings and from His dialogue with Pontius Pilate, the Church has long recognized that the Church and the State have different but complementary roles to play in the world: "[t]he two spheres are distinct, yet always interrelated."[12] Within public life, the aim of the Church, as Benedict articulates quite well, is to teach and contribute to what is just.

The Church's social teaching argues on the basis of reason and natural law, namely, on the basis of what is in accord with the nature of every human being. It recognizes that it is not the Church's responsibility to make this teaching prevail in political life. Rather, the Church wishes to help form consciences in political life and to stimulate greater insight into the authentic requirements of justice as well as greater readiness to act accordingly, even when this might involve conflict with situations of personal interest. Building a just social and civil order, wherein each person receives what is his or her due, is an essential task which every generation must take up anew. As a political task, this cannot be the Church's immediate responsibility. Yet, since it is also a most important human responsibility, the Church is duty-bound to offer, through the purification of reason and through ethical formation, her own specific contribution towards understanding the requirements of justice and achieving them politically.

The Church cannot and must not take upon herself the political battle to bring about the most just society possible. She cannot and must not replace the State. Yet at the same time she cannot and must not remain on the sidelines in the fight for justice. She has to play her part through rational argument and she has to reawaken the spiritual energy without which justice, which always demands sacrifice, cannot prevail and prosper. A just society must be the achievement of politics, not of the Church. Yet the promotion of justice through efforts to bring about openness of mind and will to the demands of the common good is something which concerns the Church deeply.[13]

For its part, in modern, secular democracies the State ought to ensure freedom of religion for its citizens. The Second Vatican Council defines religious freedom as a human right whereby "all men are to be immune from coercion on the part of individuals or of social groups and of any human power, in such wise that no one is to be forced to act in a manner contrary to his own beliefs, whether privately or publicly, whether alone or in association with others, within due limits."[14] Religion is our formal expression of the faith relationship we have with God. The State's support for religious freedom helps to build up the common good because responding to God's call in faith is part of our inherent nature and dignity as human beings in search of the truth. Hence freedom of religion is a natural right, not a privilege granted by the State, as is, say, driving a car or opening a business. Religious freedom is as fundamental to our humanity as life, liberty, and the pursuit of happiness.

But today efforts are being made not only to push faith and faith-based moral positions out of the public square, but even to make them illegal in certain cases—again, usually in those areas pertaining to human sexuality and family life issues, as well as with issues that concern biotechnology and euthanasia. In recent years, we have seen the curtailment of religious freedom in the United States play out in a very disturbing way: Florists, cake bakers, and pro-life pregnancy centers have all been attacked through the law because they refused, on the grounds of their religious faith, to facilitate the practices of same-sex marriage or abortion.[15] In all of these cases, those attacking believers have argued that one's religious exercise ought to yield to the individual rights of others.

This deliberate attack on the free exercise of religion by American citizens is wrong.

First, violations of religious freedom commit "a radical injustice with regard to what is particularly deep within man, what is authentically human."[16] What is just conforms to the truth of human nature, and the search for and living out of a relationship with God is part of our nature. By denying the authentic exercise and expression of belief in God, these violations deny our very humanity. It is a grave injustice, therefore, to deny freedom of religion to anyone. Since the task of government is to safeguard private welfare and the common good, curtailing religious freedom impinges on the former: and when private welfare is subjugated, the discontent arising from it harms the common good as well. Faith is constitutive of our whole lives, so our free exercise of religion includes all aspects of our relationship with God, including adherence to and public support for God's commandments as found in the natural law and the Decalogue. Living according to God's commandments is one of the ways we worship Him. Hence the free exercise of religion can never be reduced to a "freedom of worship" that, according to the State, consists only of prayers spoken in a private home or church building.

Second, as St. John Paul points out, there is no reason that secular arguments should have pride of place in the public square over religiously-based ones. In the absence of an overarching truth or standard to which we can appeal—a standard whose existence secularists deny—there is no way to prize one form of argument over another. "It is therefore difficult, even from a 'purely human' point of view, to accept a position that gives only atheism the right of citizenship in public and social life, while believers are, almost by principle, barely tolerated or are treated as second-class citizens or are even—and this has already happened—entirely deprived of the rights of citizenship."[17]

And this is precisely what has happened in our own secular society. Now that the once-dominant American worldview that was based on Christian and Enlightenment principles has been replaced by a relativistic, secular one, the legality of issues pertaining to religious faith and religiously-based morals is subject to the whim of judicial courts of appeal. As the florist, baker, and volunteers at crisis pregnancy centers have painfully learned, our natural human right to exercise our religious faith has become subsumed under the power of the State.

In the face of this alarming situation, believers must resist the oppression of their rights. Archbishop Chaput urges believers to use every political means available to ensure that our religious rights are protected. This includes both seeking legislative and judicial recourse as well as making arguments to the broader public about the authentic truth of the human being and the inalienable rights of the Church and of her members to exercise their faith. At the same time, we should also work for a renewal of Catholic thinking about truth, freedom, nature, the human person, and marriage that challenges more directly our secular interlocutors.[18] Such thinking should not be limited to rational arguments and op-ed pages: it should include contributions from artists, film-makers, and creative writers who can present these truths through fiction and visual media, all while helping to foster the building of a Catholic counterculture to the secularist narrative.

As we work at ensuring our God-given right to religious freedom, we should also be mindful that, be it in individual court battles or in the broader political and cultural arena, believers may suffer real defeats—defeats that have serious consequences: fines, jail time, loss of businesses or property, or even death. This is not meant as an alarmist or apocalyptic prognostication. Sadly, the two-thousand-year history of Christianity bears this out: from ancient Rome, to Northern Africa in the Middle Ages, to Protestant England, to the New World, to the insidious regimes of Hitler and Stalin, to the Middle East today, Catholics have faced the cruelest forms of discrimination, torture, and death at the hands of political regimes who denied their citizens the free exercise of their religion. It is not easy to say, but, fight as we must according to the proper channels, there is no guarantee of a happy ending for believers in the political and social arena. Our faith does not promise happiness or security in this life. The battle over religious freedom is a sobering reminder of what—and where—our ultimate destiny lies.

Jesus Himself predicted that his disciples would face persecution at the hands of others and at the hands of the State (Matt. 10:16–25): "Behold, I send you out as sheep in the midst of wolves... Beware of men; for they will deliver you up to councils, and flog you in their synagogues, and you will be dragged before governors and kings for my sake." Immediately Jesus identifies why they will endure this: "to bear testimony before them and the Gentiles." Jesus then stated plainly that "you will be hated by all for my name's sake.... If they have called the master of the house Beelzebul, how much more will they malign those of his household."

This is the lot of those who have faith in God. This faith can bring great joy to our lives, but, at the same time, it can bring suffering and death as a direct result of it. When dealing with the challenges of secularity—not just the small ones but also the real ones that place our lives and livelihoods on the line—we find solace not in a guaranteed political victory, but in the words of Jesus Himself to those in danger: "[D]o not fear those who kill the body but cannot kill the soul.... [E]very one who acknowledges me before men, I also will acknowledge before my Father who is in heaven; but whoever denies me before men, I also will deny before my Father who is in heaven" (Matt. 10:28, 32-33).

❧ Chapter 10

Faith, Evil, and Suffering

The harsh reality of evil and suffering in the world presents faith's most formidable challenge. Nothing else comes close. The horrors of war-torn societies, of innocents suddenly killed by terrorists amidst an otherwise ordinary moment, of children killed in schools or stricken by disease, of imminent threats of violence within one's own community, of storms that destroy lives and property, are ever-present to us all to one degree or another. In the face of these atrocities, we ask questions, sincere yet beguiling questions that have long stumped believers and nonbelievers alike: How is the existence of evil and of suffering in the world compatible with a God who loves and cares deeply for his creatures? Why does God not snuff out evil and put an end to suffering, or is He not, in fact, omnipotent? Is creation really good if there is so much evil within it?

The confounding existence of evil and of suffering in the world has confronted the greatest minds and saints in the Church. St. Paul, for one, acknowledged both the presence of evil in creation, which we call physical evil, with its natural disasters and storms; and the mysterious ability of human beings to carry out evil actions, which we call moral evil.[1] Try as he did, Paul was no closer to producing a fully satisfying explanation of why evil exists than we are today. Yet our rational, restless nature seeks answers none-theless. Evil and suffering put faith to the test like no other. And it is through them that faith is truly lived and best understood.

Like God Himself, evil is a mystery. The dictionary describes evil as "anything that causes displeasure, injury, pain, or suffering; misfortune; calamity; mischief; injury; moral depravity; the nega-tion or contrary of good."[2] It is this last that has for centuries been the core of the Catholic understanding of evil. Evil is not a force of its own: there is no creating evil spirit, nor is there an evil power that pervades the world. There is only the God of the Bible who creates and sustains the world, and all of what He creates is good in itself. Evil, then, does not come from God, yet He allows it to exist within His providence.[3]

Evil is an absence or privation of good that should be present but is not. Hence evil does not possess its own reality, as Joseph Ratzinger explains: rather, it "consists of negation, eating away at the substance of creation…. [E]vil is not a kind of creature but it is more like a parasitic plant. It lives on what it takes out of the other being, and in the end it kills itself off, just as surely as a parasitic plant does when it completely dominates its host and kills it."[4]

If we consider our own experiences, we see the truth of this defi-nition. When a loved one dies, we experience pain at her absence. When a person performs an evil deed inexplicably, we wonder what has come over him, what is eating away at him. When we experi-ence physical, mental, or spiritual pain of any kind, it is because the health that should be there is absent. When we read and see in our news sources the evils of disease, war, famine, and natural disasters, we see how the good of creation has been negated by the wrongful acts of human beings and the hostile turnings of nature. To be sure, evil is a parasite intent on destroying the beauty of creation and the lives of human beings.

At the same time, while evil may not be its own entity, our suffering from it is real and often extremely acute. The disease that afflicts us, for example, may well be, officially, the absence of good health, but the pain we experience as a result of it is an intense reality. Here we see right away one of the great challenges in coming to grips with evil: our intellectual understanding of it in the abstract can never measure up with the intensity with which evil strikes us. This is also the first sign that reason alone cannot sufficiently answer the challenge that evil presents to us.

Just as every parasite has to come from somewhere, evil has to have an origin. Evil, we learn from the Book of Genesis, is the tragic byproduct of one of our greatest gifts, the one that we have from being created in God's own image and likeness: freedom. Freedom is our ability to choose by our own volition what it is we want. In its proper sense, freedom is correctly exercised when we choose the good and what conforms with the truth of God's creation. Without freedom, we would not have the capacity to love or to do good for another person. Without freedom, we would not be able to have faith in God.

But within freedom's power, Joseph Ratzinger identifies an internal threat that "always develops in this way: the greater a being is, the more it wants to determine its own life. It wants to be less and less dependent and, thus, more and more itself a kind of god, needing no one else at all. This is how the desire arises to become free of all need, what we call pride."[5]

We saw earlier that pride and a lack of trust in God caused Adam and Eve to commit the first sin. They misused their freedom by choosing deliberately the opposite of God's will: they wanted to determine their own lives independent of God. And so they sinned: they disobeyed God. That human freedom has the ability to knowingly reject its own author and model shows just how powerful it is.

The subsequent fate of Adam and Eve shows how damaging misused freedom is. Evil entered the world through Adam's decision, as St. Paul saw so clearly.[6] By spurning God, Adam rejected the infinite love with which God had showered him at creation. Knowing this helps us understand why God punished Adam—and all his descendants—by expelling him from the garden and depriving him of his original justice, wholeness, and holiness: If Adam preferred himself over God's love, why should God continue to preserve him in the special garden of His love?

In addition to concupiscence, our weakened human condition that leaves us inclined toward the seven deadly sins, physical evil is also the result of Adam's original sin. As the *Catechism* describes it, "[h]armony with creation is broken: visible creation has become alien and hostile to man. Because of man, creation is now subject to its bondage to decay... Death makes its entrance into human history."[7] The plight we experience at the hands of nature—storms, avalanches, earthquakes, floods, draughts, pestilences—are all the result of Adam's sin. God made creation for us; so when Adam chose himself over God, he caused permanent friction between humanity and nature. Original sin thus left its stain on creation as much as on humanity. And despite all the calamities we experience in nature, none is greater than death, the ultimate privation. God did not make death, the most terrifying of evils: we chose it for ourselves by sinning against Him.

In a secular age that has trivialized sin, the punishment of Adam—and of all human beings subsequently—seems harsh, if not vindictively cruel. Why should so much evil be present in the world as a result of one seemingly small sin? Is not death an extreme punishment? Through more careful reflection, we learn that death is, in fact, a just punishment: death is the opposite, the privation, of life, and God is the very author of life itself. Each time we sin by choosing our way over God's, we negate life. Every act of evil freely chosen is a choice for death over life. As with the reality of Hell, we see that it is not a vindictive God punishing us out of anger, but it is we ourselves who seal our own fate and get what we want for ourselves with every sin we commit.

Descending from Adam, the entire human race is linked together, just as each member of the Church is linked by baptism into the one body of Christ. A sin by one person affects all of us. This leads us to another disturbing reality: because evil is in the world, both physical and moral, we can encounter suffering even as passive bystanders: victims of street violence, car accidents, "collateral damage" in warfare, raging storms, and horrific diseases that arise seemingly from nowhere. Although we may not be guilty of evil at the particular moment of affliction, the fact that we are all sinners brings the sobering and unpleasant reminder that none of us is wholly innocent, and no one is so good as to be exempted from suffering for sin in the world—not even Christ, who was without sin.

We also learn from the Book of Genesis that we can be tempted to misuse our freedom by an external influence: Satan, the devil himself. Satan is not an anti-God with powers that rival God. Like human beings, Satan is one of God's creatures, a fallen angel who remains in permanent rebellion against God. As an angel, Satan is subordinate to God, but more powerful than human beings, whom he induces to follow his lead in rejecting God by making evil things appear as goods. In doing so, he seeks our solidarity with him in his rebellion against God. His action, the *Catechism* tells us, "may cause grave injuries—of a spiritual nature and, indirectly, even of a physical nature," but it "cannot prevent the building up of God's reign" here on earth.[8]

The fruit of sin and evil, of Satan and of misused freedom, is suffering, the pain we experience in reaction to an injury or offense. Suffering can be physical, stemming from illness or bodily harm, and it can be spiritual, when our minds and souls experience torment in response to a host of possibilities. The quantity and quality of suffering vary wildly from one person to another: some people are perfectly healthy while others face daily a number of physical struggles; some are financially well off while others worry anxiously about making enough money to survive; some are blessed with a multitude of family and friends while others have lost family members and live alone.

Evil and suffering force us to look beyond ourselves for answers. The real difficulty with them, as Martin Cothran points out, is not necessarily the rational questions about what evil is, as difficult as they are. It is really the existential questions—the "why" questions that most deeply touch us as human beings—that are so difficult to face. "What most disturbs us about [evil] is its seeming absurdity—that it seems a morally orderless abomination in what we think should be a morally ordered world.... It is the *meaning*, the thing we really desire to know, that we most fail to see."[9]

Contemporary secularity, as a direct consequence of its denial of the purposefulness of life, has abdicated the quest to find the meaning of evil and of suffering. Richard Dawkins, as we saw earlier, declared "why" questions as silly and having no meaning. For Dawkins and his peers, we suffer in vain. And when our suffering becomes extreme and we see no meaning in it, there is little motivation to endure it for the sake of a purposeless life. The best we can do is medicate the suffering away. And, as Viktor Frankl points out from the perspective of a clinical psychologist, the contemporary "drug scene is one aspect of a more general mass phenomenon, namely the feeling of meaninglessness resulting from a frustration of our existential needs which in turn has become a universal phenomenon in our industrial societies."[10]

In recent years the drug scene that stems from this nihilistic philosophy has taken a horrifying twist: in an action euphemistically labelled as "aid in dying" or "physician-assisted dying," a doctor can legally prescribe a fatal prescription for a suffering patient close to death. Suffering is miserable and senseless, the argument goes, so we might as well hasten death to make the suffering stop. In this act, we run away from the existential questions rather than attempt an answer. It is as if we have joined Satan in exclaiming, "So farewell hope; and with hope farewell fear; farewell remorse: all good to me is lost. Evil, be thou my good."[11]

Even in a culture where faith's influence is fading, not everyone is willing to follow this secularist logic to its vicious conclusion. There are still men and women who seek a silver lining in the dark cloud of suffering, meaning in the midst of pain. Frankl reasons that "[i]f there is a meaning in life at all, then there must be a meaning in suffering. Suffering is an ineradicable part of life, even as fate and death. Without suffering and death human life cannot be complete."[12]

Yet when we are confronted by evil on the visceral, existential level—when parents watch as a pall is placed over their child's funeral casket, when the parent of young children receives a cancer diagnosis, when a family is hastily forced to leave behind everything it has because of a storm or threat of violence—the question of suffering's meaning becomes pointed and pressing. In these moments, philosophical and rational arguments ring hollow. It is only when we turn to God in faith that we can find some small comfort in the midst of our intense grief.

To this end, it is noteworthy that Jesus Himself occasionally spoke of evil and suffering, yet he never once addressed their philosophical essence. Nor did He address why evil or suffering exist. In fact, He took them both as given. In His parable of the weeds among the wheat (Matt. 13:24–30), Jesus makes clear that His mission is not to remove evil from the earth at this stage. When weeds somehow appear alongside the wheat in the householder's field, the servants are astonished: "Sir, did you not sow good seed in your field? How then has it weeds?" The householder deemed "an enemy" as the cause of the weeds. When he was then asked by his servants whether they should remove the weeds, the householder replies, "No; lest in gathering the weeds you root up the wheat along with them. Let both grow together until the harvest; and at harvest time I will tell the reapers, 'Gather the weeds first and bind them in bundles to be burned, but gather the wheat into my barn.'"

This brief parable gives flesh to the Catholic understanding of evil. Evil comes not from God, but from an enemy, Satan, who tempted our first parents to misuse their freedom. Evil is now part of human existence: it coexists alongside the good, and it will do so until the end of time, when Christ will come again to judge the living and the dead, the good and the evil. The good will be rewarded, gathered into the barn of Heaven, while the bad will be burned in the unquenchable fire of Hell.

Jesus did not come to teach us how to think in the abstract: He came to answer the existential questions concerning meaning by showing us how to live in the present, with two eyes looking toward the future of eternal life with God in Heaven. Living in the present means dealing with all the challenges of human life, and suffering is our foremost difficulty. God's revelation shows us how to accept suffering, and how to find authentic meaning in it.

The story of Job is the Bible's answer to how we ought to accept suffering in the world and in our lives. Job was a righteous and faithful man blessed with a beautiful family and with material wealth. Then Satan intervenes and dares God: if Job's family and wealth should be taken from him, surely, the devil bets, he will curse God. God consents to Satan's challenge, and in a single day Job loses all his livestock, possessions, and even his children. After hearing the news of these successive events, "Job arose, and tore his robe, and shaved his head, and fell upon the ground, and worshiped. And he said, 'Naked I came from my mother's womb, and naked shall I return; the Lord gave, and the Lord has taken away; blessed be the name of the Lord.' In all this Job did not sin or charge God with wrong" (1:20–22).

Dismayed by Job's continued faithfulness to God, Satan doubles down: if Job should be afflicted with physical maladies, he will curse God. Then Satan afflicted him from head to foot with painful sores that made him unrecognizable to his friends. Job's wife instructs him in his misery, "Curse God and die" (2:9). But Job, who still was able to worship God after this latest round of hardships, replies, "'Shall we receive good at the hand of God, and shall we not receive evil?' In all this Job did not sin with his lips" (2:10).

Job is now utterly miserable, even as he tries to remember God as the cause of all good, including the good just taken from him. Three friends come to console him, but their efforts quickly turn into confrontation. They want a rational answer to the same question we still ask today: Why do bad things happen to good people? One then puts Job to the test: "But oh, that God would speak, and open his lips to you, and that he would tell you the secrets of wisdom!" (11:5–6).

Job, in reply, again expresses the depths of his sorrow: "I am a laughingstock to my friends… If I speak, my pain is not assuaged, and if I forbear, how much of it leaves me? Surely now God has worn me out; he has made desolate all my company…. My spirit is broken, my days are extinct, the grave is ready for me" (12:4;

16:6–7; 17:1). Yet he still manages to express his trust in God: "For I know that my Redeemer lives, and at last he will stand upon the earth, and after my skin has been thus destroyed, then from my flesh I shall see God, whom I shall see on my side, and my eyes shall behold, and not another" (19:25–27).

After the friends cease arguing, God calls to Job and challenges him to consider creation as a whole: "Where were you when I laid the foundation of the earth? Tell me, if you have understanding. Who determined its measurements—surely you know?... Has the rain a father, or who has begotten the drops of dew? From whose womb did the ice come forth, and who has given birth to the hoarfrost of heaven?... Who can number the clouds by wisdom?... Do you give the horse his might?...Is it by your wisdom that the hawk soars?" (38:4–5, 28–29, 37; 39:19, 26).

In this sweeping series of questions, "God gives Job the poetic vision of an ordered world, a world which is completely under His control, a control that Job, as a mere man, cannot himself see. It is a world in which evil does not have an explanation, but a *place*—a place in a poetic order."[13] After this vision, it is Job's task—and ours—to have faith in God, to trust that He is, in fact, in control of universe, even when we feel our lives spiraling out of control. The goodness of the world gives us reason to assent to the truth of God's love and care for us, even when circumstances make it seem that we have been abandoned.

While the story of Job puts evil and suffering in their proper context, it is not does not provide meaning for our suffering. The meaning comes from God's final revelation to us, the incarnation of His Son. With the incarnation we encounter God's greatest work—and the one most incomprehensible to human ways of thinking. We cry out to God to remove evil and suffering from our lives. Rather than remove them, He enters the world to experience both of them Himself in a real and profound way. It is on the cross, one of most sinister causes of suffering that men can devise, that God vanquished evil by suffering evil's epitome—death itself. This is how God, in a strange way, shows His love: not by taking away suffering, but by showing us how to handle it.

Before He was nailed to the cross, Jesus gave instructions about what the cross means for us: "If any man would come after me, let him deny himself and take up his cross and follow me. For whoever would save his life will lose it; and whoever loses his life for my sake and the gospel's will save it" (Mark 8:34–35). Jesus Himself willingly took up His cross and gave His life for our sakes. To follow Jesus, therefore, includes accepting suffering in our lives with a willing heart. And we must not only accept the sufferings that are a normal part of human life: we also must accept the sufferings that come from being His disciple: "[T]hey will deliver you up to tribulation, and put you to death; and you will be hated by all nations for my sake" (Matt. 24:9).

Faith was never intended by God to be solely a means of feeling good and of personal security, although these are legitimate effects of authentic faith. Faith in God includes hardship, and there are few things more challenging than freely surrendering our wills in a given situation. The closest human example is entering into holy matrimony: The spouses freely give their lives to each other in mutual faith, without knowing what the future may bring. Often, when both spouses sacrifice themselves to each other, great joy and happiness ensues. But simultaneously there can be great challenges that cause serious sufferings, such as when one spouse becomes gravely ill, when finances become strained, or when a child's behavior becomes precarious. If we are to experience the fullness of God's love for us, if we are to enter more deeply into our relationship with Him, we have to walk with Christ on the road to Calvary.

When it comes to suffering, Jesus is not teaching abstractions from an ivory tower. His teachings have real import because He Himself suffered horribly. His sufferings were physical: He was tortured by captors, His flesh was scourged and torn violently from His body, He was laden with the weight and rough splinters of the cross, He was pierced through His limbs by nails, He suffocated to death over a period of three hours. His sufferings were psychological: He was betrayed by one of his followers, abandoned by his closest friends, hanged naked for bystanders to see, all while knowing He was a completely innocent victim. Most of all, His sufferings were spiritual: on the cross He cried out, "My God, My God, why have you forsaken me?" (Mark 15:34).

Jesus' spiritual sufferings are particularly instructive for us as we experience evil and suffering in our own lives. Jesus, the Son of God, feels abandoned by God on the cross, and He expresses His anguish aloud to Him. We, too, may do the same. But as we do so, we must also be mindful of the context in which Jesus expressed these words: He was quoting Psalm 22, which are most certainly the words of someone suffering horribly and wondering where God is. "My God, my God, why have you forsaken me? Why are you so far from helping me, from the words of my groaning? O my God, I cry by day, but you do not answer; and by night, but find no rest" (1–2). The very next breath, however, expresses confidence in God: "Yet you are holy, enthroned on the praises of Israel. In you our fathers trusted; they trusted, and you delivered them. To you they cried, and were saved; in you they trusted, and were not disappointed" (3–5).

In the midst of pain and suffering, even as the Psalmist feels that "I am a worm, and no man" (6), he still asks God for help and maintains his faith in Him: "But you, O Lord, be not far off! O my help, hasten to my aid!... I will tell of your name to my brethren;

in the midst of the congregation I will praise you… For he has not despised or abhorred the affliction of the afflicted; and he has not hidden his face from him, but has heard, when he cried to him" (19, 22, 24).

The relationship of faith that we have with God is not without drama on our end. As with any other sustained relationship, there are periods of great joy and there are times of trial. During the latter, there is nothing wrong with expressing our dismay at our plight and our wonder where God is during it, just as the Psalmist did. It is even okay to be angry with God, just as we can be angry with a spouse, parent, child, or other person whom we love. The expression of anger can on occasion be helpful for both sides in a relationship as a vehicle for promoting healing. The key, however, is not to allow anger to harden into resentment. It is then that a relationship begins to suffer. Resentment toward God deadens faith by tempting us to give up on God. Then, when we begin to brood over our given situation, that "God didn't heal my daughter," "God didn't save my job," or "God didn't stop that man from robbing us," we harden our hearts and withdraw from Him, because we think, wrongly, that He has withdrawn from us.

During periods of intense suffering, anger with God is healthy when, after its intensity subsides, we take control of our senses and ask Him for forgiveness, just as we would do in a human relationship when we act out because of anger. Forgiveness of our sins is the reason that Christ suffered His horrific death on the cross. If Christ was willing to suffer for our salvation, He will forgive us when we act out because of our own suffering. Receiving forgiveness after intense suffering can be one of the most spiritually enriching experiences we can have as believers.

We know that by dying Christ destroyed death and vanquished the power of evil over us. It is easy to forget, however, that Christ's victory plays out in eternity and not according to the standards of the world. Christ's victory does not magically make our sufferings and future deaths disappear. Death and evil continue to exist in the world nearly two thousand years after the resurrection as they have since Adam's first sin. The difference now is that death is not the final word: Through faith in Christ and with the help of His grace we have genuine hope that we will one day be delivered from sin, evil, and suffering and brought to share in eternal life with God, our Father and creator. For the faithful death becomes not the privation of life, but an unpleasant passageway to a new, greater life. So even if we experience the most intense sufferings and the most excruciating death, we know through faith that these awful events can lead us to the God who consented to be subjected to the same fate.

Evil, too, has been vanquished, although it is easy to forget that as we look at the world. Again, Christ's victory is not played out in the daily events of this life, as the seeming success of evildoers reminds us. It is evident in eternity, when evildoers have to withstand the judgment of God, who will separate the good from the evil as a shepherd separates the sheep and the goats: the former will go to their eternal reward while the latter will endure the everlasting punishment that they have meted out for themselves by their conduct.

Christ's victory on the cross, His conquering of sin and evil, is how suffering gains meaning for us. Jesus Himself explains this to us simply: "Was it not necessary that the Christ should suffer these things and enter into his glory?" (Luke 24:26) Suffering on the cross was the means by which evil was defeated, and the means for the glorification of Christ in His resurrection. In other words, without the suffering of the cross there could be no resurrection. The suffering of Christ was redemptive: it redeemed us from sin and brought us back into union with God.

We find meaning in suffering when, by an act of the will, we unite our plight to His. Suffering is the means by which we follow Christ into Heaven. Any suffering we experience, whether it be as small as a toothache or as large as a terminal illness, can be made redemptive for us. To make it so, we make an act of the will, a conscious decision that we will endure our sufferings as God allows them in the hope that they purify our minds and make us worthy of eternal life with Christ who suffered for us. That is, we make our suffering a prayer. In this, Jesus again provides us a model from His own sufferings: "Father, if you are willing, remove this chalice from me; nevertheless not my will, but yours, be done" (Luke 22:42).

In the midst of suffering, to pray, "thy will be done," is the first step toward making our suffering redemptive. With this prayer, we can then consciously "offer up" our sufferings in union with Christ. We can offer them for our own salvation, or for the salvation of others, just as we would offer any other prayer or sacrifice. In this way our suffering becomes redemptive for ourselves and for others. At the same time, we may certainly continue to pray that we be delivered from our sufferings, just as Jesus taught us: "deliver us from evil." But we do so now with more confidence in God and less self-pity, knowing that whatever we endure, we endure for God. Such awareness can even be a source of joy, as it was for the apostles who were beaten for preaching about Jesus immediately after the resurrection (Acts 5:40–42). St. Peter's instructions to his followers who were suffering echo this experience he had with his fellow apostles: "[R]ejoice in so far as you share Christ's sufferings, that you may also rejoice and be glad when his glory is revealed" (1 Peter 4:13).

When suffering is meaningless, it is all too easy for us to wallow in our own misery. Redemptive suffering gives purpose to our pain: It helps us endure it for the far greater good of the salvation of souls.

St. Paul reminds us that Jesus Christ is the center and purpose of our lives and all of our sufferings: "We are afflicted in every way, but not crushed; perplexed, but not driven to despair; persecuted, but not forsaken; struck down, but not destroyed; always carrying in the body the death of Jesus, so that the life of Jesus may also be manifested in our bodies. For while we live we are always being given up to death for Jesus' sake, so that the life of Jesus may be manifested in our mortal flesh. So death is at work in us, but life in you" (2 Cor. 4:8–12).

To have the faith to embrace our own crosses in imitation of the cross of Christ is a tremendous challenge. St. Paul knew well that doing so runs contrary to our sensibilities and expectations: "[W]e preach Christ crucified, a stumbling block to Jews and folly to Gentiles" (1 Cor. 1:23). Yet from all we have learned from God's revelation, from the life of Christ, and from the testimony of Christ's greatest followers, we have every reason to trust that Christ crucified is indeed God's plan for the world and for us: "He is the source of your life in Christ Jesus, whom God made our wisdom, our righteousness and sanctification and redemption" (1 Cor. 1:30).

When we accept in faith that suffering is redemptive, we begin to see the evil and suffering in the world in a new light. They indeed have their place, as we said earlier, but they cannot dictate the course of the world unless we despair and turn away from God. Their role, most importantly, is to set the stage for the greatest possible redemption that we could imagine. God could have redeemed us from sin in an infinite number of ways. He could have made our debt disappear through an unfeeling pardon of some kind. But this was not His way. He chose instead to illustrate His love and care for us in the most manifest way possible: He Himself entered the world, took on our human condition, and suffered as one of us, all so we can be one with Him.

Believers who have received religious instruction may know this teaching about our redemption, but, familiar with it as we are, rarely do we pause to allow the grandeur of it to overtake us. Our redemption should not ring as a mathematical theorem or engineering blueprint. We must allow this undeserved and wondrous prize to resonate deep within our hearts. God used our sins as the cause for His unfathomable self-revelation. We commemorate this immense paradox in a special way in the Easter Vigil: "Our birth would have been no gain, had we not been redeemed. O wonder of your humble care for us! O love, O charity beyond all telling, to ransom a slave you gave away your Son! O truly necessary sin of Adam, destroyed completely by the Death of Christ! O happy fault that earned so great, so glorious a Redeemer!"

St. Thomas Aquinas teaches that "God allows evils to happen in order to bring a greater good therefrom."[14] Only with faith can we share this view. Often we are too grieved to see the subsequent good, or we wonder how good can be possible in the midst of such suffering. What good can come from watching one's child suffer and die? What good can come from losing a relative to disease or violence? What good can come from watching a storm destroy one's home? We must accept that sometimes we will not see the good in this life: God's workings surpass ours, and, like Job, we will not have access to the bigger picture until we are with God. In the meantime, we must accept our sufferings and try our best to offer them up to God, even as we feel as if we are drowning. Then, we pray simply with St. Peter sinking into the sea, "Lord, save me" (Matt. 14:30).

But with the eyes of faith, when the intensity of our grief subsides, and when we have asked God for help in seeing His will in our sufferings, we can begin to see good coming from evil, even as our pain lingers. When a child's death prompts a colossal show of support and unity from a family and community, when the victim of disease or violence inspires a foundation dedicated to eradicating that evil, when an entire country mobilizes billions of dollars in assistance along with legions of generous volunteers, we see that evil does not have the last word. But without faith, we will never see.

Catholics can always look to the saints for guidance and inspiration in enduring sufferings. The saints were not endowed with superhuman powers. They were men and women like us. What made them saints is that, despite the pain they felt on a human level, they maintained faith that their suffering has a place in God's plan, that they ought to accept God's will even if it was painful to do so, and that the love of God is far greater than anything they could imagine. We will look briefly at two examples of how the saints faithfully and heroically endured some of the worst types of sufferings.

First, while losing anyone dear through death is never easy, the death of a child is considered by many to be the hardest parting of all. St. Elizabeth Ann Seton, the first American-born canonized saint, experienced this intense grief at the death of her daughter Anna. Her pain was so crippling that she recollected to a friend, "For three months after Nina was taken I was so often expecting to lose my senses, and my head was so disordered, that unless for the daily duties always before me, I did not know much what I did or what I left undone."[15] She even had moments that tested her faith, such as when, sitting beside Anna's grave, she saw a snake slithering nearby: the thought entered her mind that Anna was now "the companion of snakes and reptiles! And the beautiful soul, *where?*"[16] On the first anniversary of Anna's death, St. Elizabeth writes in a letter to a friend: "Dear Anna, was ever the beauty of the soul so pictured as on that dying face? How faithfully represented by memory. You would not believe the love of a mother could increase as mine has since she is gone."[17]

St. Elizabeth expressed how she was trying to cope with her sufferings in faith in a letter to Archbishop John Carroll, the first bishop in the United States: "I have had a great many hard trials, my father... Indeed it has at times burnt so deep that the anguish could not be concealed. But by degrees custom reconciles pain itself, and I determined, dry and hard as my daily bread is, to take it with as good grace as possible. When I carry myself before the Lord sometimes, He makes me laugh at myself and asks me what other kind I would choose in the valley of tears, than that which Himself and all His followers made use of."[18]

It was not until sometime later, while using a stick to push away her dog, who kept following her until he began licking her feet, that St. Elizabeth had the spiritual breakthrough she needed. She expressed this moment in a prayer: "Yes, my beloved Savior, my adorable Master, I too shall kiss the stick raised to strike me and I shall clasp those feet that are ready to trample upon me.... 'I will submit myself to the will of those toward whom I feel the greatest aversion and dislike. I will put myself under the feet of all.'"[19]

We learn from Mother Seton that the grief and sorrow at the loss of a child never goes away. What can go away, and it may take some time before it does so, is our downtrodden disposition, which we can offer up to God when we choose to carry this horrific cross for ourselves and with Christ—rather than attempt to endure it alone.

Second, all of us are afflicted at one time or another with physical pain. Whether it be a short-term illness or a long-term hardship, we turn to God in our anguish and ask for Him to provide us relief. All too often, the immediate reprieve we earnestly desire does not follow, and we are forced to persevere through the ailment. One saint of many who teaches us how we can make our suffering redemptive is Franciscan priest Maximilian Kolbe. As a young man, he became stricken with tuberculosis, the effects of which would plague him for the rest of his life. Despite his weakened constitution, he founded a Catholic magazine and a house for Franciscans in Poland. He also traveled to Japan for the sake of preaching the Gospel there. One companion related how St. Maximilian conducted himself through his physical hardship:

> Father Maximilian always tried to keep it to himself if he was feeling bad so as not to discourage the rest of us. He always hid his sufferings that came from his poor health. Because he had only one lung he had difficulty breathing and this caused him to have tremendous headaches almost constantly, but you never heard it from him. He never complained. On the other hand, if one of us got sick, he would stay with him twenty-four hours if necessary to see he got every possible attention.[20]

St. Maximilian was later martyred in the Holocaust at Auschwitz, where he gave his life in the place of another prisoner designated for death. Witnesses described him as constantly encouraging his fellow prisoners to hope and to offer up their sufferings to God: "Take Christ's hand in one of yours and Mary's in the other. Now even if you are in darkness you can go forward with the confidence of a child guided by its parents."[21]

St. Maximilian's advice is equally apt for us during our own physical trials: as hard and as unpleasant as they may be, if we extend our hand to Christ and to His Blessed Mother in our time of need, they will help us persevere. With their help, the physical burden does not lighten, but the mental and spiritual one that comes with it does.

The death of a child and physical illness are just two of a limitless list of causes of suffering and pain. Regardless of the cause or the specific suffering, our response must be the same. As Ronda Chervin advises, rather than run from our pain, we can, like the saints, run toward Christ; rather than escape into addiction, we can long for intimacy with Christ; rather than "sinking in self-pity," we can offer our sufferings for others, "believing that Christ will use those offerings to build his kingdom."[22] To do this, we must make an act of the will to remain faithful to Christ, just as we did when we first accepted His invitation to faith. And just as when we made our initial acceptance of faith, the only way we can remain faithful during the trials of suffering is if we beg for and receive His divine grace to help us.

Hence when we consider pain, evil, and suffering, we return to the very essence of faith: our trust in God who invites us into a relationship with Him. To enter this relationship, we first need His grace; then we make a free decision to assent to all that God has revealed about Himself through His holy Church.

But God never promises that this relationship will be easy for us. Instead, He flips our expectations by sending His Son into the world not as a triumphant king, but as a suffering servant. On the cross, it is as if Jesus were saying to each of us, "I am doing this for you, so that you may be with me and my Father, now and forever. Will you now take up your cross in imitation of me?" Suffering is repugnant, yet it is the means by which God redeemed the world. With that redemption, our suffering, too, becomes redemptive, provided that we trust Him, that we have faith in Him.

In the midst of suffering, doubt and difficulties creep into our minds more than at any other time. Emotions and contrary voices from the world attack us and our beliefs acutely. All of our professed beliefs are put to the test. It is in these moments that we see how dependent we are on God, and how free we are to choose Him or to walk away from Him. This is the drama of faith.

We can look around and see the secular world collapsing from the weight of its own purposeless doctrine. We can see that when meaning is expelled from our lives, all that remains are emptiness and despair.

Each of us has been given challenges, crosses, and sufferings to overcome. Each of us has been given grace from God Himself to bear them in a manner worthy of the salvation He won for us. God tests our faith in Him, our love for Him, and He gives us the freedom to exercise this faith and this love. As we celebrate the good moments of life and struggle through its challenges, we remember that by baptism Christ became both our savior and our friend. We have been given the grace to turn to our divine Friend whenever we are in need, and when we do so, we make the prayer to Jesus of the grieving father whom we saw earlier our own: "I believe; help my unbelief!" (Mark 9:24).

❧ Epilogue

"When the Son of Man Comes, Will He Find Faith on Earth"?

And Jesus told them a parable, to the effect that they ought always to pray and not lose heart. He said, "In a certain city there was a judge who neither feared God nor regarded man; and there was a widow in that city who kept coming to him saying, 'Vindicate me against my adversary.' For a while he refused; but afterward he said to himself, 'Though I neither fear God nor regard man, yet because this widow bothers me, I will vindicate her, or she will wear me out by her continual coming.'" And the Lord said, "Hear what the unrighteous judge says. And will not God vindicate his elect, who cry to him day and night? Will he delay long over them? I tell you, he will vindicate them speedily. Nevertheless, *when the Son of Man comes, will he find faith on earth*?" (Luke 18:1–8)

Two thousand years later, Jesus's parable, intended to reassure us, strikes us, paradoxically, as chilling. Yes, God promises vindication to those who, like the persistent widow, cry to Him daily to seek His aid. He encourages us to keep praying, to not lose heart, to trust Him, to believe He has a plan for us, to remain steadfast in our faith.

Yet God does not promise that our tasks will be easy. The certain city that is the modern world not only does not fear God, but it has set itself up as judge over believers, whom it deems adversaries to its misguided vision of progress. The speedy vindication that God promises to believers never seems to happen on an earthly timetable.

And then there is that harrowing question: "When the Son of Man comes, will he find faith on earth?"

It is all too easy to interpret our Lord's mysterious question as a prophecy that our own age is the final age before His return. Modern secularity rapidly and rapaciously has dislodged the faith of countless people worldwide. Our churches have emptied. Our young parents are indifferent. Our children are unchurched. Our governments now prosecute believers and sanction immorality. Even some of our clergy have yielded to horrific sin and vice. As Benedict XVI soberly summarizes, "the real crisis facing the Church in the western world is a crisis of faith."[1]

We would be wrong, however, to read our current situation as the prophesized end times. From the first days after Pentecost through to our own day, believers have been all too eager to match the "signs of the times" to Jesus's words. In every instance of what becomes human prophecy, we make two errors: we exalt our own historical moment to privileged status over all prior epochs, and we force God to see the world as human beings see it.

Our historical moment is indeed in crisis, but so has been every moment before our own. In each, the faith itself has been imperiled by any variety of forces and situations. And through each, the faith has endured, thanks to the heroic witness of the saints, many of whom gave their lives so that we might believe through their sacrifice to God our Father. In their prayer, in their trials, and in their sufferings, the saints, by choosing not to lose heart, proved their faith; and by it, they brought stability and confidence to their epochs and to their fellow believers.

Twenty-first-century secular America, and the twenty-first-century Catholic Church, are in desperate need of saints to help us through these trying times. And we need not look around to find them: we should first look in the mirror to ourselves.

All Catholics, by virtue of their baptism, are given the means they need to become saints. That is sanctifying grace, which we receive in the sacraments, deepen in prayer, exercise in works of charity, and fortify through sacrifice. Sacraments, prayer, charity, sacrifice—if we frequent and practice these, we will remain steadfast in our faith in God the Father, in Jesus Christ His Son, and in the Holy Spirit. And if we remain steadfast in faith, we, too, can become saints.

To do this is our choice. Our life of faith begins with one critical "yes" to God and to His invitation to a relationship with Him. It continues thereafter with thousands of smaller "yeses," each and every day, to whatever it is that God is calling us at a particular moment. To pray more. To leave behind our sins and bad habits. To die to self rather than to answer back harshly. To fast and do acts of penance in reparation for our sins. To invite a wayward Catholic back to Mass. To volunteer to teach religious education. To participate in parish devotional events, from holy hours to pro-life vigils. To support Catholic education by financial donations. To initiate conversations about the faith with family, friends, and colleagues, and to share books and other Catholic resources with them. We do not need to do fantastic things in order to become saints. Rather, following the advice of Saint Theresa of Calcutta, we can do small things with great love.

Only with this type of committed faith can we convince those who do not believe, or those who once believed but have fallen away, to form their own friendships with the one true God and to turn back the tide of secularization. To convert an entire civilization is a slow work that will take decades, but it has happened in the past and it can happen again, one soul at a time. Such a work depends first and foremost on the faith of individual members of the Body of Christ, not on programs, committees, or documents. As Benedict XVI cautions, "If we do not find a way of genuinely renewing our faith, all structural reform will remain ineffective."[2]

The vindication promised by Jesus in the parable is not one in earthly terms, with conflicts removed and comforts restored. Rather, our vindication necessarily is that of our Lord's: earthly humiliation for heavenly exaltation. This is where our faith is put to the test most severely: Knowing what we have learned about God through the witness of others, do we trust Him enough to pick up our cross and follow Him?

If our answer is yes, then we ought to pray earnestly the words our Savior gave us: "Thy will be done, on earth as it is in Heaven."

❧ Notes

Chapter 1

1. John Henry Newman, *Parochial and Plain Sermons*, Vol. 1 (London: Rivingtons, 1868), p. 191.

2. Ibid., p. 193. Emphasis in original.

3. Pew Research Forum, *Global Christianity: A Report on the Size and Distribution of the World's Christian Population*, December 2011.

4. Pew Research Forum, *America's Changing Religious Landscape*, May 12, 2015.

5. Ibid.

6. Pew Research Forum, *"Strong" Catholic Identity at a Four-Decade Low in U.S.*, March 13, 2013.

7. R. R. Reno, "The New Secular Moral Majority," *First Things* (December 2012), p. 3.

8. Pew Research Forum, *America's Changing Religious Landscape*, and Elizabeth Drescher, "The Gospel According to the 'Nones,'" *America*, June 8–15, 2015, pp. 16-20.

9. Pew Research Forum, *"Nones" on the Rise*, October 9, 2012.

10. Mark M. Gray, "Catholic Population Steady, Despite Pew Report," *Our Sunday Visitor*, May 31, 2015.

11. Pew Research Forum, *America's Changing Religious Landscape*.

12. Ibid.

13. All Scripture quotations are taken from the Revised Standard Version.

14. John Paul II, Homily delivered for the Finnish Faithful in the Cathedral Church of Christ the King, Reykjavik, Iceland, June 4, 1989. Emphasis in original.

15. Both quotations come from the FAQ page of the Freedom from Religion Foundation's website, www.ffrf.org (accessed December 1, 2018).

16. See the National Secular Society's webpage, www.secularism.org.uk, under the "What Is Secularism?" tab (accessed December 1, 2018). Emphasis in original.

17. Ronald Rolheiser, O.M.I., *Secularity and the Gospel* (New York: The Crossroad Publishing Company, 2006), p. 39.

18. Harvey Cox, *The Secular City* (New York: The Macmillan Company, 1966), p. 2.

19. Tom Flynn, "Secular Humanism Defined," available at www.secularhumanism.org (accessed December 1, 2018).

20. Charles Taylor, *A Secular Age* (Cambridge, MA: The Belknap Press, 2007), pp. 19–20.

21. Ibid., p. 12.

22. Ibid., p. 13.

23. Ibid., p. 13.

24. Ibid., p. 542.

25. Ibid., p. 18.

Chapter 2

1. Bernard L. Marthaler, *The Creed* (New London, CT: Twenty-Third Publications, 2007), pp. 53–69.

2. Joseph Ratzinger, "*In the Beginning...*": *A Catholic Understanding of the Story of Creation and the Fall*, trans. Boniface Ramsey (Grand Rapids, MI: William B. Eerdmans Publishing Co., 1995), pp. 17–18.

3. Irenaeus, *Adversus Haereses*. Quoted in the *Catechism of the Catholic Church* (*CCC*), §460.

4. St. Thomas Aquinas, *Summa Theologica* (hereafter, *ST*) I, q. 21, a. 2.

5. Etienne Gilson, *Thomist Realism and the Critique of Knowledge*, trans. Mark A. Wauck (San Francisco: Ignatius Press, 1986), pp. 190–93.

6. *CCC*, §1954.

7. *Planned Parenthood of Southern PA vs. Casey*, 505 U.S. 833, 851 (1992).

8. John Paul II, *Veritatis Splendor*, §35.

9. John Paul II, *Centesimus Annus*, §46. Emphasis added.

10. Joseph Ratzinger, *The Nature and Mission of Theology*, trans. Adrian Walker (San Francisco: Ignatius Press, 1995), pp. 83–84.

11. Steven Pinker, "Science Is Not Your Enemy," *The New Republic*, August 6, 2013. All subsequent citations are from the online version of this essay.

12. Ibid. Emphasis added.

13. Joseph Ratzinger, *Introduction to Christianity*, trans. J. R. Foster (San Francisco: Ignatius Press, 2004), pp. 64–65.

14. Ratzinger, *"In the Beginning...",* p. 23.

15. Howard P. Kainz, *The Existence of God and the Faith-Instinct* (Cranbury, NJ: Susquehanna University Press, 2010), pp. 36–37.

16. Ibid, p. 38.

17. John Paul II, *Fides et Ratio*, Introduction.

18. Ibid., §46.

19. Ibid., §56.

20. Benedict XVI, *Deus Caritas Est*, §28.

21. Ibid., §28.

22. *CCC*, §215.

23. John Paul II, *Fides et Ratio*, §34. Emphasis in original.

24. Ibid., §48.

Chapter 3

1. Vatican I, *Dei Filius*, DH 3001, 3004. Cited in Henry Denzinger, *Compendium of Creeds, Definitions, and Declarations on Matters of Faith and Morals*, 43rd ed., ed. Peter Hünermann (San Francisco: Ignatius Press, 2012).

2. *ST* I, q. 2, a. 2.

3. *CCC*, §27.

4. Cardinal Avery Dulles, S.J., *The New World of Faith* (Huntington, IN:

Our Sunday Visitor, Inc., 2000), pp. 31–34. Dulles only lists the first four approaches; he does not consider religious experience.

5. Ibid., p. 31.

6. Richard Dawkins, *The God Delusion* (New York: Houghton Mifflin Company, 2006), p. 77.

7. Ibid., pp. 77, 120.

8. Ibid., p. 153.

9. Stanley Jaki, *The Purpose of It All* (Washington, DC: Regnery Gateway, 1990), pp. 101–102. Quoted in Kainz, *The Existence of God and the Faith Instinct*, p. 22.

10. Ratzinger, *"In the Beginning..."*, p. 23.

11. Dawkins, *The God Delusion*, p. 118.

12. Ibid., p. 116.

13. Ibid., p. 136. In a footnote on p. 145, Dawkins cites one physicist who says the anthropic principle "is hated by most physicists." He then adds, "I can't understand why. I think it is beautiful—perhaps because my consciousness has been raised by Darwin."

14. Ibid., p. 144.

15. Ibid., p. 145.

16. Ibid., p. 143.

17. Ibid., p. 155.

18. Ibid., p. 137.

19. Ibid., p. 137.

20. A whole team of scientists has intelligently designed a study that that may reproduce the molecule that first allowed for cells to divide successfully. It is not a bit ironic that these scientists *created* the conditions for evolution to occur. See Carl Zimmer, "Recreating the Road to Multicell Life," *The New York Times*, January 12, 2016.

21. Genesis 2:7 states that "the Lord God formed man of dust from the ground, and breathed into his nostrils the breath of life; and man became a living soul." This does not tell us the exact process whereby man came to be from the earth, only that he is so composed. Following the *Catechism of the Catholic Church* (§362), we

know that God deliberately made human beings; there is no way to say *how exactly* God formed man from the dust of the ground. We can only say that He did so.

22. Pius XII, *Humani Generis*, §36: "For these reasons the Teaching Authority of the Church does not forbid that, in conformity with the present state of human sciences and sacred theology, research and discussions, on the part of men experienced in both fields, take place with regard to the doctrine of evolution, *in as far as it inquires into the origin of the human body as coming from pre-existent and living matter—for the Catholic faith obliges us to hold that souls are immediately created by God*. However, this must be done in such a way that the reasons for both opinions, that is, those favorable and those unfavorable to evolution, be weighed and judged with the necessary seriousness, moderation and measure, and provided that all are prepared to submit to the judgment of the Church, to whom Christ has given the mission of interpreting authentically the Sacred Scriptures and of defending the dogmas of faith." Emphasis added.

23. Leo XIII, *Providentissimus Deus*, §23.

24. Stacy A. Trasancos, *Particles of Faith: A Catholic Guide to Navigating the Sciences* (Notre Dame, IN: Ave Maria Press, 2016), p. 46. Emphasis added.

25. Ratzinger, *"In the Beginning..."*, p. 50. Emphasis added. Quoted in Michael Chaberek, *Catholicism and Evolution* (Kettering, OH: Angelico Press, 2015), p. 257.

26. Dawkins, *The God Delusion*, p. 61.

27. Richard Dawkins, *The Blind Watchmaker* (New York: Norton, 1986), 6. Quoted in Chaberek, *Catholicism and Evolution*, p. 232, n. 30.

28. Dulles, *The New World of Faith*, p. 33.

29. Ibid., p. 34.

30. Dawkins, *The God Delusion*, p. 214–33.

31. John Henry Newman, *An Essay in Aid of a Grammar of Assent* (Notre Dame, IN: University of Notre Dame Press, 1979), pp. 98–107.

32. Ibid., p. 101.

33. Dawkins, *The God Delusion*, pp. 220–21.

34. Dulles, *The New World of Faith*, p. 34.

35. John Paul II, *Redemptor Hominis*, §18.

36. Augustine, *Confessions*, trans. Henry Chadwick (New York: Oxford University Press, 1998), p. 3.

37. William James, *The Varieties of Religious Experience* (New York: Collier Books, 1961), p. 62.

38. This sister is a personal friend of the author. She is the source of this story.

39. Dawkins, *The God Delusion*, p. 88.

40. Ibid., pp. 91–92. Dawkins dismissed the event at Fatima on the grounds that nowhere else in the world was the sun reported to dip. But if God is powerful enough to make the sun fall, could he not also be powerful enough to localize the experience?

41. Ibid., p. 59.

42. Matthew Bunson, "Mother Theresa to Be Canonized Sept. 4," *Our Sunday Visitor*, March 27, 2016. See also, John Thavis, *The Vatican Prophecies* (New York: Viking, 2015), pp. 191–93.

43. Thavis, *The Vatican Prophecies*, p. 197.

44. Bruno Sammaciccia, *The Eucharist Miracle of Lanciano, Italy*, trans. Anthony E. Burakowski (Trumbull, CT: Rev. Francis J. Kuba CP, 1976).

45. Joseph Ratzinger points out these assumptions and responds as follows in *Introduction to Christianity*, pp. 143–48.

46. Adam Gopnik, "Bigger Than Phil," *The New Yorker*, February 17 and 24, 2014. Emphasis in original. This citation is from the online version of the article, http://www.newyorker.com/magazine/2014/02/17/bigger-phil (accessed October 9, 2018).

47. Ratzinger, *Introduction to Christianity*, p. 146.

48. Ibid., p. 159.

49. John 1:1. This summary follows Ratzinger's analysis of the relationship of reason, Exodus, and John's Prologue in *Introduction to Christianity*, pp. 116–90.

50. *Gaudium et Spes*, §22.

51. G. K. Chesterton, *The Everlasting Man* (San Francisco: Ignatius Press, 1993), pp. 186–98.

52. On revelation as a pulling back of a veil, see Joseph Ratzinger, *Milestones: Memoirs 1927–1977*, trans. Erasmo Leiva-Merikakis (San Francisco: Ignatius Press, 1998), pp. 108–109.

53. Dawkins, *The God Delusion*, pp. 183–84.

54. Dawkins made this comment on the television show *Q & A* on October 4, 2012, in a debate with Cardinal George Pell of Australia. A recording of the show can be found at https://www.youtube.com/watch?v=tD1QHO_AVZA (accessed October 9, 2018).

55. Aristotle, *Physics*, 194b17–20, in *The Basic Works of Aristotle*, ed. Richard McKeon (New York: Random House, 1941), p. 240.

56. Gopnik, "Bigger Than Phil."

Chapter 4

1. Video Message of His Holiness Pope Benedict XVI for the Initiative "10 Squares for the 10 Commandments," September 8, 2012.

2. Ratzinger, *Introduction to Christianity*, pp. 72–73.

3. Ibid., p. 73.

4. Ibid., p. 69.

5. Pope Benedict XVI, *Jesus of Nazareth, Part Two: Holy Week: From the Entrance into Jerusalem to the Resurrection*, trans. Philip J. Whitmore (San Francisco: Ignatius Press, 2006), p. 85.

6. Pope Francis, *Lumen Fidei*, §18.

7. Henri de Lubac, *The Christian Faith*, trans. Richard Arnandez (San Francisco: Ignatius Press, 1986), pp. 145–47. Emphasis in original.

8. *Dei Filius* 3, DH 3008. *CCC*, §156.

9. *CCC*, §157.

10. Pope Francis, *Lumen Fidei*, §8.

11. Hebrews 11:8 and *CCC*, §145.

12. Josef Pieper, *Faith, Hope, Love* (San Francisco: Ignatius Press, 1997), p. 42.

13. DH 3542. Quoted in Reinhard Hütter, "What Is Faith? The Theocentric, Unitive, and Eschatologically Inchoative Character of Divine Faith," *Nova et Vetera*, Vol. 11, No. 2 (2013), pp. 331–32, n. 32.

14. Avery Dulles, S.J., *The Assurance of Things Hoped For: A Theology of Christian Faith* (New York: Oxford University Press, 1994), p. 51.

15. Pieper, *Faith, Hope, Love*, p. 37. Emphasis in original.

16. *ST* I-II, q. 55, a. 2.

Chapter 5

1. Benedict XVI, *Friendship with Jesus: Pope Benedict XVI Speaks to Children on their First Holy Communion*, ed. Amy Welborn (San Francisco: Ignatius Press, 2011), p. 12.

2. John Hardon, S.J., *History and Theology of Grace* (Ann Arbor, MI: Sapientia Press, 2005), p. 249.

3. Quoted in *CCC*, §1847.

4. *CCC*, §1236.

5. *CCC*, §1250.

6. G. K. Chesterton, *Orthodoxy* (San Francisco: Ignatius Press, 1995), p. 19.

7. International Theological Commission, *The Hope of Salvation for Infants Who Die Without Being Baptized*, April 19, 2007. The report was sensationalized by the media. See Ian Fisher, "Vatican City: Pope Closes Limbo," *The New York Times*, April 20, 2007.

8. *CCC*, §1261.

9. Dulles, *The Assurance of Things Hoped For*, p. 242.

10. *CCC*, §1257.

11. *CCC*, §1260. Emphasis in original.

12. *ST* I-II, q. 112, a. 4, *sed contra*.

13. *Lumen Gentium*, §14.

14. DH 1305. Cf. John Hardon, S.J., *The Catholic Catechism* (New York: Doubleday, 1975), p. 262.

15. *Lumen Genium*, §§39–40.

16. *CCC*, §1257.

17. Letter of St. Francis Xavier to St. Ignatius Loyola, in *The Liturgy of the Hours: Advent and Christmas Seasons* (New York: Catholic Book Publishing Co., 1975), Office of Readings, December 3.

18. John Paul II, Homily on the Beatification of Father Kuriakose Elias Chavara and Sister Alfonsa Muttathupandathu, Kottayam, India, February 8, 1986.

19. Charles J. Chaput, *Strangers in a Strange Land* (New York: Henry Holt and Company, 2017), p. 116.

20. De Lubac, *The Christian Faith*, p. 238.

21. *CCC*, §1210.

22. Center for Applied Research in the Apostolate (CARA), *Sacraments Today: Belief and Practice Among U.S. Catholics* (Washington, DC: Georgetown University, 2008), p. 54.

23. Thomas Aquinas, *Adoro Te Devote*. Translation by the author.

24. *CCC*, §1324.

25. Pope Benedict XVI, *Deus Caritas Est*, §31.

26. *CCC*, §2096.

27. *The Life of St. Theresa of Jesus*, trans. David Lewis, ed. Benedict Zimmerman (New York: Benziger Brothers, 1916), p. 41.

28. Pope Benedict XVI, Address to Pupils, St. Mary's University College, September 17, 2010.

29. *The New Saint Joseph Baltimore Catechism*, No. 2 (New York: The Catholic Book Publishing Co., 1969), p. 9.

30. Thomas Aquinas, *Compendium of Theology*, trans. Richard J. Regan (New York: Oxford University Press, 2009), p. 18.

31. Pope Benedict XVI, *Spe Salvi*, §10.

32. Canon 1752.

33. Pope Benedict XVI, *Spe Salvi*, §12.

Chapter 6

1. Henri de Lubac, *The Splendor of the Church*, trans. Michael Mason (San Francisco: Ignatius Press, 1999), p. 45.

2. Pius XII, *Mystici Corporis Christi*.

3. Karl Adam, *The Spirit of Catholicism*, trans. Justin McCann (New York: Image Books, 1954), p. 21.

4. *Lumen Gentium*, §39.

5. Ibid., §39.

6. Ibid., §39.

7. Ratzinger, *Introduction to Christianity*, pp. 342, 343.

8. Ibid., p. 342.

9. Ibid., pp. 342–43.

10. De Lubac, *The Splendor of the Church*, p. 232.

11. Ratzinger, *Introduction to Christianity*, p. 343.

12. De Lubac, *The Splendor of the Church*, p. 235.

13. *Lumen Gentium*, §§20, 21.

14. Ratzinger, *Introduction to Christianity*, p. 346.

15. The Church's reservation of the priesthood to men only remains a major cause of controversy in the modern world, and even faithful Catholics have difficulty understanding this teaching. Detailed discussion of this matter lies beyond the scope of this book. It is worth noting briefly that St. John Paul II definitively settled this issue in his 1994 apostolic letter *Ordinatio Sacerdotalis*, which stated that the priesthood is reserved to men only because Christ chose men only to be priests, and the Church is bound to follow the practices established by Christ. By way of comparison, the Church applies the same understanding to the sacraments: for the physical elements of the sacraments, she can only authorize the use of what Christ Himself used and established, e.g., water for baptism and bread and wine for the Eucharist.

16. *ST* II-II, q. 33, a. 4, ad 2.

17. Adam, *The Spirit of Catholicism*, p. 25.

18. De Lubac, *The Splendor of the Church*, pp. 82, 83.

19. Joseph Ratzinger makes this point, using a meteor as his example, in *Milestones: Memoirs 1927–1977*, p. 127. The following observation concerning faith residing within believers as the Church's living Tradition comes from Ratzinger's "The Question of the Concept of Tradition: A Provisional Response." *God's Word: Scripture, Tradition, Office*, ed. Peter Hünermann and Thomas Söding, trans. Henry Taylor (San Francisco: Ignatius Press, 2008), pp. 41–89.

20. Adam, *The Spirit of Catholicism*, p. 31.

21. The Church teaches that to obtain salvation "it is not always required that [a

person] be incorporated into the Church actually as a member" (DH 3870). At the same time, the Church also teaches that "separated churches and communities...derive their efficacy from the very fullness of grace and truth entrusted to the Church" (*Unitatis Redintegratio*, §3).

22. Pope John Paul II, *Ecclesia de Eucharistia*, §26.

23. Ibid., §23.

24. Ibid., §40.

25. Ibid., §35. Emphasis in original.

26. *Dei Verbum*, §10. Emphasis added.

27. *CCC*, §89.

28. Establishing dogma as an obstacle to charity is a favorite caricature of those who despise the former. See, for example, Nicholas Kristof, "A Church Mary Can Love," *The New York Times*, April 17, 2010, and "What Religion Would Jesus Belong To?" *New York Times*, September 4, 2016.

29. Congregation for the Doctrine of the Faith, *Doctrinal Commentary on the Concluding Formula of* Professio Fidei, §11.

30. Ibid.

31. Ibid., §§6–7.

32. *CCC*, §§2331–2400.

33. Ibid.

34. John XXIII, *Mater et Magistra*, §1.

35. *Unitatis Redinegratio*, §3.

36. Pope Benedict XVI, *Last Testament: In His Own Words*, trans. Jacob Phillips (New York: Bloomsbury Continuum, 2016), p. 241.

37. *Lumen Gentium*, §14.

38. Benedict XVI, Lecture at the University of Regensburg, September 12, 2006.

39. C. S. Lewis, *Mere Christianity* (New York: HarperOne, 2001), p. 52.

40. Reza Aslan, *Zealot: The Life and Times of Jesus of Nazareth* (New York: Random House, 2014).

41. Alister McGrath, *C. S. Lewis—A Life: Eccentric Genius, Reluctant Prophet* (Carol Stream, IL: Tyndale House Publishers, 2013), p. 227.

42. Bart Ehrman, *How Jesus Became God* (New York: HarperOne, 2015).

43. Thomas Kocik, *The Fullness of Truth: Catholicism and the World's Major Religions* (Pine Beach, NJ: Newman House Press, 2013), p. 200.

44. Ibid.

45. Newman, *Grammar of Assent*, p. 201.

Chapter 7

1. *ST* II-II, q. 4, a. 8, and Dulles, *The Assurance of Things Hoped For*, pp. 230–31.

2. Ibid., p. 230.

3. Newman, *Grammar of Assent*, p. 181.

4. Ibid., p. 186. The following observations are all taken from Newman's *Grammar of Assent*, Chapter 7, pp. 173–208.

5. Ibid., p. 181.

6. Dulles, *The Assurance of Things Hoped For*, p. 233.

7. Ibid., p. 234.

8. Newman, *Grammar of Assent*, p. 180.

9. Dulles, *The Assurance of Things Hoped For*, p. 231.

10. Ibid., pp. 231, 232.

11. Ibid., p. 232.

12. Ibid., p. 233.

13. Ibid., p. 234.

14. Pieper, *Faith, Hope, Love*, p. 50. Pieper's use of this term is also quoted in Dulles, *The Assurance of Things Hoped For*, p. 232.

15. John of the Cross, *Ascent of Mount Carmel*, trans. E. Allison Peers (London: Burns & Oates, 1993), p. 67.

16. Ibid., p. 68.

17. Ibid., p. 69. The citation is from Isaiah 7:9, which in the RSV reads, "If you will not believe, surely you shall not be established." A footnote to the text adds that John was likely using the Septuagint.

18. Ibid., p. 80.

19. Thomas Aquinas, *Quaestiones Disputatae de Veritate*, q. 14, a. 1. Quoted in

Pieper, *Faith, Hope, Love*, p. 52.

20. John Henry Newman, *Apologia Pro Vita Sua* (New York: Penguin Classics, 1994), pp. 214-15.

21. *Oxford English Dictionary*, 2nd ed., s.v. "doubt."

22. Ibid.

23. Ibid.

24. *Gaudium et Spes*, §16.

25. *CCC*, §1778.

26. Emphasis added.

27. *Lumen Gentium*, §16.

28. Pope John Paul II, *Veritatis Splendor*, §59.

29. Ibid., §62.

30. *Dignitatis Humanae*, §14

31. Pope John Paul II, *Veritatis Splendor*, §64.

32. Ibid., §60.

33. Joseph Ratzinger, *On Conscience* (San Francisco: Ignatius Press, 2007), p. 38.

34. This is the familiar line often used in the Mass as a responsorial psalm verse. The translation in the RSV reads, "O that today you would listen to his voice! Harden not your hearts."

35. Blaise Pascal, *Pensées*, ed. Anthony Levi, trans. Honor Levi (New York: Oxford University Press, 1999), p. 158.

Chapter 8

1. Victor Frankl, *Man's Search for Meaning*, trans. Ilse Lasch (Boston: Beacon Press, 2006), p. 66.

2. Friedrich Schleiermacher, *The Christian Faith*, 3rd ed. (New York: Bloomsbury T&T Clark, 2016), pp. 68, 70. Emphasis added.

3. Gabriel of St. Mary Magdalen, *Divine Intimacy* (Rockford, IL: TAN Books and Publishers, Inc., 1996), p. 1091.

4. Joseph Ratzinger, *The Spirit of the Liturgy*, trans. John Saward (San Francisco: Ignatius Press, 2000), p. 168.

5. Ibid., 165.

6. Romano Guardini, *The Spirit of the Liturgy*, trans. Ada Lane (Providence, RI: Cluny Media, 2018), pp. 8, 9.

7. Ibid., pp. 13, 14.

8. Ibid., pp. 51–52.

9. Ibid., p. 53.

10. Ibid., p. 32.

11. Ibid., p. 54.

12. *Sacrosanctum Concilium*, §90.

13. Guardini, *The Spirit of the Liturgy*, p. 10.

14. Thérèse of Lisieux, *Story of a Soul: The Autobiography of St. Thérèse of Lisieux*, 3rd ed., trans. John Clarke (Washington, DC: ICS Publications, 1996), pp. 211–12.

15. Ibid., p. 212.

16. Ibid., p. 213.

17. The following insights about spiritual aridity come from Gabriel of St. Mary Magdalen, *Divine Intimacy*, pp. 458–60, 464–72.

18. Ibid., p. 459.

19. Ibid., p. 460.

20. Thérèse of Lisieux, *Story of a Soul*, p. 213. Emphasis in original.

21. Quoted in Gabriel of St. Mary Magdalen, *Divine Intimacy*, p. 466.

22. Francis de Sales, *Introduction to the Devout Life*, trans. and ed. Allan Ross (Charlotte, NC: Saint Benedict Press, 2006), pp. 62–63.

23. Ibid., pp. 63–64.

24. *CCC*, §365.

25. *CCC*, §996.

26. *ST* II-II, q. 44, a. 1.

27. Gabriel of St. Mary Magdalen, *Divine Intimacy*, p. 1043.

28. John of the Cross, *Dark Night of the Soul*, trans. and ed. E. Allison Peers (New York: Image Books, 1990), p. 38.

29. Ibid., pp. 39–60.

30. Ibid., p. 61.

31. Gabriel of St. Mary Magdalen, *Divine Intimacy*, p. 1050.

32. Ibid., pp. 1050–1051.

33. Ibid., p. 1051.

Chapter 9

1. De Lubac, *The Christian Faith*, p. 300.

2. Pope Leo XIII, *Immortale Dei*, §3.

3. *CCC*, §1898.

4. *CCC*, §§1905–1909.

5. Pope John Paul II, *Christifideles Laici*, §42. Cf. Congregation for the Doctrine of the Faith, *Doctrinal Note on Some Questions regarding the Participation of Catholics in Political Life*, §1. Original in italics.

6. Congregation for the Doctrine of the Faith, *Doctrinal Note on Some Questions regarding the Participation of Catholics in Political Life*, §1.

7. Ibid., §4.

8. Chaput, *Strangers in a Strange Land*, p. 237.

9. Martin Luther King, Jr., *Why We Can't Wait* (New York: Mentor, 1964), p. 82.

10. *Gaudium et Spes*, §45.

11. Pope Benedict XVI, *Deus Caritas Est*, §28.

12. Ibid.

13. Ibid.

14. *Dignitatis Humanae*, §2.

15. *Arlene's Flowers v. The State of Washington*, No. 17-108, concerned the refusal to sell flowers for a same-sex wedding; the Washington State Court ruled against the florist for discriminating against a potential customer in 2017, but this decision was vacated by the U.S. Supreme Court in 2018. *Masterpiece Cakeshop v. The Colorado Civil Rights Commission*, No. 16-111, concerned the refusal to bake a cake for a same-sex wedding; the Colorado Court of Appeals ruled against the baker, also for discrimination, but this decision was also vacated by the U.S. Supreme Court on the grounds that the Colorado Court of Appeals showed reli-

gious animus to the baker. *National Institute of Family Life Advocates v. Becerra*, No. 16-1140, concerned a California state law that required pro-life pregnancy centers to provide their clients information on abortion; the U.S. Supreme Court ruled the law a violation of the First Amendment of the Constitution in 2018.

16. John Paul II, *Redemptor Hominis*, §17.

17. Ibid.

18. Chaput, *Strangers in a Strange Land*, pp. 238–41.

Chapter 10

1. Cf. Rom. 8:22 and 7:19–20.

2. *Webster's New Twentieth Century Dictionary of the English Language* (1954), s.v. "evil."

3. See, for example, Isaiah 45:7, which shows us that God is in control of all things in the universe—good and evil. He does not, however, cause sin, the ultimate evil.

4. Joseph Ratzinger, *God and the World*, trans. Henry Taylor (San Francisco: Ignatius Press, 2002), p. 128.

5. Ibid., p. 125.

6. Cf. above, p. 106.

7. *CCC*, §400.

8. *CCC*, §395.

9. Martin Cothran, "Light to the Darkness: How Literature Puts Evil in Its Place," *The Classical Teacher* (Summer 2016), p. 38. Emphasis in original.

10. Frankl, *Man's Search for Meaning*, pp. 139–40.

11. John Milton, *Paradise Lost*, Book IV, ll. 108–110.

12. Frankl, *Man's Search for Meaning*, p. 67.

13. Cothran, "Light to the Darkness," p. 38. Emphasis in original.

14. *ST* III, q. 1, a. 3, ad 3. Cf. *CCC*, §412.

15. Joseph I. Dirvin, *The Soul of Elizabeth Seton: A Spiritual Portrait* (San Francisco: Ignatius Press, 1990), p. 29.

16. Joan Barthel, *American Saint: The Life of Elizabeth Seton* (New York: Thomas Dunne Press, 2014), p. 168.

17. Robert Seton, ed., *Memoir, Letters, and Journal of Elizabeth Ann Seton: Convert to the Catholic Faith and Sister of Charity*, Vol. II (New York: P. O'Shea, Publisher, 1869), p. 143.

18. Mary Coyle O'Neil, *Mother Elizabeth Ann Seton* (Emmitsburg, MD: Mother Seton Guild, 1940), p. 87.

19. Ibid., p. 88.

20. Ronda Chervin, *Avoiding Bitterness in Suffering* (Manchester, NH: Sophia Press, 2015), p. 210.

21. Ibid., pp. 211–12.

22. Ibid., pp. 234–35.

Epilogue

1. Benedict XVI, Meeting with the Council of the Central Committee for German Catholics (*ZDK*) in the Seminary Hörsaal, Freiburg im Breisgau, September 24, 2011.

2. Ibid.

❧ Glossary of Terms

ARIDITY: A spiritual condition in which the believer does not experience any emotion or spiritual consolation in prayer. This condition is also referred to as spiritual dryness.

ASSENT: To accept something as true.

CATECHUMEN: The name for an adult in the process of converting to the Catholic faith.

CERTITUDE: State of mind that is established when an individual deliberately assents to a truth after careful reasoning.

CONCUPISCENCE: The irregular attraction, experienced by all human beings as a result of original sin, toward sin.

CONSCIENCE: The inner voice of human beings that makes them aware of God's presence and of right action in a given situation.

CREED: A statement of belief. The creed most well known to Catholics is the Nicene Creed recited at Mass each Sunday.

DARK NIGHT OF THE SOUL: An intense experience of spiritual purification in which the soul is deprived of God's consolation with the intention of purifying it from imperfections and earthly concerns.

DIVINE ECONOMY: God's providential work of creating, redeeming, and guiding the world. "Economy" comes from the Greek *oikonomia*, meaning the ordering of a household.

EMPIRICAL: Relating to what can be known by experience, experiment, or measure.

EVANGELIZATION: The preaching of the gospel of Jesus Christ.

FAITH: The personal relationship of trust that exists between human beings and the invisible God, who invites us to accept Him and His word with freedom and generosity. This relationship is manifested in a friendship with Jesus Christ, the Son of God. As a virtue faith is sustained over time through our continued assent to God and the truth about Him, on account of the grace communicated by God to us, and through our continued responses to Him.

GRACE: A free and supernatural gift from God to human beings whereby God communicates His divine life to us so that human beings may respond to His will. Theologians classify grace into two headings depending on its function in the lives of human beings. Actual grace is given to human beings to help them in a particular situation. Sanctifying, or habitual, grace is received from the seven sacraments and makes us holy by dwelling within us during our lives.

INFALLIBILITY: A gift given to the Church by God to teach without error on matters of faith and morals.

INDEFECTIBILITY: A gift given to the Church by God that protects her holiness from ceasing or failing.

IMMANENT: That which pertains to what is internal and inherent. An "immanent frame" is a worldview that considers only what is natural and inherent within the world, as opposed to what is supernatural and transcendent, as real.

INDIVIDUALISM: The belief that each individual is the ultimate arbiter of his or her own existence, behavior, and decisions.

KERYGMA: The proclamation of belief in the resurrection of Jesus Christ. It is the Greek word for preaching.

MATERIALISM: The belief that only what is physical and tangible has any real significance for our lives.

NATURAL LAW: The law given by God to all human beings whereby they use reason to discern what is good and what is evil, what is true and what is false, according to the ends, found in nature, for which things and human beings are created.

NIHILISM: The belief that nothing really exists or can be known.

OBJECTIVE: Pertaining to what is determined by factors that exist in the world, in contrast to an individual person's own subjective, internal understanding of how things are.

Soul: A spiritual, immaterial substance made directly by God that is the animating principle of the human being. The soul is distinct from the body yet integral to it; the union of body and soul forms a single nature.

Subjective: Pertaining to what is perceived and determined internally by the individual person, as opposed to what is objective, or exists external from the person within the world.

Pluralism: The belief that different groups can express their respective opinions without reference to a common whole or common truth, with each group demanding respect and tolerance for its own ideas and practices within the public square by virtue of its existence, not by the validity of its ideas.

Realism: The belief that the world as it exists and is experienced is determinate of reality and of truth.

Relativism: The belief that moral claims can apply only to individuals or groups, not to humanity as a whole, and these claims are determined by subjective criteria, such as emotion, preference, or cultural standards.

Scientism: The belief that only what can be measured by science is real.

Skepticism: The belief that no knowledge is certain and that truth cannot be known.

Secular: That which belongs to this world.

SECULARISM: The belief that only the realities of the natural world should have any bearing on our conduct and political life.

SECULARIST: A person who espouses secularity as an ideal way of living.

SECULARITY: The status or condition of a world that considers only what is of the demonstrable natural order as constitutive of society and public life.

SECULARIZATION: Literally "the process of becoming secular," the process of transitioning from a situation of religious influence to one where the state or some other nonreligious entity becomes the dominant influence.

WORLDVIEW: A theory about the meaning and philosophical underpinnings of life and of the world.

 BIBLIOGRAPHY

Documents from the Second Vatican Council

Dei Verbum

Lumen Gentium

Sacrosanctum Concilium

Unitatis Redintegratio

Documents from the Congregation for the Doctrine of the Faith

Doctrinal Commentary on the Concluding Formula of Professio Fidei

Doctrinal Note on Some Questions regarding the Participation of Catholics in Political Life

General Bibliography

Adam, Karl. *The Spirit of Catholicism.* Translated by Justin McCann. New York: Image Books, 1954.

Aristotle. *The Basic Works of Aristotle.* Edited by Richard McKeon. New York: Random House, 1941.

Aslan, Raza. *Zealot: The Life and Times of Jesus of Nazareth.* New York: Random House, 2014.

Augustine. *Confessions.* Translated by Henry Chadwick. New York: Oxford University Press, 1998.

Barthel, Joan. *American Saint: The Life of Elizabeth Seton.* New York: Thomas Dunne Press, 2014.

Benedict XVI. *Deus Caritas Est.*

———. *Friendship with Jesus: Pope Benedict XVI Speaks to Children on their First Holy Communion.* Edited by Amy Welborn. San Francisco: Ignatius Press, 2011.

———. *Jesus of Nazareth, Part Two: Holy Week: From the Entrance into Jerusalem to the Resurrection.* Translated by Philip J. Whitmore. San Francisco: Ignatius Press, 2006.

———. *Last Testament: In His Own Words.* Translated by Jacob Phillips. New York: Bloomsbury Continuum, 2016.

———. Lecture at the University of Regensburg. September 12, 2006.

_____. *Spe Salvi*.

_____. Video Message of His Holiness Pope Benedict XVI for the Initiative "10 Squares for the 10 Commandments." Rome. September 8, 2012.

Bunson, Matthew. "Mother Theresa to Be Canonized Sept. 4." *Our Sunday Visitor*. March 27, 2016.

Catechism of the Catholic Church.

Center for Applied Research in the Apostolate (CARA). *Sacraments Today: Belief and Practice Among U.S. Catholics*. Washington, DC: Georgetown University, 2008.

Chaberek, Michael. *Catholicism and Evolution*. Kettering, OH: Angelico Press, 2015.

Chaput, Charles J. *Strangers in a Strange Land: Living the Catholic Faith in a Post-Christian World*. New York. Henry Holt and Company, 2017.

Chervin, Ronda. *Avoiding Bitterness in Suffering*. Manchester, NH: Sophia Press, 2015.

Chesterton, G. K. *Orthodoxy*. San Francisco: Ignatius Press, 1995.

_____. *The Everlasting Man*. San Francisco: Ignatius Press, 1993.

Code of Canon Law.

Cothran, Martin. "Light to the Darkness: How Literature Puts Evil in Its Place." *The Classical Teacher* (Summer 2016): pp. 36–38.

Cox, Harvey. *The Secular City.* New York: The Macmillan Company, 1966.

Dawkins, Richard. *The God Delusion.* New York: Houghton Mifflin Company, 2006.

Denzinger, Henry. *Enchiridion symbolorum definitionum et declarationum de rebus fidei et morum—Compendium of Creeds, Definitions, and Declarations on Matters of Faith and Morals,* 43d ed. Edited by Peter Hünermann, Robert Fastiggi, and Anne Englund Nash. San Francisco: Ignatius Press, 2012.

Dirvin, Joseph I. *The Soul of Elizabeth Seton: A Spiritual Portrait.* San Francisco: Ignatius Press, 1990.

Drescher, Elizabeth. "The Gospel According to the 'Nones.'" *America,* June 8–15, 2015: pp. 16–20.

Dulles, Avery. *The Assurance of Things Hoped For: A Theology of Christian Faith.* New York: Oxford University Press, 1994.

_____. *The New World of Faith.* Huntington, IN: Our Sunday Visitor, Inc., 2000.

Ehrman, Bart. *How Jesus Became God.* New York: HarperOne, 2015.

Francis. *Lumen Fidei.*

Frankl, Viktor. *Man's Search for Meaning*. Translated by Ilse Lasch. Boston: Beacon Press, 2006.

Gabriel of St. Mary Magdalen. *Divine Intimacy*. Rockford, IL: TAN Books and Publishers, Inc., 1996.

Gilson, Etienne. *Thomist Realism and the Critique of Knowledge*. Translated by Mark A. Wauck. San Francisco: Ignatius Press, 1986.

Gopnik, Adam. "Bigger than Phil." *The New Yorker*, February 17 & 24, 2014.

Gray, Mark M. "Catholic Population Steady, Despite Pew Report." *Our Sunday Visitor*, May 31, 2015.

Guardini, Romano. *The Spirit of the Liturgy*. Translated by Ada Lane. Providence, RI: Cluny Media, 2018.

Hardon, John. *History and Theology of Grace*. Ann Arbor, MI: Sapientia Press, 2005.

_____. *The Catholic Catechism*. New York: Doubleday, 1975.

James, William. *The Varieties of Religious Experience*. New York: Collier Books, 1961.

John of the Cross. *Ascent of Mount Carmel*. Translated by E. Allison Peers. London: Burns & Oates, 1993.

_____. *Dark Night of the Soul*. Translated and edited by E. Allison Peers. New York: Image Books, 1990.

John XXIII. *Mater et Magistra.*

John Paul II. *Centesimus Annus.*

———. *Christifideles Laici.*

———. *Ecclesia de Eucharistia.*

———. Homily on the Beatification of Father Kuriakose Elias Chavara and Sister Alfonsa Muttathupandathu. Kottayam, India. February 8, 1986.

———. Homily delivered for the Finnish faithful in the Cathedral Church of Christ the King. Reykjavik, Iceland. June 4, 1989.

———. *Ordinatio Sacerdotalis.*

———. *Redemptor Hominis.*

———. *Veritatis Splendor.*

Kainz, Howard P. *The Existence of God and the Faith Instinct.* Cranbury, NJ: Susquehanna University Press, 2010.

Kocik, Thomas. *The Fullness of Truth: Catholicism and the World's Major Religions.* Pine Beach, NJ: Newman House Press, 2013.

Kristof, Nicholas. "A Church Mary Can Love." *The New York Times,* April 17, 2010.

———. "What Religion Would Jesus Belong To?" *The New York Times,* September 4, 2016.

Leo XIII. *Immortale Dei.*

Lewis, C. S. *Mere Christianity.* New York: HarperOne, 2001.

King, Jr., Martin Luther. "Letter from Birmingham Jail." *Why We Can't Wait.* New York: Mentor Books, 1964.

De Lubac, Henri. *The Christian Faith.* Translated by Richard Arnandez. San Francisco: Ignatius Press, 1986.

_____. *The Splendor of the Church.* Translated by Michael Mason. San Francisco: Ignatius Press, 1999.

Marthaler, Bernard L. *The Creed.* New London, CT: Twenty-Third Publications, 2007.

The New Saint Joseph Baltimore Catechism, No. 2. New York: The Catholic Book Publishing Co., 1969.

McGrath, Alister. *C. S. Lewis—A Life: Eccentric Genius, Reluctant Prophet.* Carol Stream, IL: Tyndale House Publishers, 2013.

Milton, John. *Paradise Lost.* London: Cassell and Company, 1894.

Newman, John Henry. *An Essay in Aid of a Grammar of Assent.* Notre Dame, IN: University of Notre Dame Press, 1979.

_____. *Apologia Pro Vita Sua.* New York: Penguin Classics, 1994.

_____. *Parochial and Plain Sermons,* Vol. I. London: Rivingtons, 1868.

O'Neil, Mary Coyle. *Mother Elizabeth Ann Seton*. Emmitsburg, MD: Mother Seton Guild, 1940.

Pascal, Blaise. *Pensées and Other Writings*. Translated by Honor Levi. Edited by Anthony Levi. New York: Oxford University Press, 1999.

Pew Research Forum. *America's Changing Religious Landscape*. May 12, 2015.

_____. *Global Christianity: A Report on the Size and Distribution of the World's Christian Population*. December 2011.

_____. *"Nones" on the Rise*. October 9, 2012.

_____. *"Strong" Catholic Identity at a Four-Decade Low in U.S.* March 13, 2013.

Pieper, Josef. *Faith, Hope, Love*. San Francisco: Ignatius Press, 1997.

Pinker, Steven. "Science Is Not Your Enemy." *The New Republic*, August 6, 2013.

Ratzinger, Joseph. *God and the World*. Translated by Henry Taylor. San Francisco: Ignatius Press, 2002.

_____. *"In the Beginning...": A Catholic Understanding of the Story of Creation and the Fall*. Translated by Boniface Ramsey. Grand Rapids, MI: William B. Eerdmans Publishing Co., 1995.

_____. *Introduction to Christianity*. Translated by J. R. Foster. San Francisco: Ignatius Press, 2004.

_____. *Milestones: Memoirs 1927-1977.* Translated by Erasmo Leiva-Merikakis. San Francisco: Ignatius Press, 1998.

_____. *On Conscience.* San Francisco: Ignatius Press, 2007.

_____. *The Nature and Mission of Theology.* Translated by Adrian Walker. San Francisco: Ignatius Press, 1995.

_____. "The Question of the Concept of Tradition: A Provisional Response." *God's Word: Scripture, Tradition, Office.* Edited by Peter Hünermann and Thomas Söding. Translated by Henry Taylor. San Francisco: Ignatius Press, 2008.

_____. *The Spirit of the Liturgy.* Translated by John Saward. San Francisco: Ignatius Press, 2000.

Reno, R. R. "The New Secular Moral Majority." *First Things* (December 2012): pp. 3–5.

Rolheiser, Ronald. *Secularity and the Gospel.* New York: The Crossroad Publishing Company, 2006.

De Sales, Francis. *Introduction to the Devout Life.* Translated and edited by Allan Ross. Charlotte, NC: Saint Benedict Press, 2006.

Sammaciccia, Bruno. *The Eucharist Miracle of Lanciano, Italy.* Translated by Anthony E. Burakowski. Trumbull, CT: Rev. Francis J. Kuba CP, 1976.

Schleiermacher, Friedrich. *The Christian Faith.* 3rd ed. New York: Bloomsbury T&T Clark, 2016.

Seton, Robert, ed. *Memoir, Letters, and Journal of Elizabeth Ann Seton: Convert to the Catholic Faith and Sister of Charity*, Vol. II. New York: P. O'Shea, Publisher, 1869.

Taylor, Charles. *A Secular Age*. Cambridge, MA: The Belknap Press, 2007.

Teresa of Jesus. *The Life of St. Theresa of Jesus*. Translated by David Lewis. Edited by Benedict Zimmerman. New York: Benziger Brothers, 1916.

Thavis, John. *The Vatican Prophecies*. New York: Viking, 2015.

Thérèse of Lisieux. *Story of a Soul: The Autobiography of St. Thérèse of Lisieux*. 3rd ed. Translated by John Clarke. Washington, DC: ICS Publications, 1996.

Thomas Aquinas. *Compendium of Theology*. Translated by Richard J. Regan. New York: Oxford University Press, 2009.

_____. *Summa Theologica*. Translated by the Fathers of the English Dominican Province. New York: Benziger Brothers, Inc., 1947.

Trasancos, Stacy A. *Particles of Faith: A Catholic Guide to Navigating the Sciences*. Notre Dame, IN: Ave Maria Press, 2016.

Wade, Nicholas. *The Faith Instinct: How Religion Evolved and Why It Endured*. New York: The Penguin Press, 2009.

Weigel, George. *Witness to Hope*. New York: HarperCollins, 1999.

Xavier, Francis. Letter to Ignatius Loyola, 1542 and 1546. *The Liturgy of the Hours: Advent and Christmas Seasons.* New York: Catholic Book Publishing Co., 1975.

Zimmer, Carl. "Recreating the Road to Multicell Life." *The New York Times*, January 12, 2016.

CLUNY MEDIA

Designed by Fiona Cecile Clarke, the CLUNY MEDIA *logo
depicts a monk at work in the scriptorium,
with a cat sitting at his feet.*

*The monk represents our mission to emulate
the invaluable contributions of the monks
of Cluny in preserving the libraries of the West,
our strivings to know and love the truth.*

*The cat at the monk's feet is Pangur Bán, from the
eponymous Irish poem of the 9th century.
The anonymous poet compares his scholarly
pursuit of truth with the cat's happy hunting of mice.
The depiction of Pangur Bán is an homage to the work
of the monks of Irish monasteries and a sign
of the joy we at Cluny take in our trade.*

"Messe ocus Pangur Bán,
cechtar nathar fria saindan:
bíth a menmasam fri seilgg,
mu memna céin im saincheirdd."

Made in the USA
Middletown, DE
15 April 2019